Commercial Club (Geneva Historical Society)

THE Kane County Bar Association

1858–2008

150 YEARS
KCBA
1858-2008

THE
DONNING COMPANY
PUBLISHERS

THE Kane County *Bar Association*

1858–2008

The Donning Company Publishers
184 Business Park Drive, Suite 206
Virginia Beach, VA 23462

Steve Mull, General Manager
Barbara Buchanan, Office Manager
Heather Floyd, Editor
Lori Wiley, Graphic Designer
Derek Eley, Imaging Artist
Lori Porter, Project Research Coordinator
Tonya Hannink, Marketing Specialist
Pamela Engelhard, Marketing Advisor

Dennis N. Walton, Project Director

Library of Congress Cataloging-in-Publication Data

Beck, Bill, 1945-
The Kane County Bar Association / by Bill Beck.
p. cm.
Includes bibliographical references.
ISBN 978-1-57864-533-6 (hardcover : alk. paper)
1. Kane County Bar Association (Kane County, Ill.)--History. 2. Bar associations--Illinois--Kane County--History. 3. Lawyers--Illinois--Kane County--Biography. I. Title.
KF334.K35K3543 2008
340.06'077323--dc22
2008040658

Printed in the United States of America at Walsworth Publishing Company

Table of Contents

7	Acknowledgments	
9	Foreword	
11	Chapter 1	*In the Beginning*
29	Chapter 2	*The Early Bench and Bar*
49	Chapter 3	*Into the Modern Era: 1908–1958*
65	Chapter 4	*The Association Reborn: 1959–1965*
81	Chapter 5	*The Growth of the Legal Community: 1965–1970*
97	Chapter 6	*The Bar Association Comes of Age: 1971–1979*
109	Chapter 7	*Growth Years: 1980–1989*
125	Chapter 8	*A Generation in Transition: 1990–1999*
139	Chapter 9	*The Association in the Twenty-first Century: 2000–2008*
157	Chapter 10	*The Association Today and Tomorrow: 2008*
176	Sponsors	
178	Appendix	*Chronology of Kane County Judiciary*
180	Endnotes	
186	Index	
192	About the Author	

150
KCBA
Organized 1858
YEARS
1858-2008

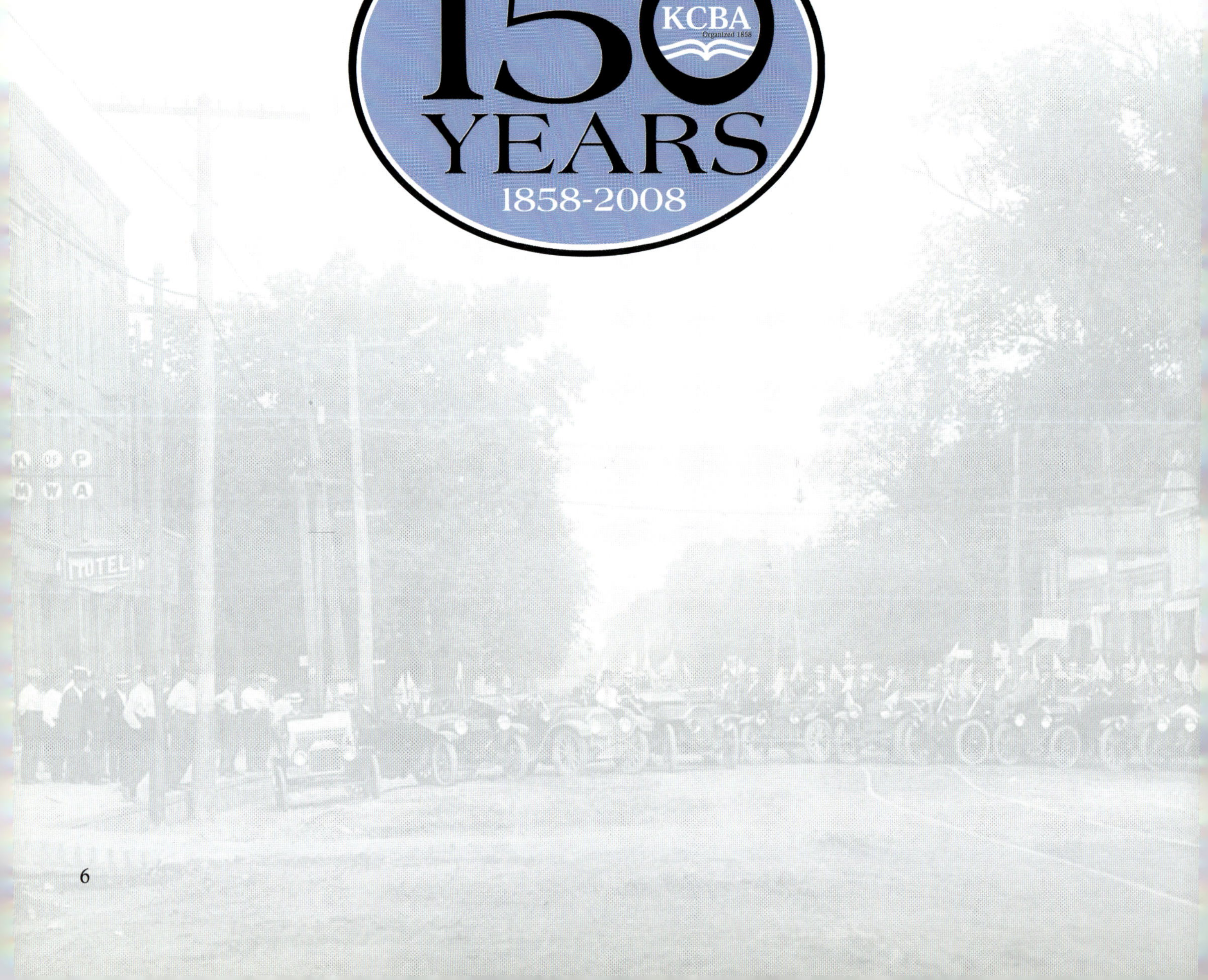

Acknowledgments

No book is produced without help. That help is particularly meaningful and necessary in a book from a nonprofit membership organization with limited resources and personnel. The KCBA has benefited from the assistance of many people and entities in the production of this book.

We are grateful for the resources and staff of the Aurora, Batavia, Geneva, and Elgin History Centers, especially the professionalism and expertise of Ron Rawson of Geneva, whose patience and cooperation were exemplary. These centers are essential to preserving the history of our local communities and they deserve our thanks and support. Thanks is also due to Illinois Supreme Court Librarian Amanda Ciaccio, who graciously researched and provided many details.

We also thank the many KCBA members who contributed time, photographs, and memories, whose names are too numerous to mention. Their interest and commitment have made this a better book. Particular thanks are extended to William C. Murphy, John P. Callahan, Jr., Judge Don Anderson, Maggie Mayer, and Gregory H. Booth. Appreciation is likewise due to the staff of the KCBA: Jan Wade, executive director; Carolyn Jones, membership services and CLE coordinator; and Deb Cook, publications coordinator. Much of the professionalism we have achieved as an organization is due to their reliable and tireless support. We thank as well the members listed on pages 176 and 177, whose financial support made this book possible.

Our largest debt is owed to members Patrick M. Flaherty (President 2007–2008), Julie L. Cibulskis (President 2009–2010), and Scott G. Richmond. They formed the book committee of the KCBA and were responsible for the planning, direction, and oversight of the project. They volunteered countless hours researching, interviewing, editing, obtaining photographs, writing captions, and developing storylines. This book exists because of the vision and dedication of these three members.

Kane County Bar Association

KANE CO COURT HOUSE

Foreword

The practice of law is about passion: passion for principles and ideals; passion for advocacy and debate; passion for critical thinking and intellectual exchange; passion for language and words; and passion for creativity and ideas. But most of all, at its core, it is about passion for helping people.

The Kane County Bar Association begins in 2008 a celebration of 150 years of helping people. We celebrate this anniversary, not simply to recognize an organization, but to honor what it represents: the enormous contribution of members to the prosperity and decency of the communities they serve. It is a celebration of the life work of lawyers and judges who have comprised the KCBA and promoted the rule of law through twenty-nine presidents, eight disclosed wars, and profound social and technological change.

This book tells the story of our Association on the occasion of this anniversary, and in so doing, tells the story of the people, events, and communities that form its soul. These distinguished men and women, past and present, represent a tradition of honor, service, and professionalism of which we can all be proud. It is impossible to cover every contribution made by every member over the past fifteen decades, and the many notable omissions are due to limitations of resources rather than importance. Nonetheless, it is not an overstatement to say that every step forward in our communities, every advance in the private and public arena, has benefited from the industry and imagination of the local legal profession.

We hope that you enjoy the history and nostalgia this book provides. The lasting importance of this story, however, is that it offers a resource for future generations of lawyers. Here they will see how the legal profession in Kane County grew and prospered, how members played a vital role in the development of Fox Valley communities, and how our Association faithfully nurtured the ideals and traditions of a noble profession. On behalf of the KCBA, we entrust to our successors the guardianship of this very special heritage. May we continue to invest the same dignity, vision, and vitality our predecessors were so careful to provide.

Patrick M. Flaherty
President
2007–2008

David C. Camic
President
2008–2009

William C. Murphy
President
1972–1973

Aurora

Batavia

Big Rock

Blackberry

Burlington–Plato

Campton

Dundee

Elgin

Eleven murals depicting early scenes throughout Kane County decorate the walls of the current courthouse in Geneva. (Geneva Historical Society)

CHAPTER 1

In the Beginning

Geneva

Mill Creek

St. Charles

Every city, county, and state arises from humble beginnings, and Kane County, Illinois, was no exception. For much of its history, the fertile glacial plain drained by the Fox River was home to Native Americans, most notably the Potawatomi. Wigwams and campfires could be found along the Fox River from Aurora to Dundee. Encampments existed on the west side of the river in Aurora north of Indian Trail, along the east side of the river between Butterfield Road and Batavia, and along the river south of Dundee.[1] Tribes fished and hunted here during warm months and followed game south and west during winter. They produced leaders still recognized today, including Chief Shabbona and Chief Waubonsie.[2]

The natives referred to this area as "Valley of the Foxes." It is known today simply as the Fox Valley.[3]

Before Kane County would host the first meeting of its bar association in 1858, there would be more than a century of European exploration and sixty years of settlement during the formative years of the American Republic. The earliest recorded history of the region begins with the first white explorers in the late seventeenth century. Frenchmen Father Jacques Marquette and Louis Joliet traveled down the Mississippi River from the Great Lakes and what is now the upper peninsula of Michigan in 1673. On their return north the next year, the pair followed the Mississippi River to the mouth of the Illinois River and then explored the region along the Illinois in a shortcut back to the Great Lakes. Although there is no evidence they entered the Fox River, all of Illinois—and much of the modern Midwest—was later claimed for France by explorer Robert LaSalle.

An 1882 bird's-eye view of Aurora looking northeast. The Chicago, Burlington & Quincy Railroad Roundhouses are shown northeast of Stolp Island. (Aurora Historical Society)

This broad expanse remained under French rule until the Treaty of Paris ceded it to the British at the conclusion of the French and Indian War in 1763. The British, in turn, lost control of the area to a young United States in 1778, when Colonel George Rogers Clark captured Kaskaskia and Cahokia (Illinois cities southeast of St. Louis) during the Revolutionary War. Congress later established the Northwest Territory in 1787, which encompassed all lands northwest of the Ohio River. In 1809, the Illinois Territory was created by Congress, and in 1818, Illinois was admitted to the Union as the twenty-first state with Kaskaskia as its first capital.

Kane County would likely have seen more settlement in the early 1830s had it not been for the onset of the Blackhawk War of 1832. Hundreds of Sac and Fox, led by a fiercely independent Blackhawk, moved from the Iowa Territory back into their homelands in northern Illinois, homelands mostly west and north of Kane County which had been lost in a disputed treaty in 1804. Illinois Governor John Reynolds proclaimed it "an invasion" and state militia and federal troops intervened. Panicked white settlers fled east toward Chicago.[4] Potawatomi Chiefs Waubonsie and Shabbona did not support Blackhawk, and there is no evidence that battles occurred in Kane County. Battles did, however, occur south, west, and north, including one in Ottawa, where fifteen white settlers died in what became known in the white community as the Indian Creek Massacre. Blackhawk and his followers were successfully evicted west of the Mississippi, and most of the remaining native population was removed to reservations in Iowa, Kansas, and Oklahoma by 1836.

On January 16, 1836, the Illinois legislature established Kane County from land that had formerly been included as part of LaSalle County. The new county included what is now DeKalb and the northern portions of Kendall County. It was named after Elias Kent Kane, an attorney from southern Illinois who had helped draft the state's first constitution, was its first secretary of state, and was later a U.S. congressman and senator. DeKalb County was carved out of Kane County in 1837, and Kendall County was established in 1841, leaving Kane with its present boundaries and dimensions. Kane County is thirty miles north to south, eighteen miles east to west, and 522 square miles. In 1837, there were about 5,000 residents farming the Fox River Valley and the prairies to the west of the river.[5] Today, in 2008, the population is estimated to be 501,000.

Early Life

Farmers, millwrights, and other craftsmen and entrepreneurs arrived in the unspoiled wilderness of the Fox Valley several years before the first lawyers. Most settlers came from the East and South, and most came by wooden-wheeled wagons over hard and uneven dirt trails in journeys that took months. Housing consisted of temporary handmade lean-tos, followed weeks later by hand-cut and split one-room log cabins through the crevices of which blew the cold and snow of piercing winter winds. Food was grown or killed and cooked over wood-stoked fires. Light was by handmade candles and heat by hand-cut timber. The only transportation was by foot or horse over trails that were poorly defined and often impassable in snow and heavy rain.

An 1869 bird's-eye view of Geneva looking northwest. The 1856 courthouse on Third Street is located four blocks west of the river and four blocks north of the railroad tracks. (Geneva Historical Society)

The first settler in Kane County was Christopher Payne in 1832. He came by ox team from Pennsylvania and settled in Batavia. Batavia was also the site of the first store, saw mill, and log schoolhouse in 1834, the first church in 1835, and the first flour mill in 1837. The first taverns were in Aurora, Geneva, and Elgin in 1836, and the first library was in Aurora in 1837. The first newspaper was in St. Charles in 1841 (*St. Charles Patriot*). Interestingly, the first medical school in Illinois was founded in St. Charles in 1842. The Franklin Medical School operated at the northeast corner of First Avenue and Main Street for

An 1871 bird's-eye view of Elgin looking east from the Fox River (Elgin Historical Society)

seven years before it closed following community violence over student theft of cadavers from local cemeteries.[6]

The first road into Kane County was Army Trail Road, created by General Winfield Scott's troops traveling from Fort Dearborn (Chicago) to the Mississippi River during the Blackhawk War in 1832. Army Trail Road survives today in part and enters Kane County through the Village of Wayne, terminating at Route 25. The first surveyed road was Galena Road between Chicago and Galena, which ran through Aurora in 1834. A northern route was created through Elgin in 1836. A remnant of the southern route is Galena Road in Montgomery/Aurora. A stagecoach began between Aurora and Elgin and between Chicago and Galena in 1837. Initial mail delivery for the county was by horseback to Geneva once every two weeks. In those early days, a wagon ride from Elgin to Chicago took eight hours.[7]

Joseph McCarty, the first settler in Aurora in 1834, purchased a neighbor's claim of 400 acres for $60. By 1840, the price of an acre of land was 25¢ to $1.25 and by 1908 it was $90 to $125. One hundred and sixty acres was thought to make a good farm. Horses cost $50 to $80, and oxen and cows $25 to $30 in 1837. Wages for general labor were $1.25 per day. A teacher could make $14 to $20 per month for three to four months in the winter.

Early County Government

A committee of three members of the Illinois legislature selected the Village of La Fox (Geneva) as the Kane County Seat because James Herrington's log Tavern and Inn, located on the corner of State and River streets facing the Fox River, had the only post office in the county. Herrington's Tavern also served as the site of the first court proceedings. On June 4, 1836, 180 men gathered at Herrington's Tavern to elect officials for the new county: three commissioners, a sheriff, a recorder of deeds, a coroner, and a surveyor.[8]

The first circuit court session was held at Herrington's on June 19, 1837. Judge John Pearson presided. He was the first judge of the circuit that included Kane, but he was not a county resident. The first court term lasted three days, during which there were five jury trials, fourteen judgments entered, twenty cases continued, and five dismissed. The first jury trial was that of *Wilson v. Wilson* (no relation to each other) for what today would be false imprisonment. The jury assessed damages at $4,160.66, likely an amount equal to all the money in circulation in the county at that time.[9] The case was tried for the plaintiff by John Dean Caton, a lawyer from Ottawa who would later serve on the Illinois Supreme Court from 1842 to 1864. He sat as a circuit judge in Kane County on occasion during those early years when Supreme Court justices traveled to county seats and "held circuit."

In 1837, the county offices were moved out of Herrington's Tavern into a new log courthouse on the northeast corner of Fourth and State streets in the renamed community of Geneva. The total construction cost for this courthouse was $3,000. Seven years later, Kane County had outgrown these quarters and a new courthouse, constructed of quarry stone, was built on the site of the present Geneva City Hall on the west side of what is now Illinois Route 31.[10] The second courthouse cost approximately $3,000 to build and equip.[11] As was common in the day, the courthouse included all county offices and records, including the sheriff and jail.

The Illinois Constitution of 1848 empowered counties to change their form of government, and the residents of Kane County, mostly from New England, chose the county-township form, with sixteen townships created as a result.[12] Eleven of those sixteen townships are depicted in murals gracing the third floor of the current (fourth) courthouse on Third Street in Geneva.

Kane County's first courthouse was built in 1837 at the northeast corner of Fourth and State streets in Geneva. (Geneva Historical Society)

Top: Kane County's first court session was held above Herrington's Tavern on June 19, 1837. Herrington's Tavern was located on the corner of State and River streets facing the Fox River. (Geneva Historical Society)

The First Attorneys

With the establishment of county government, attorneys began to arrive in the Fox Valley to practice law in the frontier community. The first lawyer in

Kane County constructed its second courthouse of quarry stone in 1844 on the site of the present Geneva City Hall on the west side of Route 31 between James and State streets. (Geneva Historical Society)

Kane County's third courthouse was built between 1854 and 1856 on the site of the current Third Street courthouse. (Geneva Historical Society)

Drawing of the 1856 courthouse (Geneva Historical Society)

Kane County was Benjamin F. Fridley (1810 to 1898) who arrived in Aurora in 1835 and built a log cabin along the Fox River south of Ashland Avenue. He was followed in 1837 by Caleb A. Buckingham, H. N. Chapman, and S. S. Jones in Geneva and St. Charles and in 1839 by A. R. Dodge in Aurora. Fridley also was the first elected sheriff of Kane County in 1836 and later served as state's attorney for nine years in a district that included Kane and eleven other counties.

The first elected resident judge for the county was Isaac G. Wilson, who began his term as a judge of the circuit court in the summer of 1851. Wilson was the model of a frontier judge. A native of Middlebury, New York, and the son of a judge, he earned his undergraduate degree at Brown University in 1838, moved to Chicago to join his father, and then went back east to Harvard College to study law. He passed the Massachusetts Bar in 1841, returned to Illinois and began practicing law in Elgin. In practice for ten years, he was elected judge in 1851 and served for nearly seventeen years in a district that included multiple counties.[13]

At Aurora—James G. Barr, O. M. Bates (law student), S. W. Brown, O. D. Day, S. N. Dickinson, B. F. Fridley, A. C. Gibson, John Little (law student), Charles J. Metzner, R. G. Montony, William R. Parker, Samuel Parker (law student), B. F. Parks, E. A. Prichard, A. E. Searles, N. J. Smith, James Van Allen (law student), L. R. Wagner.

At Batavia—Judge Samuel D. Lockwood, Thomas C. Moore, Charles Wheaton.

At Elgin—John Calvert, F. Colby, Edmund Gifford, A. B. Phiney.

At Geneva—Judge Isaac G. Wilson, Augustus M. Herrington, J. H. Mayborne, W. B. Plato.

At Lodi Station (now Maple Park)—William J. Brown, who was also postmaster.

At St. Charles—Alonzo H. Barry, Judge William D. Barry, D. L. Eastman, John F. Farnsworth, J. H. Ferguson, S. S. Jones.

List of practicing attorneys in Kane County in 1858 (Joslyn and Joslyn, History of Kane County, Illinois*)*

Riding Circuit

Not all communities had experienced lawyers in the 1830s and 1840s. Attorneys capable of conducting trials and handling important cases were in demand, and they would travel between nearby counties to represent clients. Judges and state's attorneys were assigned to districts that included multiple counties, and they would likewise travel from one county seat to the next. Circuit riders would set out by horseback, frequently putting twenty-five or thirty miles behind them by nightfall, crossing streams at fords or swimming if necessary. The difficulty of travel varied depending on weather, trail conditions, and the health of the horses. At the end of the day, accommodations would be sought in log cabin taverns or in the log cabin homes of area residents, who commonly made room for weary travelers.

S. S. Jones arrived in Kane County in 1837. (Geneva Historical Society)

The evening for circuit riders was often a social event. Occasionally music would be played or a mock trial presented, but storytelling was clearly the most common activity. "Frequently a quite ordinary incident would be dressed up and so embellished as to be exceedingly ludicrous and amusing," one circuit rider recalled. Abraham Lincoln was said to have sharpened his reputation for storytelling in nighttime revels on the Illinois circuit.[14]

Circuit practice was said to require a "quickness of thought and rapidity of action." Lawyers would be presented with new cases upon arrival at the county seat and often had to complete documents or pleadings or proceed immediately with hearing or trial, learning about the case as it progressed.[15]

As a vestige of the days of circuit practice, the courthouse for the Second District Appellate Court in Elgin, built in 1966, includes on the second floor four bedrooms and a kitchen to accommodate justices required to travel long distances.

Thomas Ford served as governor of Illinois from 1842 until 1846. (Geneva Historical Society)

Early Crime and Early Punishment

Criminal activity in the fledging days of the county reflected the economic realities of the era. Horse thievery, claim jumping, log cabin burning, and lar-

The home of Isaac G. Wilson was built in 1876 at 328 South Second Street in Geneva. Wilson was the first resident circuit judge in Kane County and served from 1851 to 1869 in that capacity. (Geneva Historical Society)

ceny were common offenses. At a time when horses were essential for transportation and farming and often served as payment for legal services, stealing horses was one of the worst crimes one could commit. Kane County had an early law offering a $50 reward (approximately three months' pay) for the apprehension and conviction of persons "stealing a horse, mare, or mule within the limits of Kane County." Horse thieves were punished at a whipping post behind the courthouse or by terms in the penitentiary, then located in Alton.[16]

Isaac G. Wilson served as Kane County's first resident circuit judge, commencing in 1851. (Geneva Historical Society)

A story is told that in Vandalia (the second state capital), an adjournment for dinner was called just after a man was convicted of horse-stealing and just before his motion for a new trial was heard. Before leaving the bench, the judge whispered to the sheriff, "Take that rascal out behind the courthouse and give him forty lashes . . . and tell him if he is ever caught again. . . you will give him twice as much." The whipping was administered and the defendant released. Court resumed after dinner, and the defense attorney made his argument for a new trial not knowing that his client had already been punished. A horrified defendant heard the plea and cried out, "For God's sake, don't get a new trial." The judge explained what had happened but encouraged the attorney to continue because, "I am inclined to be with you and I think another whipping would do him good."[17]

The first death penalty in Kane County was carried out in 1855, when John Collins was hung from gallows constructed several blocks southwest of the second courthouse on Route 31 and just north of the present Chicago & Northwestern railroad tracks. The sheriff escorted the prisoner from the courthouse jail to the gallows where a large crowd had gathered. The

EARLY KANE COUNTY JUDGES AND LAWYERS.

R. G. MONTONY.	P. N. BOTSFORD.	B. F. PARKS.
J. F. FARNSWORTH.	I. G. WILSON.	B. F. FRIDLEY.
E. S. JOSLYN.	A. M. HERRINGTON.	J. H. MAYBORNE.
A. H. BARRY.	F. G. GARFIELD.	SYLVANUS WILCOX.

Above and opposite page: Portraits of early Kane County judges and lawyers prior to 1900 (Joslyn and Joslyn, History of Kane County, Illinois*)*

EARLY KANE COUNTY JUDGES AND LAWYERS.

S. D. LOCKWOOD.	J. G. BARR.	A. S. BABCOCK.	L. R. WAGNER.
O. D. DAY.	R. M. IRELAND.	LUTHER DEARBORN.	W. F. LYNCH.
JAMES COLEMAN.	S. S. JONES.	A. G. M'DOLE.	T. E. RYAN.
CHARLES WHEATON.	J. W. RANSTEAD.	E. C. LOVELL.	J. S. WILCOX.

atmosphere was like a "Fourth of July celebration." The sheriff cut the rope with a hatchet, dropping a heavy iron weight that swiftly jerked Mr. Collins a foot off the wooden platform. He was pronounced dead after hanging thirty minutes. Collins had been charged with killing his wife while intoxicated. The execution was carried out two months after his conviction.[18]

The Klink Wagon Shop at 301 West Main Street in St. Charles is also believed to be one of several stations of the underground railroad. Antique Market II currently occupies the building.

Joseph Whelpley Churchill, Esq.

One of the early attorneys to practice in the county was Joseph Whelpley Churchill, a Vermont native who settled in Batavia as its first lawyer in 1838. Then thirty-seven years old, Churchill married Delia Wilson, the daughter of a Kane County pioneer and sister of Judge Isaac G. Wilson of Geneva. At a time when Kane County and northern Illinois were undergoing a land rush, it was of little surprise that Churchill's first client was VanNortwick, Barker, House & Company, a group of eastern investors interested in purchasing land in Kane County. Congressional passage of the Distribution Preemption Act of 1837, a measure designed to jump-start the economy in the wake of the Panic of 1837, allowed settlers to purchase up to 160 acres of land at no more than $1.25 an acre.[19] The legislation was a real boon to the legal community in northern Illinois, and Churchill was very busy from 1838 to 1843 buying parcels of land, arranging for surveys under federal legislation passed in 1842, registering deeds, and handling debt collections related to the purchases.[20]

Churchill established a tradition of Kane County attorneys serving their fellow citizens in legislative and political positions. Churchill, a Democrat, served in the Eleventh General Assembly in the House of Representatives at the Illinois capital of Vandalia from early December 1838 to March 1839. Churchill was elected with 231 votes to represent the area that became DeKalb, Kane, and LaSalle counties. He served the second session of his term from December 9, 1839, to February 3, 1840, at the capital in Springfield.[21]

In 1841, Isaac Wilson, Churchill's brother-in-law and later a judge, was named Geneva's first postmaster. Wilson set up shop in Churchill's law office downtown. By 1850, Churchill was the second-richest person in Batavia, behind John VanNortwick, the area's leading industrialist and Churchill's long-time client.[22]

In his later years with the bar, Churchill practiced in Kane County's third courthouse. When the community outgrew the 1844 courthouse, the county board let bids for a new building on Third Street in Geneva. Designed by John M. Van Osdel of Chicago, the three-story limestone building with its ornate cupola towered over the Kane County countryside. Van Osdel, regarded as the first Chicago architect, also designed the Palmer House in Chicago, the Illinois Executive Mansion in Springfield, and the old McHenry County Courthouse.[23]

The construction of the new courthouse had been precipitated by an 1852 political row over moving the county seat from Geneva to St. Charles. One local newspaper charged that the 1844 courthouse in Geneva was "quite inadequate to the wants of the county, and the jail is a disgrace to humanity."[24]

The Lincoln Factor

What little is known about the practice of law in Kane County and northern Illinois in the middle years of the nineteenth century is because Abraham Lincoln enjoyed a successful legal career in the area during the 1840s and 1850s prior to his 1860 election to the White House. An Indiana native who grew up in Kentucky, America's sixteenth president spent most of his adult life in Illinois before leaving Springfield for Washington in the spring of 1861.

By 1858, Abraham Lincoln had been a practicing attorney for twenty-two years. After he lost the 1832 election for the Illinois General Assembly, Lincoln considered a career in law but decided against it because he thought he needed more education to succeed as a lawyer. In 1834, he won election as a representative for Sangamon County to the state legislature, and during legislative sessions in Vandalia, he was encouraged by fellow legislator John Todd Stuart to study law. One of Lincoln's colleagues in the General Assembly from 1838 to 1840 was Joseph Whelpley Churchill of Batavia.

In the early nineteenth century, aspiring attorneys typically studied with established members of the bar or served as clerks in law offices to prepare

Bellevue Institute at 333 South Jefferson Street in Batavia was a private sanitarium. In 1875, Mary Todd Lincoln was committed there by her son after a jury declared her insane ten years after the assassination of her husband, President Abraham Lincoln. (Batavia Depot Museum)

Slavery

The single most controversial issue in Illinois and the rest of America in the middle years of the nineteenth century was slavery. It consumed American politics and our culture.

The people of Kane County were largely opposed to slavery and strongly condemned the Fugitive Slave Act passed by Congress in 1850, a law that criminalized helping slaves to freedom with penalties of fines and imprisonment and that required residents of free states to return slaves to their owners.[31]

One reflection of that spirit was the Kane County Anti-Slavery Society, founded in 1842. It had 180 members actively advocating for abolition. Meetings were held and resolutions were adopted opposing slavery and its extension. One prominent abolitionist to speak in Aurora was Frederick Douglass. He was scheduled to speak opposite U.S. Senator Stephen A. Douglas, but Stephen Douglas took ill, disappointing the large crowd at the First Congregational Church. In another instance, a series of abolition lectures was delivered at the 1856 Kane County Courthouse. Pro-slavery men threatened to disrupt the speaker. Local attorneys John F. Farnsworth of St. Charles and Issac Preston of Aurora guarded the anteroom of the courthouse with lead "slugshots" encased in old socks in the event the crowd tried to interfere.[32]

Another reflection of that spirit was the contribution of Kane County anti-slavery activists to formation of the Republican Party, whose birth was predicated on slavery opposition. On August 10, 1850, a Whig party meeting was held in Geneva at which resolutions were passed opposing the extension of slavery in any manner and supporting various anti-slavery candidates and positions. Just over four years later, on August 19, 1854, with the Whig party fracturing over slavery, a Republican county convention was held in Geneva followed by a Republican congressional convention in Aurora. Both conventions resulted in emphatic resolutions and platforms opposing slavery and its expansion. It was these meetings that led some to claim that Kane County was the true birthplace of the Republican Party.[33]

A further reflection of the abolitionist spirit in Kane County was the existence of the underground railroad, believed to have run through the Fox Valley. A loose network of people and places active in helping slaves to freedom in Canada, the underground railroad helped many African Americans who fled slavery. Those who helped were referred to as "conductors," and the temporary hideouts were called "stations." One historian described it as a strange road whose charter came from God. The conductors were volunteers whose reward would come not in this life but in the next.[34]

Although many safe houses in Kane County are unknown, several have been identified as likely hosts to fleeing slaves. Several of the structures have tunnels, false doorways, or small hideouts. In Aurora, one such location was the 518 South Lake Street home of John Wagner, a member of the strong anti-slavery First Congregational Church. Another station was the home of Deacon William Strong at the intersection of New York Street and Eola Road.[35]

The activities in Kane County reflected the debates taking place nationally. No slavery debate was more famous than the Lincoln-Douglas debates in 1858, a series of formal political debates between Abraham Lincoln and Stephen A. Douglas. Both gentlemen were engaged in a campaign for one of Illinois' two United States Senate seats. At the time, U.S. senators were elected by state legislatures.

Stephen Douglas, a Democrat, had served as Illinois' U.S. Senator since 1847. Along with Whig Senator Daniel Webster, he had guided the Compromise of 1850 through Congress, a series of laws that attempted to resolve the territorial and slavery controversies arising from the Mexican-American War of 1846–1848.[36]

With this wealth of legislative experience garnered in his years in the Senate, Douglas appeared poised to sweep the series of debates against Lincoln, the small-town lawyer who had served only one term in Congress and had not sponsored any significant legislation during his time there. The debates underscored the importance of the 1858 legislative elections in Illinois, and the resulting selection of a U.S. senator from the state. Then, as today, Congress was almost equally divided between the two major parties, and one senatorial vote was deemed of paramount importance.

The debates were held in seven Illinois towns: Ottawa, Freeport, Jonesboro, Charleston, Galesburg, Quincy, and Alton. They began on August 21 in Ottawa and ended on October 15 in Alton with the main issue discussed in all seven debates being slavery, especially the expansion of slavery into new territories. The debates also mirrored the issues that Lincoln would face in his campaign for the presidency in 1860.

While it is generally agreed that there was no clear winner during the course of the debates, one debate does stand out in terms of its impact on American history. That is the one that was held at Freeport on August 27, which was closely watched by members of the Kane County Bar Association who were in attendance.

At the debate at Freeport, Lincoln forced Douglas to choose between two options, either of which would damage Douglas' popularity and chances of getting reelected. Lincoln asked Douglas to reconcile popular sovereignty with the Supreme Court's *Dred Scott* decision, which returned a slave to slavery who had accompanied his owner to a free state. Douglas responded that the people of a territory could keep slavery out even though the Supreme Court said that the federal government had no authority to exclude slavery, simply by refusing to pass a slave code and other legislation needed to protect slavery.[37]

At the debate in Ottawa, Douglas accused Lincoln and the Republicans of being radical abolitionists and of drafting an anti-slavery platform, which Lincoln had endorsed. In actuality, the "radical" abolitionist resolutions that Douglas referred to were those drafted by the convention held in Kane County.[38] Among those invited by Lincoln to attend the Ottawa debate was Potawatomi Chief Shabbona.

In the fall election, the Democrats won a narrow majority of seats in the Illinois General Assembly and then proceeded to re-appoint Douglas to the United States Senate. Although Lincoln lost the 1858 senate race, the debates placed him squarely in the national spotlight. And that newly won prominence would lead to his election as president of the United States two years later and ultimately to the Emancipation Proclamation in 1863.

The Durant House located at 100 South Third Street in St. Charles is believed to have been a station on the underground railroad in the 1850s. It has undergone several renovations and is now the Norris Funeral Home. (Preservation Partners of the Fox Valley)

for a legal career. Churchill, who had graduated from Vermont's Middlebury College in the early 1830s, studied law under the son of Revolutionary War hero Ethan Allen.

Lincoln had no such opportunity in New Salem on Illinois' frontier. Instead, he borrowed law books from Stuart's law office in Springfield and read them while the legislature was not in session.[25] Like most of his contemporaries, Lincoln read *Blackstone's Commentaries* and various legal pleading and practice treatises to become familiar with the forms of action and the legal system. On March 24, 1836, the Sangamon County Circuit Court in Springfield certified that Lincoln was a person of good moral character. This certification was the first of several steps to becoming a lawyer in Illinois. On September 9, 1836, the Illinois Supreme Court examined Lincoln's competence and issued him a license to practice law in all of the courts in the state, which was the final step to becoming an attorney in nineteenth-century Illinois.[26]

Lincoln's legal career encompassed three successive formal partnerships. From 1837 to 1841, he was a junior partner with John Todd Stuart; from 1841 to 1844, he practiced as a junior partner with Stephen T. Logan; and from 1844 to 1861, he formed a practice with William H. Herndon with himself as senior partner.

During Lincoln's association with John Stuart, his practice consisted primarily of debt-related matters—much as Churchill's practice in Batavia involved land debt—and he also handled a variety of legal actions in the criminal, common law, and chancery divisions. Stuart and Lincoln both traveled the First Judicial Circuit, and when Sangamon County became part of the newly formed Eighth Judicial Circuit in 1839, Lincoln rode that circuit as well.

Lincoln in Aurora

Abraham Lincoln was known to represent clients in the frontier community of Aurora as early as 1851. Pioneer Charles Hoyt, who ran a grocery store on River Street and also owned the Black Hawk Flour Mill on the Fox River, retained Lincoln to represent him in a water rights lawsuit involving several other mill owners along the river.

Isabelle Landry, a longtime Aurora resident, was a seven-year-old girl in 1851 when Lincoln visited the Hoyt store to confer with the owners about the riparian rights suit. Landry was in the store that day when Lincoln came in, accompanied by Judge Columbus Pinney of Aurora. "This little girl can sing," Hoyt told his two guests, "and she can sing in French, too." Judge Pinney lifted Landry onto a chair, and she sang an operatic aria, "Little Flower of the Wood."[27]

Landry remembered that Lincoln was exceedingly tall with a tall stovepipe hat, but that the sleeves of his coat were much too short. After she had finished singing, Lincoln took Landry's hand and helped her down. He asked what kind of candy she liked, and when Landry replied that she loved horehound, Lincoln instructed Hoyt to make up a pound of horehound for the little girl and charge it to his account. Not to be outdone, Judge Pinney told Hoyt to put a pound of stick candy into a sack for the little girl.[28]

The case that brought Lincoln to Aurora involved responsibility for maintaining the dams at the north end of Stolp Island in Aurora, as well as the mill race that bisected the island. Lincoln eventually prevailed in the case with the federal court in nearby Chicago.[29]

The Founding of the Kane County Bar Association

Lincoln's practice, while perhaps not typical of most Kane County attorneys in the 1850s, was a model to which the successful attorney in Illinois aspired. The practice of law in nineteenth-century Illinois, even for a lawyer as successful as Abraham Lincoln, was a solitary affair. Most attorneys in the state at the time were sole practitioners; Lincoln himself never had more than one partner in all the years he practiced in the state.

The solitary nature of practice in a day before telephones and e-mail placed a premium on intelligent discourse, and it is little wonder that Kane County's growing corps of attorneys sought the opportunity to socialize with their colleagues up and down the Fox River Valley. In 1858, twenty years before one hundred attorneys from around the nation gathered in Saratoga, New York, to found the American Bar Association, a group of attorneys founded the Kane County Bar Association.

Regarding the formation of the KCBA, J. E. Alschuler, a well-known attorney from Aurora, wrote at the turn of the twentieth century that "so far as the date of the organization of the Kane County Bar Association is concerned, I have to say that it is not truly known. It must have been organized before the admission to the Bar of all of the oldest living members, none of whom can recall the date, even approximately. When we were admitted, it was just there!"[30]

Regardless of the ambiguity of the Association's founding date, it is generally accepted that by 1858 there was an organization catering to the needs of the Kane County attorneys. There were thirty-two lawyers and four law students practicing in Kane County at the time. By forming the KCBA, those thirty-two attorneys embarked upon a mission to develop and promote the practice of law in Kane County, a mission that would ebb and flow over the next 150 years, but would ultimately succeed beyond the most optimistic expectations.

Home of attorney, congressman, and civil war general John F. Farnsworth in St. Charles in 1871. The house was built on the west side of Route 31 on the site that later became Mount St. Mary Academy. (Geneva Historical Society)

CHAPTER 2

The Early Bench and Bar

For the legal community in the Fox River Valley, the defining event of the second half of the nineteenth century was the Civil War. For four long years, from 1861 to 1865, the nation's energies were channeled into a great battle that would settle decades-long questions concerning slavery and states' rights.

Members of the Kane County Bar, present and future, would take their worldview from places most Americans had never heard of prior to 1861: Pea Ridge, Perrysburg, Chancellorsville, Gettysburg, Chickamauga, The Wilderness. The crucible of war would dictate the course of Kane County, Illinois, and American politics for the next fifty years.

Kane County's attorneys and attorneys-to-be flocked to the Union colors in 1861 and 1862.

Attorney, physician, and civil war soldier Alexander C. Little of Aurora was admitted to the bar in 1867. (Geneva Historical Society)

Alexander C. Little of Aurora, who had aspired to become a doctor and who actually completed his studies at Iowa College in Keokuk just before the Confederates fired on Ft. Sumter, decided to put aside all business and personal considerations and enlisted in the Union Army in July 1862. He became a member of the 127th Illinois Volunteer Infantry, which was assigned to General William Tecumseh Sherman's division. Little saw action at the Battle of Chickasaw Bayou and Arkansas Post and then went to Vicksburg to serve with General Ulysses Grant. Upon completion of that campaign, he again served under General Sherman during his march to Atlanta and at the battle of Kenesaw Mountain. He ended the war serving with the Second Missouri Engineer Corps of the Army of the Tennessee. Little was finally mustered out of the service on June 5, 1865, and returned to Aurora to complete his schooling at Antioch College. He took up the study of law and was admitted to the Kane County Bar in 1867.[1]

John F. Farnsworth, who was admitted to the practice of law in 1843, located to St. Charles in that same year to begin his professional career. In 1856, he was elected to the first of two terms in Congress, and at the 1860 Republican convention in Chicago, he helped nominate Abraham Lincoln for president.

When the Civil War began, Farnsworth left St. Charles in October 1861 in command of the Eighth Illinois Cavalry, a regiment of 1,200 soldiers. In November 1862, Colonel Farnsworth was promoted to the rank of brevet brigadier general and served at the Battle of Fredericksburg the next month. He left the service for medical reasons and resigned his commission in March 1863. Re-elected to Congress in 1862, Farnsworth resumed his old seat in Washington and served in the U.S. House of Representatives until 1872. After his defeat in the election of 1872, Farnsworth resumed his law practice, eventually moving from St. Charles to Chicago.[2]

The home of attorney, circuit clerk, and civil war major Charles Brown Wells was built in 1850 at 220 South Third Street in Geneva. The house later became Geneva's first hospital. (Geneva Historical Society)

Charles Brown Wells of Geneva was elected circuit clerk in 1848, serving until 1852. In 1859 and 1860, he also represented Geneva Township on the board of supervisors. After the war broke out, Wells enlisted as a private in Company I, Fifty-second Regiment of the Illinois Volunteers. Promoted to lieutenant and then captain, he served with General Ulysses Grant at the capture of Fort Donelson and during various engagements around the Confederate rail center at Corinth, Mississippi, culminating in the siege and capture of Vicksburg. Wells was later attached to General William T. Sherman's army and participated in the capture of Atlanta, Georgia, in 1864 and the subsequent "March to the Sea." In July 1865, Wells was honorably discharged with the rank of

The home of prominent attorney Augustus M. Herrington was constructed in 1851 at 416 South First Street in Geneva. A. M. Herrington was the son of James and Charity Herrington, Geneva's founding family. (Geneva Historical Society)

major. Following the war, he returned to Geneva and resumed his law practice.[3]

Terence E. Ryan served as a member of the 141st Illinois Volunteer Infantry before his admission to the bar in 1871. (Joslyn and Joslyn, History of Kane County, Illinois*)*

Another young man who answered the call, albeit briefly, was Terence E. Ryan, who enlisted in 1864 when he was seventeen years of age. He served as a member of the 141st Illinois Volunteer Infantry, serving as a corporal until the end of the war. After discharge, he studied law under William D. Barry at St. Charles and was admitted to the bar in October 1871.[4]

Back home, other members of the Kane County Bar provided for the smooth running of county government during a time of war. The Kane County Board of Commissioners appointed a War Committee in the summer of 1861 to appropriate money for horses, equipment, bounties, and benefits of the families of local soldiers.[5]

Members of the Kane County legal community, such as Little, Farnsworth, Wells, Ryan, and dozens like them, were typical of the young men who answered President Lincoln's call for volunteers to serve in the Union Army during the sectional crisis that rent the nation asunder. They served their country to the best of their abilities. Many never came back. More than 600,000 Union and Confederate soldiers died during the four years of the Civil War, a number equivalent to six million today.[6] Elgin, a village in 1860, lost sixty-six of its sons to battle casualties and disease during the war.

Home of county judge Richard Botsford at 111 North Channing Street in Elgin. The home was built for $10,000 in 1871, which is the equivalent today of almost $1,000,000. (Elgin Historical Society)

When the fighting was finished and peace had been restored, they came home to either begin or resume legal careers. The Kane County that they returned to was changing rapidly, and the relentless march of industrialization would mark Kane County's history for the next half-century.

The Gilded Age

Historians call the second half of the nineteenth century "the Gilded Age." In the forty years after the Civil War, America evolved from a rural, agrarian society into one of the world's industrial powerhouses, marked in many quarters by extravagant displays of wealth. Steel mills, coal mines, and railroads all contributed to this rapid industrialization.

Kane County typified the national march to industrial prominence. Aurora in the southern end of the county and Elgin in the north became two of the more heavily industrialized cities in the state of Illinois during the latter years of the nineteenth century and the early years of the twentieth century.

The initial tie that began to bind the cities of Kane County together was provided by the railroads. The first railroad serving Kane County was the Galena and Chicago Union Railway (later the Chicago & Northwestern), which initially went through Elgin in 1848. The Aurora Branch Railroad (later the Chicago, Burlington & Quincy) connected to the Chicago-Galena line at West Chicago in 1851. The current main line of the Chicago & Northwestern (now the Union Pacific) from Geneva to Chicago was completed in 1853. The current main line of the Burlington (now Burlington Northern Santa Fe) from Aurora to Chicago was built in 1864. Rail transportation reduced the travel time to Chicago from eight hours to one hour and twenty-five minutes.

St. Charles, by contrast, was without a railroad until 1871, when a branch line from Geneva was constructed. The city, however, remained without a direct connection to Chicago until the 1880s, when the Chicago Great Western Railway reached the Fox River Valley. By 1896, streetcar or trolley lines ran about forty miles along the Fox River connecting Carpentersville to Yorkville and also connecting the street car systems in Aurora and Elgin. With

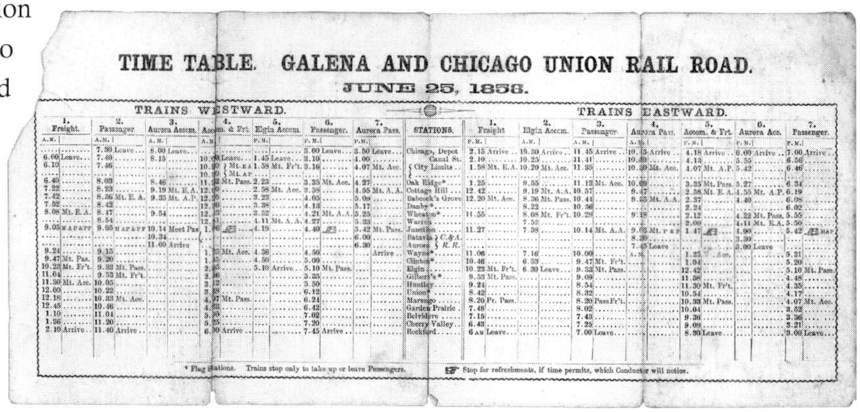
TIME TABLE. GALENA AND CHICAGO UNION RAIL ROAD.
JUNE 25, 1856.
TRAINS WESTWARD. TRAINS EASTWARD.

The Galena and Chicago Union Railroad timetable from June 25, 1856. The Galena and Chicago Union was the first railroad to serve Kane County. It later became the Chicago & Northwestern and is now the Union Pacific. (Geneva Historical Society)

Chicago & Northwestern train crossing the Fox River in Geneva, c. 1900 (Geneva Historical Society)

An 1884 Chicago & Northwestern Railway ticket between Geneva and Chicago for a Republican rally, including the presidential race between Republican James Blaime and Democrat Grover Cleveland. (Geneva Historical Society)

the addition of this means of transportation, St. Charles was now brought into the "community" of towns in Kane County, enabling attorneys to travel more easily to the county courthouse in nearby Geneva.

Nineteenth-century Illinois residents believed that if a city was to grow and prosper, a manufacturing base must become an integral part of a municipality's development, and Aurora was no exception. One of the earliest and largest manufacturing facilities to be located in the area was the repair shops of the Chicago, Burlington & Quincy Railroad, which opened in 1855. By 1910, the shops covered seventy acres and employed 2,400 people.

Other businesses in Aurora ran the gamut of the manufacturing spectrum. The Aurora Silver Plate Manufacturing Company was founded in 1870 for the purpose of making silver-plated tableware. The Chicago & Aurora Smelting & Refining Company started operations in North Aurora in 1882, bringing bullion from western mines and separating the gold and silver from the lead and other waste metals. The Love Brothers Foundry commenced operations in 1878 as a general foundry with a specialty in architectural iron.

In contrast, the most important new venture started in Elgin in 1864 was the Elgin National Watch Company, which eventually became the world's largest watch manufacturing complex, spreading the name of Elgin across much of the industrialized world. By 1908, the company employed 3,500 people and produced 2,500 watches daily.[7]

The railroad was also instrumental in establishing Kane County as a prominent dairy region around this time. The Chicago hotels were a major consumer of the milk, butter, and cheese from the northern Kane County area, and the railroads provided rapid transportation for the fresh dairy products that were shipped daily into the city. The Elgin Board of Trade even established butter prices throughout the entire country.[8]

Chicago & Northwestern Railway Geneva depot, c. 1900 (Geneva Historical Society)

Train crew inside one of two roundhouses at the Chicago, Burlington & Quincy yards in Aurora, c. 1870 (Aurora Historical Society)

Elgin National Watch Company became the world's largest watch manufacturer. It operated from 1866 to 1964 on the east side of the river between National Street on the north and May Street on the south. (Elgin Historical Society)

W. H. Howell Sadiron Works foundry workers pose with a coal delivery. The foundry was located on the west bank of the Fox River near the State Street bridge in Geneva, c. 1880. (Geneva Historical Society)

In 1866, Gail Borden built a condensed milk factory whose products became widely known. Borden had originally obtained a patent in 1856 for condensing milk, and when the Civil War intensified the demand for powdered milk, he opened plants in Connecticut, New York City, and Elgin, Illinois.

Other Elgin industries included a large shoe factory and a number of grain mills. In 1872, the city attracted a major state institution, the Northern Illinois Hospital for the Insane, known for years simply as Elgin State Hospital.[9] The Dundee Brick Company was established in 1852. It later evolved into Haegar Brick and now Haegar Pottery and was a major supplier of brick for rebuilding Chicago after the Great Fire in 1871.[10]

As the nineteenth century evolved into the twentieth century, it was clear that Kane County had established its own identity with its manufacturing base and developing legal community. In the years to come, that prominence would grow and enable the Kane County Bar Association to take its place as one of the preeminent bar associations in the State of Illinois.

Dealing With Growth

The industrialization of Kane County in the years following the Civil War brought a sudden increase in population as people came to the area looking

State Street in Geneva looking east from Third Street during the 1890s (Geneva Historical Society)

for jobs in mills and factories. With the migration of industry to the northern and southern ends of the county, the tri-cities areas of Geneva, Batavia, and St. Charles remained largely rural.

The population and industrial growth in the county created a corresponding growth in practice opportunities for the legal community. The growth of railroads and manufacturing facilities created new or expanded work in corporate law, property rights, commercial transactions, patent and trademark, and passenger and employee safety. With the advent of the automobile at the dawn of the twentieth century, accidents at crossings and elsewhere greatly expanded the field of litigation, a field in which Kane County attorneys would become well respected.

Shareholder suits were also becoming more common as groups of shareholders, unhappy with their boards of directors, began to flex their collective muscles to force improvements in the operation of companies in which they held an interest. The growth of population likewise contributed to the expansion of practice in such fields as real estate, estates and trusts, family matters, and land-use planning as property gradually changed from farming to commercial, industrial, and residential use.

Downtown Aurora in 1893, looking east along Downer Place from the top of the City Hall and Court of Common Pleas building (Aurora Historical Society)

The 1856 courthouse was located at the site of the current courthouse on South Third Street in Geneva. (Geneva Historical Society)

A New Courthouse

Enthusiasm about the growth of the legal community was pushed aside on the night of March 13, 1890, when the Kane County Courthouse burned to the ground. The *Beacon News* reported two days later that "Kane County's venerable Temple of Justice, which has been the repository of the county records for the last thirty-four years, and whose walls have oft resounded with the eloquence of the learned expositors of the law, now lies a mass of blackened ruins."[11] Although the cause of the fire was never determined, speculation included a prisoner, a lawyers' party, and spontaneous combustion. Fortunately, the records of the recorder, the county clerk, and the circuit clerk were locked in fireproof vaults and were not damaged.[12] For the next two years, the county rented a house at Second and

A fire on March 13, 1890, destroyed the 1856 courthouse, which was the third courthouse built in Kane County. (Geneva Historical Society)

Campbell streets. Clerks were crowded into various rooms and judges coped by holding court in the dining room until the new and current courthouse was completed on the same Third Street site in 1892.[13]

Construction of the massive four-story courthouse, regarded as one of the finest in Illinois, signaled a new and expanded era in the practice of law in Kane County. The Kane County Board reached out to the Chicago architectural firm of Edbrooke and Burnham to design the courthouse, with its massive square dome towering over the enclosed rotunda. Willoughby Edbrooke and Franklin Burnham were best known for their work on the Georgia State Capitol Building in Atlanta in 1889. The two also designed the U.S. Post Office Building in Washington, D.C., and several buildings on the campus of Notre Dame University.[14] Inside the $195,000 Kane County Courthouse, decorative ironwork railings encircle each floor, and eleven murals of scenes from the county decorate the interior arches of the dome on the fourth floor.[15]

As was the tradition, the new courthouse contained all county offices in addition to the courts. The north hall on the first floor contained the Probate Court on the west side (where the current Chancery Court is) and the probate clerk's office on the east side (where the current Small Claims Court is). The south hall on the first floor contained county offices such as treasurer and recorder of deeds. The sheriff was located on the west side of the first floor (where the circuit clerk is now). The north hall on the second floor contained the Board of Supervisors on the west side and the county clerk's office on the east side (both of these are now occupied by the Mediation Center). The south hall on the second floor contained the superintendent of schools' office on the west side and the circuit clerk's office on the east side.

After the 1890 courthouse fire, the George Patten house on South Second Street in Geneva served as the Kane County Courthouse until the completion of the new courthouse in 1892. (Geneva Historical Society)

The third floor contained the office of the state's attorney on the east side and the law library on the west side. The north side of the third floor (where courtrooms 310 and 320 currently are) was originally one large room housing the County Court. The south side of the third floor (where courtrooms 340 and 350 currently are) also was originally one large space and housed the courtroom for the Circuit Court. Those two large rooms were divided into the present four courtrooms in the mid-1970s, after the county moved into the present Government Center at Route 31 and Third Street in Geneva. The drop ceiling installed during renovations conceal the arched windows and the decorative ceiling work in all four rooms.

The Kane County Legal Community in 1908

By 1908, the Kane County Bar Association had completed its first fifty years of existence. By then, Colonel George Fabyan had built his magnificent estate and game preserve along the west bank of the Fox River in Geneva in 1905, President Teddy Roosevelt had visited Aurora in that city's largest parade in 1903, and Frank Lloyd Wright had built three homes in Geneva and one in Batavia in 1906 and 1907, respectively. The legal community at the time was already composed of a mix of family and corporate firms, some of which traced their roots to the county's earliest days.

The Joslyn family, for example, enjoyed a long history of practicing law in Elgin. Colonel Edward S. Joslyn was described by his contemporaries as one of the ablest lawyers who ever practiced in the courts of Kane County. He served as mayor of Elgin in 1861 and as an alderman from 1855 to 1878. The senior Joslyn also was a member of the Board of Education and city attorney. In addition, he was one of the early state's attorneys of Kane County. A colleague at the time noted that "with his upright honor and integrity, he did much to establish the standard of legal ethics and practice among lawyers that made the word of a Kane County lawyer trustworthy."[17]

President Theodore Roosevelt at the Geneva depot on May 10, 1905 (Geneva Historical Society)

Below, top: Frank W. Joslyn (Joslyn and Joslyn, History of Kane County, Illinois*)*

Below, bottom: R. Waite Joslyn (Joslyn and Joslyn, History of Kane County, Illinois*)*

Colonel Joslyn's two sons, Frank W. and R. Waite, were both attorneys in the city of Elgin. Their partnership was one of the largest practices in the city. Frank W. Joslyn studied law in the office of his father and was admitted to the bar at Ottawa, Illinois, in 1883. He served two terms as Elgin's city attorney and two terms as state's attorney. He also had an enviable record as a criminal lawyer.[18] His brother, R. Waite Joslyn, studied law at the University of Michigan, graduating in 1891 with the degree of Master of Laws. He then practiced in Chicago for ten years before returning to Elgin and forming a law practice with his brother. He was the author of several law books, including *Joslyn on Personal Injuries* and *Corporation Law in Illinois*.[19]

The name of Alschuler has been associated with Kane County legal affairs for almost the entire history of the Bar Association. Samuel Alschuler, who studied law at Aurora, was admitted to the bar before the appellate court at Ottawa in December 1880 and began his practice in 1881. Alschuler made an enviable reputation as an attorney and became affiliated with the firm of Kraus, Alschuler & Holden in Chicago, although he did reside in Aurora. He later ran unsuccessfully for governor of Illinois on the Democratic ticket and served as a judge on the U.S. Seventh Circuit Court of Appeals from 1915 through 1936.

Alschuler's first partner, John C. Murphy, was another bulwark of the legal community in 1908. A native of Grundy County, Illinois, Murphy read law under M. O. Southworth and spent much of the 1880s as a U.S. attorney in Dakota Territory. He returned to Aurora in 1890, entered into a partnership with Samuel Alschuler, and took in Alschuler's brother, Benjamin, when Samuel Alschuler left for practice in Chicago.[20]

Many attorneys of the time practiced law as a side job, engaging in farming, banking, insurance, or real estate as their principal source of income. William Moffett Mercer was typical. One of nine children who grew up on a farm in DeKalb County, Mercer was educated in a seminary in Michigan and then spent much of the 1880s in business in Nebraska. He returned to Kane County as an investor in numerous farms and agricultural enterprises, earned his law degree at Northwestern University Law School in 1901, and moved to Aurora to practice.[21]

O. A. Holcomb, another Aurora attorney, was admitted to the bar in 1889. By 1908, he was one of the better-known real estate investors in the county. "He has devoted much time to other interests," a 1908 biography noted, "being the owner of valuable farming property and also making farm loans. He does an extensive land business in all the surrounding states, handling much valuable property and placing many investments. He also owns real estate in the city and has built several houses here, the rental thereof bringing him a gratifying annual income."[22]

By the turn of the twentieth century, the practice of law in Kane County was beginning to undergo a pronounced change. With the growth of formal law schools, attorneys were becoming much more professional in their practice. And the growth of the nearby metropolis of Chicago was already beginning to spill northwest into Kane County.

Drawing of the 1892 courthouse located on South Third Street in Geneva (Geneva Historical Society)

A 1900 photo of the fourth and current Kane County Courthouse. The decorative balusters along the roofline and the miniature turret caps surrounding the dome no longer exist today. (Geneva Historical Society)

At the same time the courthouse was constructed, a jail was built as a separate structure immediately west of the courthouse, close to the easterly edge of the current parking lot. An underground passage connected the cell block to the basement of the court building. The jail was torn down in approximately 1979, shortly after the new Correctional Center was completed on Fabyan Parkway.

The completion of the new courthouse occurred in the nick of time, because Kane County and northern Illinois were quickly impacted by the onset of the Panic of 1893. Economic conditions in the county, particularly in the manufacturing strongholds of Elgin and Aurora, were slow to recover and manufacturing payrolls were not back to pre-Panic levels until 1895 or later.

Kane County's population doubled between 1870 and 1900, with most of the growth concentrated along the Fox River. What had a generation before been a bucolic farming community light years from the metropolis of Chicago was becoming itself a metropolitan area of nearly 80,000 people by the turn of the new century.[16]

Kane County clerk's office, c. 1890 (Geneva Historical Society)

The Practice of Law a Century Ago

Kane County attorneys in the late nineteenth century had none of the office equipment that their twenty-first-century counterparts have come to rely upon. There were no computers, no Internet, and no multi-function printers and copiers. In fact, most law offices in the county would not acquire typewriters until the early twentieth century. While we are living in an era of unprecedented technological change, those early lawyers witnessed the invention of the light bulb and the telephone. Their revolution in mass communications consisted of the laying of the first transatlantic cable. It was a society without Social Security, Medicare, health insurance, and government regulation. There was no income tax, since government revenues were raised mainly through taxes on imports, tobacco, and alcohol.

Most law firms in Kane County were typically headquartered downtown in a two- or three-story building. Central heating for the building, usually coal from downstate, was just making its presence known, with most offices heated with the legendary pot-bellied stove. Since electric lighting did not become commonplace until late in the nineteenth century, the typical law office in the county was illuminated with gas lighting, which cast a flickering glow over law books spread out on massive wooden tables.

Twelve men serve on a jury in the third-floor circuit courtroom of the current Kane County Courthouse, c. 1895. (Geneva Historical Society)

Cities such as St. Charles, Batavia, Aurora, Geneva, and Elgin all became focal points for early law firms in Kane County. Since the surrounding areas of the county were mostly rural, it made sense for the legal profession to migrate to the cities where the courts were located and the business of the law could be conducted. In addition, when automated communications were finally established, they were initially installed in the cities. The Aurora City Council, for instance, granted a franchise in 1881 to the Chicago Telephone Company to install poles and string wires for a phone system within the city limits. This type of early service was unavailable in the rural areas, providing another incentive for establishing a law practice in the city.

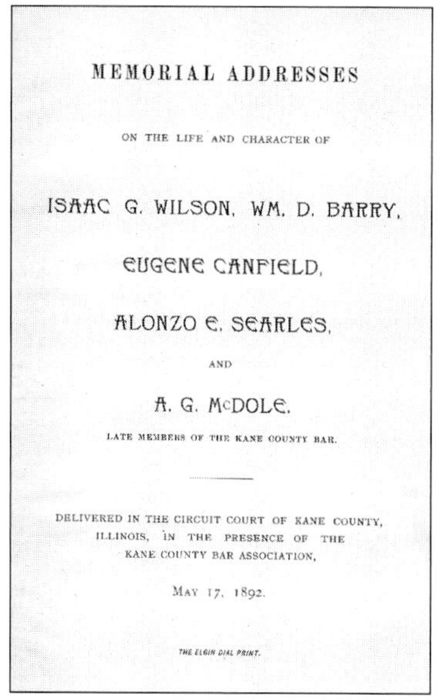

MEMORIAL ADDRESSES

ON THE LIFE AND CHARACTER OF

ISAAC G. WILSON, WM. D. BARRY,

EUGENE CANFIELD,

ALONZO E. SEARLES,

AND

A. G. McDOLE.

LATE MEMBERS OF THE KANE COUNTY BAR.

DELIVERED IN THE CIRCUIT COURT OF KANE COUNTY, ILLINOIS, IN THE PRESENCE OF THE KANE COUNTY BAR ASSOCIATION,

MAY 17, 1892.

THE ELGIN DIAL PRINT.

Transcript of the Kane County Bar Association memorial addresses from May 1, 1892

To ease the burden of travel to the only court in Geneva, a state law was passed in 1857 allowing Aurora and Elgin to establish "inferior courts," the first in Illinois. They were initially called Courts of Common Pleas and later the Aurora and Elgin City Courts. The building housing the Aurora court was completed in 1866 and contained City Hall, the post office, and the city jail. The court had jurisdiction over any case arising within the boundaries of the city. The city courts in Elgin and Aurora were discontinued in 1964, and the Aurora Courthouse was demolished later that year.

Most of the early attorneys in Kane County were self-taught in the law. With established law schools few and far between, many aspiring attorneys "read the law," meaning that they studied law in the office of a senior attorney until they were deemed competent to take the bar exam. In the early days of the legal profession and even into the early part of the twentieth century, there was no requirement that an aspiring attorney had to be a graduate of a law school. This situation changed as law schools were established at many universities by the 1920s and a degree in the study of law became a requirement to take the bar exam.

By the 1920s, lawyers were no longer required to "ride the circuit" to make a living. With the coming of mass communications, the law office was becoming the center of the attorney's practice, which enabled him to service a wider range of clients. By the 1890s, northern Illinois was crisscrossed by a network of electric street railways and interurbans that made it possible for local attorneys to venture into Chicago for a meeting or conference and be home before nightfall. The "Good Roads Movement," which began in the early 1920s and led to the construction of the federal highway system, made travel much easier for both attorney and client. Illinois Route 64 from St. Charles to Chicago was completed in 1920.

Lawyers dined at Valentine Howell's restaurant and ice cream confectionary across from the courthouse on South Third Street in Geneva, c. 1905. (Geneva Historical Society)

Aurora City Hall and Court of Common Pleas building in 1896 after several major renovations. The newly completed post office is located to the right. (Aurora Historical Society)

At the start of the twentieth century, the practice of law in Kane County was becoming a true profession stocked with many talented individuals who would lay the groundwork for the later growth of the Kane County Bar Association.

By the early 1900s, the legal system was now fully equipped to allow Kane County's citizens to air their grievances and seek justice. As the population of Kane County increased and the manufacturing base grew, the attorneys of the area would have to acquaint themselves with new aspects of legal work that were undreamed of when the Bar Association was first founded in 1858.

The dedication of Aurora City Hall and the Court of Common Pleas in 1869. The building was located on Downer Place between the Fox River and Stolp Avenue. (Aurora Historical Society)

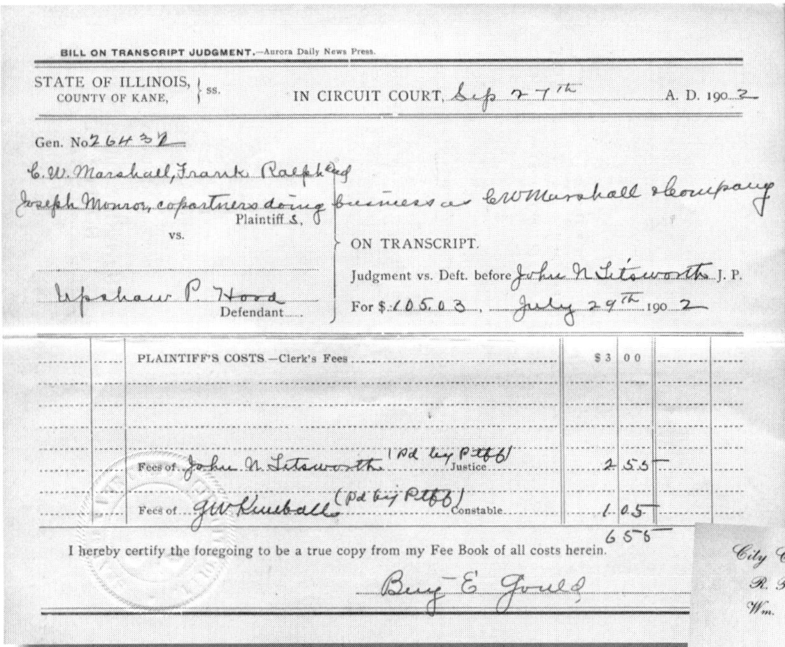

BILL ON TRANSCRIPT JUDGMENT.—Aurora Daily News Press.

STATE OF ILLINOIS, } ss. IN CIRCUIT COURT, Sep 27th A. D. 1902
COUNTY OF KANE,

Gen. No 26437

C. W. Marshall, Frank Ralph and Joseph Monroe, copartners doing business as C W Marshall & Company
Plaintiffs,

vs.

Upshaw P. Hood
Defendant.

ON TRANSCRIPT.
Judgment vs. Deft. before John N. Titsworth J. P.
For $ 105.03, July 29th 1902

PLAINTIFF'S COSTS —Clerk's Fees	$ 3 00
Fees of John N. Titsworth (Pd by Pltff) Justice	2 55
Fees of G W Kimball (Pd by Pltff) Constable	1 05
	6 55

I hereby certify the foregoing to be a true copy from my Fee Book of all costs herein.

Benj E Gould

The September 27, 1902 Bill on Transcript Judgment (Aurora Historical Society)

The Northern Illinois Hospital and Asylum for the Insane in Elgin admitted its first patient on April 3, 1872. The institution was renamed the Elgin State Hospital in 1909 and the Elgin Mental Health Center in 1975.

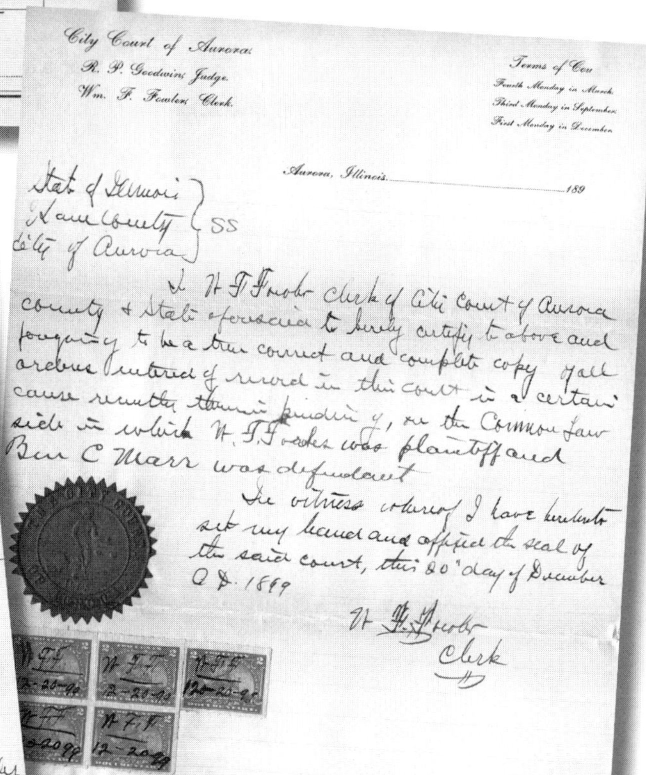

City Court of Aurora.
R. P. Goodwin, Judge.
Wm. F. Fowler, Clerk.

Terms of Court
Fourth Monday in March.
Third Monday in September.
First Monday in December.

Aurora, Illinois, 189

State of Illinois }
Kane County } SS
City of Aurora }

I H F Forbes Clerk of City Court of Aurora county & State aforesaid do hereby certify the above and foregoing to be a true correct and complete copy of all orders entered of record in this court in a certain cause remaining therein pending, on the Common Law side in which H. F. Forbes was plaintiff and Ben C Marr was defendant.

In witness whereof I have hereunto set my hand and affixed the seal of the said court, this 20 day of December A.D. 1899

H F Forbes
Clerk

City Court of Aurora order dated December 20, 1899 (Aurora Historical Society)

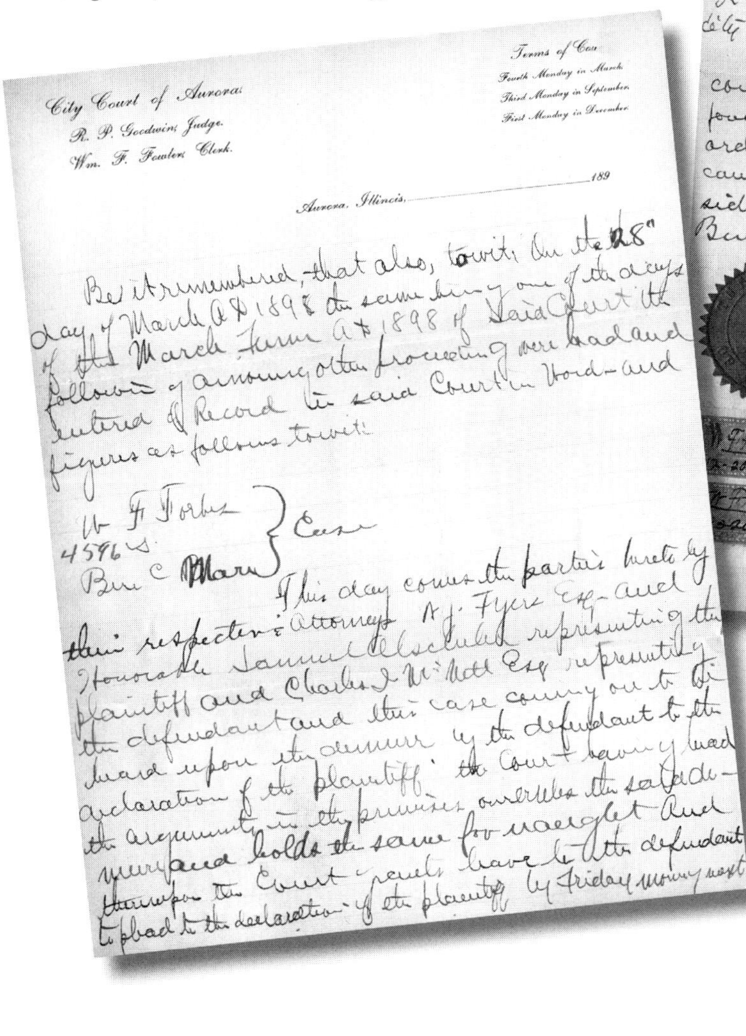

City Court of Aurora.
R. P. Goodwin, Judge.
Wm. F. Fowler, Clerk.

Terms of Court
Fourth Monday in March.
Third Monday in September.
First Monday in December.

Aurora, Illinois, 189

Be it remembered, that also, to wit: On the 28" day of March A.D. 1898 the same being one of the days of the March Term A.D. 1898 of said Court the following among other proceedings were had and entered of Record in said Court in Word and figures as follows to wit:

H F Forbes
4596 } Case
Ben C Marr

This day comes the parties hereto by their respective attorneys A. J. Fyers Esq. and Honorable Samuel Alschuler representing the plaintiff and Charles J. McNott Esq representing the defendant and this case coming on to be heard upon the demurrer of the defendant to the declaration of the plaintiff the Court having heard the argument in the premises overrules the said demurrer and holds the same for naught And thereupon the Court grants leave to the defendant to plead to the declaration of the plaintiff by Friday morning next

A City Court of Aurora order dated December 20, 1899 denies a motion to strike (demur) and orders the defendant to answer the complaint (declaration) in a case in which Samuel Alschuler represented the plaintiff. (Aurora Historical Society)

The Elgin City Hall building in 1898 also contained the City Court of Common Pleas. The building was demolished in 1969. (Elgin Historical Society)

The Love Brothers Foundry could be seen looking north along the east side of the Fox River from the New York Street Bridge. (Aurora Historical Society)

Workers of the Aurora Silver Plate Manufacturing Company (Aurora Historical Society)

Kane County Bench and Bar in 1906

A bird's-eye view of Aurora in 1921, looking northeast with the Chicago, Burlington & Quincy Railroad Roundhouses just north of the New York Street bridge on the right side of the river and the Aurora Cotton Mills on the left side (Aurora Historical Society)

CHAPTER 3

Into the Modern Era: 1908–1958

The Kane County Bar in the first decade of the twentieth century grew with Kane County and northern Illinois. New roads, new industry, and new ideas characterized the region's growth during the period, and the practice of law became a more professional, more specialized calling. Kane County weathered two world wars, an influenza pandemic, the Great Depression, and the beginnings of a cold war in the fifty short years that separated 1908 from 1958.

Kane County and northern Illinois were tied to the Windy City of Chicago during this period by a sophisticated web of electric street railways and a gas and electric utility infrastructure that was controlled by Samuel Insull of Chicago. In the 1910s, attorneys from Aurora, Elgin, and other communities in the Fox Valley could take an interurban electric car or commuter train and be in Chicago's Loop in ninety minutes or less. The Chicago, Aurora and DeKalb Railroad, the Joliet, Plainfield and Aurora Railroad, and the Elgin and Belvidere Electric Company all provided through service from Kane County to Chicago.

In the 1920s, Samuel Insull's Public Service Company of Northern Illinois strung high-voltage electric transmission lines across Kane and DeKalb counties, bringing inexpensive electric power to homes and businesses across the region. In the 1930s and 1940s, the company, now known as NICOR Gas, brought natural gas from the booming new fields of Kansas and Oklahoma to the Fox River Valley.

One big change that impacted the Kane County Bar during the 1920s and the 1930s was the gradual formalization of a law school education as a prerequisite for taking the Illinois Bar. The University of Illinois School of Law, for example, was founded in 1900 and was accorded status as a college of law in 1900.[1] Northwestern University had a law school in the 1890s, and the University of Chicago was the first university in North America to offer a Juris Doctor (J.D.) degree at the turn of the twentieth century. As a result, Progressives in Illinois, Wisconsin, and the Midwest passed legislation in the

Geneva looking east from Third and West State streets in 1911 during the Grand Army of the Republic (G.A.R.) parade commemorating the fiftieth anniversary of the beginning of the Civil War (Geneva Historical Society)

1900s and 1910s requiring attorneys to earn a degree from an accredited school and pass a bar exam in order to practice law.

The reality, however, was that the reputation of the Kane County Bar was burnished during the first half of the twentieth century by attorneys who had never set foot inside a law school classroom.

The Legend of George Carbary

Get any two veteran members of the Kane County Bar Association together and the conversation will inevitably turn to the subject of the legendary George Carbary.

Carbary, perhaps the only attorney in the history of the Kane County Bar Association to make the pages of *Time* magazine, was a legend in the local legal community. Born in May 1888, Carbary decided upon a legal career after completing his high school education. He read law in the law offices of Judge Irwin in the first decade of the twentieth century and was admitted to the Illinois Bar in 1912.

George Carbary ran for re-election in 1932 as the Republican candidate for Kane County state's attorney.

Carbary made his first run for the office of state's attorney in the 1912 elections, running on the Socialist ticket, and lost. He was finally elected state's attorney of Kane County in 1928 on a reform platform, and he served until 1936. "During the election, George Carbary got more votes for state's attorney in Kane County than FDR did for president," remarked Clarence J. Ruddy.[2]

Prohibition was the law of the land from 1920 to 1933, and Carbary pledged to dry up the county in general, and the cities of Elgin and Aurora in particular, the largest cities in Kane County then and now. Upon taking office, Carbary immediately launched a series of raids in the Elgin area. Carefully planned, they led to the arrest of more than thirty violators of the dry law and eight people accused of bookmaking, a form of

Geneva looking southeast from Third and West State streets in 1911 during the G.A.R. parade (Geneva Historical Society)

illegal sports gambling.[3] Taken as evidence were 837 gallons of wine, sixty gallons of whiskey, a large quantity of gin, assorted containers of beer, winepresses, and fifteen gambling machines. For a time, a great thirst prevailed, but the purveyors were soon back in business.[4]

And even if it was the law of the land, that did not mean all members of the Kane County legal community had the same crusading zeal about Prohibition as their colleagues. Despite George Carbary's efforts to clean up the county, Clarence Ruddy recalled years later that "during the Prohibition years, there were always places in Kane County where judges and lawyers could go and get a drink."[5]

Employees of the Kane County Home and Farm, c. 1917. The facility was located on the site of the present Kane County Correctional Center on Fabyan Parkway. Remnants of the building remain. (Geneva Historical Society)

Top: The Kane County Home and Farm was also known as the Alms House and the Poor Farm. The 1900 U.S. Federal Census classified seventy-five of the 139 inmates at the facility as "insane." Other classifications of inmates included simple-minded, idiot, feeble-minded, and foolish. (Geneva Historical Society)

400 Raids

But the operation that landed Carbary in the pages of *Time* magazine took place in Aurora in the first week of April 1929. In a raid on a home in Aurora, which was suspected of doubling as a speakeasy, the Kane County sheriff surrounded the house with deputies and rushed the door. The owner was clubbed into unconsciousness, his wife was shot and killed by a deputy, and the owner's son picked up a gun and shot the sheriff in the leg. Only one gallon of weak wine was found in the raid, with the owner claiming that he had never sold any of the output from his small winepress.[6] In the uproar that followed the raid, Reform State's Attorney Carbary came under fire, but he dismissed the criticism by saying, "The people knew I was going to make raids. I've made 400, and I'm going to make more."[7]

JURY

DEKING FAMILY COUNSEL DEMAND NEW PROSECUTOR

State's Attorney Carbary Promises to Push Case If Deputy Smith Is Indicted.

FAMILY IN OWN INQUIRY

(Picture on back page.)

State's Atty. George W. Carbary announced today that he would lay before the grand jury the complete facts hav-

The March 27, 1929 headline from the Beacon News *regarding the killing of Mrs. Lillian DeKing during a liquor raid authorized by George W. Carbary (*Beacon News*)*

Carbary was more successful in halting the spread of gambling at a dog-racing track named the 102 Ranch. After the track was sold at

Kane County Board of Supervisors inside the Third Street courthouse in Geneva, c. 1910 (Geneva Historical Society)

foreclosure in 1928, the new owners began reconditioning the track for a sixty-day meet. Carbary hit the roof, announcing that "they can open their track and run dogs, but they can't gamble." He was then asked by a deputy sheriff to attend a meeting with three unidentified men to discuss the impasse. At the meeting, one of the men was identified as Al Capone. Nothing was resolved, and after the meeting, Carbary had the deputy fired.[8] The track later burned under mysterious circumstances and was never reopened. It was never proved to be arson, and no one was ever accused of setting the fire.

Kane County Board of Supervisors inside the current Third Street courthouse in Geneva, c. 1910. The space they occupied was on the north side of the second floor in what is now the Arbitration Center. (Geneva Historical Society)

Carbary & Carbary

After George Carbary left public office in 1936, he opened a legal practice in Elgin, practicing alone until his son, Warren, passed the bar in 1949. Father and son then began a joint practice with the firm of Carbary & Carbary. George Carbary remained in practice until his death in 1973 at the age of eighty-five.[9]

Cement workers on the west side of the Third Street courthouse in Geneva (Geneva Historical Society)

During the 1950s and 1960s, Carbary was one of the best-known members of the Kane County Bar. In 1961, according to his grandson, Jonathan, also an attorney, he chaired the committee that was charged with rewriting the criminal code of the State of Illinois.[10]

For much of the 1950s and 1960s, Carbary conducted the ethics interviews of new attorneys who had passed the bar exam. Wendell Clancy recalled meeting Carbary for the first time at his interview. "When I walked in, Mr. Carbary looked at me and remarked, 'With ears that big, you must be Gates Clancy's kid. Go on and get out of here.'"[11]

East side of the Third Street courthouse, c. 1915 (Geneva Historical Society)

Interior of the first floor of the current Third Street courthouse looking southwest, c. 1920s (Geneva Historical Society)

Longtime members of the Bar Association still chuckle when they recount the story of the vagrant that Carbary was charged with defending. Ben Rifken recalled that "George and I were in Justice O'Connor's court one day as he was giving out case files for us to handle. We did that in those days because we didn't have a public defender. George got a case that involved a vagrant and was told by the judge to 'give your client your best advice.' He took the file and then went to meet his client. While George was waiting for his case to be called, he pointed to the courthouse door and advised his client to leave the courthouse, leave the city and get out of Kane County."[12]

When the case was called, Rifken told the story with relish, "Justice O'Connor asked George where his client was. George replied that he had given his client his best advice and told the judge what he had done. Justice O'Connor was known for his short temper, and he almost threw George in jail for contempt. George thought that he had done a good thing because he had spared the court the cost of a trial, they didn't have to feed his client, and the guy never came back to Kane County."[13]

Carbary's practice of the law typified the individual approach to legal affairs in Kane County during the mid-years of the twentieth century. "George Carbary was a product of reading the law in a lawyer's office," Rifken recalled. "He was a tremendous lawyer in front of a jury."[14]

Interior of the circuit courtroom on the south side of the third floor of the Third Street courthouse, c. 1920s. The space was divided into the current two courtrooms in approximately 1975. (Geneva Historical Society)

Paid With a Lawn Mower

An electric trolley passes the east side of the Third Street courthouse in Geneva, c. 1940. (Geneva Historical Society)

The practice of law in Kane County in the first half of the twentieth century was far different than it is today. Many attorneys bartered their services, many senior attorneys still had no formal university legal training, and practitioners typically used public transportation.

Ben Rifken recalled the early days of his practice when he came back from World War II. "I always hoped that my clients would have enough money to pay the bill," Rifken said. "I once defended an indigent awaiting trial on criminal charges, and I was paid with a lawn mower. Another time, I got a drum set as payment for my fee, and I gave the drums to my daughter, who was starting to learn to play them."[15]

With the courthouse centrally located in Geneva, many attorneys with offices in the outlying portions of the county often found it a challenge to make the trip to court in the 1930s and 1940s. Many young lawyers who were just starting their practices could not immediately afford a car so they had to rely on public transportation. "When I was first starting out as a lawyer, I didn't have a car," Rifken said, whose office was located in Elgin at the time. "I would wait at the bus stop, and people who knew who I was would offer

Servicemen leave the Geneva depot on their way to training camp at Fort Grant, Rockford, in September 1917. (Geneva Historical Society)

me a ride to work. When I needed to be at the courthouse in Geneva, I would call up either George Carbary or Judge Seidel and hitch a ride with them and bring all of my files. After a couple of years, I was able to pay for a car with cash. I didn't pay for a car with credit back then."[16]

Lawyers frequented the Lincoln Café on South Third Street near the courthouse in the 1920s. (Geneva Historical Society)

The Postwar Kane County Bar

As World War II ended, many Kane County attorneys who had served in the armed forces returned to resume their legal careers. Many returning veterans also used their G.I. benefits following the war to attend law school, and many attorneys honed legal skills that may have grown rusty while in military service.

Joseph Radovich, who had been admitted to the bar on January 11, 1943, was drafted into the army on March 15, 1943, and served until June 26, 1946. After being discharged, he returned to Geneva and performed title work for Chicago Title and Kane County Title for three years.[17] Working at the title companies gave him experience in real estate law, an area that he hadn't studied in law school.[18]

Many young attorneys got their start in the legal profession as sole practitioners, and Joseph Radovich was no exception. "I started a sole practice in Geneva in April 1949," Radovich remembers. "At that time, a lot of us were sole practitioners like Harry Hanson and Howard E. Smith, Sr. Daniel Schifeling was also a sole practitioner in St. Charles. He had been a B-24 pilot during World War II."[19]

E. M. Mangan ran for judge of the city courts of Aurora and Elgin in 1911. City courts were created in 1857 and abolished in 1964. (Aurora Historical Society)

The first female jurors in Illinois served in Kane County on a probate case on July 25, 1939: (left to right) Honorable Harry Daniels, Clerk Bert Gallraith, Bailiff William Kruse, Sheriff M. W. Damisch, Mrs. Rose Tazewell of Elgin, and Mrs. Winifred Dunlop of Aurora. (Geneva Historical Society)

Ben Rifken, who also began his career as a sole practitioner, remembers the postwar years as a period of optimism. "It was a great time for the country," he recalled. "We had emerged from World War II victorious and everybody who wanted to work had a job."[20]

In the years following World War II, the counties west of Chicago began to grow in population as people from Chicago began to move to the suburbs. The growth of automobile ownership made possible longer commutes from outlying counties to jobs in the city. But a permanent population loss in the Windy City also occurred as Chicagoans increasingly pulled up stakes and settled in the cities west of Chicago along the Fox River in Kane County.

If attorneys had business in Chicago in the late 1940s, it was a fairly easy journey to undertake. "To get to Chicago, you could take the interurban known as the Chicago, Aurora & Elgin (CA&E) into the Wells Street Station," recalled William Murphy. "You probably only saw three farmhouses between Aurora and Wheaton. It was very rural."[21]

You Knew Every Single Lawyer

Howard M. Smith was typical of the new breed of attorneys who set up shop in Kane County following the war. The son of a Geneva attorney, Smith attended the University of Wisconsin in Madison and then earned his J.D. at Harvard Law School. During World War II, he worked in the Office of Price Stability in Washington, D.C., and returned to Geneva to set up a practice in the early 1950s.

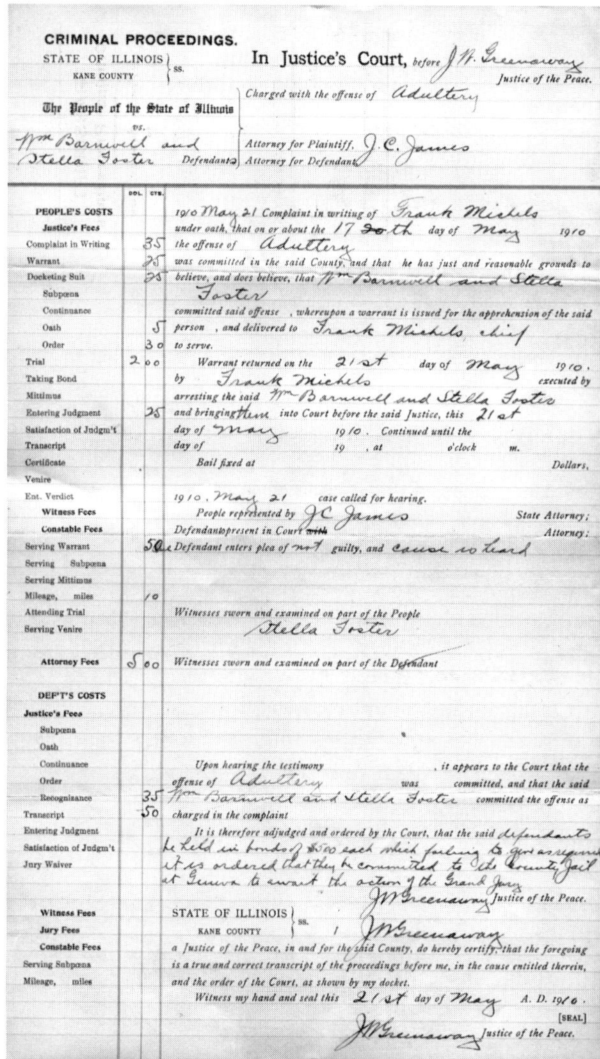

CRIMINAL PROCEEDINGS.

STATE OF ILLINOIS, KANE COUNTY } ss. In Justice's Court, before J W. Greenaway Justice of the Peace.

The People of the State of Illinois vs. Wm Barnwell and Stella Foster Defendants

Charged with the offense of Adultery

Attorney for Plaintiff, J. C. James

Attorney for Defendant

PEOPLE'S COSTS	DOL.	CTS.	
Justice's Fees			1910 May 21 Complaint in writing of Frank Michels under oath, that on or about the 17 ~~20~~th day of May 1910
Complaint in Writing		35	the offense of Adultery
Warrant		25	was committed in the said County, and that he has just and reasonable grounds to
Docketing Suit		25	believe, and does believe, that Wm Barnwell and Stella Foster
Subpœna			
Continuance			committed said offense, whereupon a warrant is issued for the apprehension of the said
Oath		5	person, and delivered to Frank Michels, chief
Order		30	to serve.
Trial	2	00	Warrant returned on the 21st day of May 1910,
Taking Bond			by Frank Michels executed by
Mittimus			arresting the said Wm Barnwell and Stella Foster
Entering Judgment		25	and bringing them into Court before the said Justice, this 21st
Satisfaction of Judgm't			day of May 1910. Continued until the
Transcript			day of 19 , at o'clock m.
Certificate			Bail fixed at Dollars,
Venire			
Ent. Verdict			1910, May 21 case called for hearing.
Witness Fees			People represented by J C James State Attorney;
Constable Fees			Defendants present in Court ~~with~~ Attorney;
Serving Warrant		50	Defendant enters plea of not guilty, and cause is heard
Serving Subpœna			
Serving Mittimus			
Mileage, miles		10	
Attending Trial			Witnesses sworn and examined on part of the People
Serving Venire			Stella Foster
Attorney Fees	5	00	Witnesses sworn and examined on part of the Defendant
DEF'T'S COSTS			
Justice's Fees			
Subpœna			
Oath			
Continuance			Upon hearing the testimony, it appears to the Court that the
Order			offense of Adultery was committed, and that the said
Recognizance		35	Wm Barnwell and Stella Foster committed the offense as
Transcript		50	charged in the complaint
Entering Judgment			It is therefore adjudged and ordered by the Court, that the said defendants
Satisfaction of Judgm't			be held in bonds of $500 each which failing to give as required
Jury Waiver			it is ordered that they be committed to the County Jail at Geneva to await the action of the Grand Jury
			J W Greenaway Justice of the Peace.
Witness Fees			STATE OF ILLINOIS, KANE COUNTY } ss. I, J W Greenaway
Jury Fees			
Constable Fees			a Justice of the Peace, in and for the said County, do hereby certify, that the foregoing
Serving Subpœna			is a true and correct transcript of the proceedings before me, in the cause entitled therein,
Mileage, miles			and the order of the Court, as shown by my docket.
			Witness my hand and seal this 21st day of May A. D. 1910. [SEAL]
			J W Greenaway Justice of the Peace.

An order by a justice of the peace found sufficient evidence of adultery to bind both participants over to a grand jury in 1910. (Aurora Historical Society)

"In the 1950s and 1960s you knew every single lawyer in Kane County," Smith said.[22]

Two local Kane County attorneys from the early 1950s who made an impression on Smith were Harry Hansen and Emil Benson. "Harry never went to law school, and he started practicing in 1919. Emil was from Batavia. Harry was either the mayor or city attorney of Geneva from the 1920s to 1954. He started his office on Third Street. They used to call him 'The Baron.' In later years, a lot of people came from the North Shore of Chicago to shop on Third Street. Emil Benson was an old curmudgeon, but he was the only game in town in Batavia. Emil represented every farmer in Kane County."[23]

Clarence Ruddy was another legendary local attorney in the 1950s. Ruddy, an Aurora native who graduated from the Notre Dame School of Law in 1927 and was the first editor of the *Notre Dame Law Review*, had been in practice for twenty-five years in Kane County when Smith hung out his shingle in 1952.[24] Ruddy practiced in Aurora with the Alschuler firm from 1930 to 1950, when he left to start his own firm in downtown Aurora.[25] He died in 2004 at the age of ninety-nine.

Clarence T. Ruddy in 1927. He later served as KCBA president in 1946–1947.

Another Aurora attorney who had been practicing since the 1930s was Zalmon Goldsmith. An Aurora native, Goldsmith grew up over a shoe store in downtown Aurora. He began practicing with Lord & Parker in Aurora in 1938, after graduating from the University of Chicago Law School. Hugh Parker handled real estate work in Aurora, and Maurice Lord "did most everything else," Goldsmith recalled. Goldsmith did probate work for Lord & Parker until he joined the U.S. Army Air Corps in 1943. For the next two years, he serviced the hydraulic gear of P-47s in the European Theatre of Operations.[26]

Right: Charles G. Seidel was the Republican nominee for Kane County state's attorney in 1940. He later served as a circuit judge of the Sixteenth Judicial Circuit for fifteen years.

In 1946, Goldsmith returned to Lord & Parker. In the 1950s, after Lord died, Goldsmith became a partner, and by the mid-1950s, had renamed the firm Goldsmith, Thielen, Schiller and Dickson. "We moved out of the Merchants Bank Building to the West Suburban Bank Building on the far west side of Aurora," Goldsmith recalled in a 2007 interview. "The firm grew until it had twelve lawyers."[27] Goldsmith celebrated seventy years as a lawyer in 2008.

The Kane County Bar Association observed its centennial anniversary in 1958. It would see more change in the next fifty years than it had in the past one hundred.

Honorable Frank W. Shepherd, probate judge from 1922 to 1926

Zalmon Goldsmith and John Petersen in January 1953

The Alschulers

No family name has figured more prominently in the long history of the Kane County Bar Association than the name of Alschuler. Brothers Samuel and Benjamin Alschuler were both influential attorneys who contributed to the early success and prolonged growth of the Kane County Bar.

Samuel Alschuler was born in 1859, and decided on a career as a lawyer when he graduated from high school in Aurora. He did not attend law school, but instead "read the law" in the office of Aurora attorney and Civil War veteran Alexander Little until he became a member of the bar in 1880. He formed the firm of Murphy and Alschuler. "My Uncle Sam took his first case at the age of twenty, so we consider that date the starting point of his legal career," recalled Sam Alschuler, a nephew of the founder. "He earned his first fee—one dollar—by arguing a poll tax case in the Justice Court in Aurora. The case was the *City of Aurora v. Rice Thompson*, who was the meanest man in town."[28]

Campaign poster for Samuel Alschuler of Aurora, the Democratic candidate for governor in 1912 (Aurora Historical Society)

Samuel's younger brother, Benjamin, was born on November 8, 1876. After graduating from Aurora East High School, he also determined that the practice of law should be his life's work. He became a student in the law office of his brother, Samuel. After passing the bar exam in 1899, he also became a partner in the Murphy and Alschuler firm.

Samuel Alschuler also served in the Illinois House of Representatives from 1896 through 1912. He was the nominee of the Democratic Party for governor of Illinois in 1912, and although he ran ahead of the rest of the ticket, he lost the election. He then moved his law practice to Chicago, where he became affiliated with the firm of Kraus, Alschuler & Holden, although he still continued to reside in Aurora. In 1915, President Woodrow Wilson appointed Alschuler a circuit court judge for the U.S. Circuit Court of Appeals, Seventh Circuit. "Uncle Sam didn't want to accept the Seventh Circuit from President Wilson because he hadn't been to college or law school," said Sam Alschuler. "He thought there were other, more qualified people, but Wilson said they were satisfied that he was the right one for the job."[29]

While on the Court of Appeals, Alschuler served as a special arbiter of labor disputes in the meat-packing industry during World War I. He awarded employees an eight-hour day, health benefits, and increased wages.

Benjamin Alschuler succeeded his older brother as senior partner of the Alschuler firm after Sam's appointment to the Seventh Circuit. The firm became increasingly prominent in the Kane County courts. A contemporary described Benjamin Alschuler as "a man who possesses a natural discrimination as to legal ethics and who never fails to recognize the main point at issue or neglects to give a thorough presentation."[30]

Following in the family tradition of public service, Benjamin was elected a judge of the Illinois Court of Claims, serving from 1913 to 1917. He also served as a delegate to the 1932 Democratic National Convention in Chicago, which resulted in the nomination of Franklin D. Roosevelt for president. He was vice-president and general counsel of Western United Gas and Electric Company and also represented the Copley Press, Copley Hospital, and the Chicago, Aurora & Elgin Railroad.

Samuel Alschuler retired from the Seventh Circuit in 1936 and passed away at the age of eighty in 1939. Benjamin continued to practice law until his retirement and died in 1967 at the age of ninety-one.

Benjamin Alschuler had two sons, Sam and Jacob, who continued the family legal tradition and became attorneys in Kane County. Both practiced with the firm that was founded by their Uncle Sam and with the successor firm, Alschuler, Funkey, Loats & Pilmer. Jacob's son, Benjamin (named for his grandfather), also practiced with the firm and later was a founder of Alschuler, Simantz and Hem. Benjamin's death in 2001 concluded a 122-year period in which a member of the Alschuler family practiced law in Aurora.

Jacob's other son, George, was a California lawyer. Sam's son, Albert, recently retired from his position as Julius Kreeger Professor at the University of Chicago Law School and took a position as professor of law at Northwestern University School of Law. One of Sam's grandchildren, Norman Hale, is a lawyer in Rhode Island.

Many members of the Kane County Bar Association still speak of the Alschuler firm with a tone of great respect. The firm became a key driver of Aurora's economic development efforts, beginning with the original construction of Stolp Island as the central part of downtown Aurora to the construction of the Fox Valley Center.[31]

Philip Ruddy, himself an Aurora attorney, remembers that "the Alschuler firm had an amazing participation in the development of Aurora."[32] Zalmon Goldsmith, who served as president of the KCBA in 1947–1948, recalls, "The major law firm in Aurora was the Alschuler firm because it represented most of the major manufacturing firms in Aurora. They were a class act, as was Benjamin Alschuler."[33] Other lawyers in Kane County also gave the firm high marks for research. Joseph Radovich recalls that "the Alschuler firm had the best law library in the county."[34]

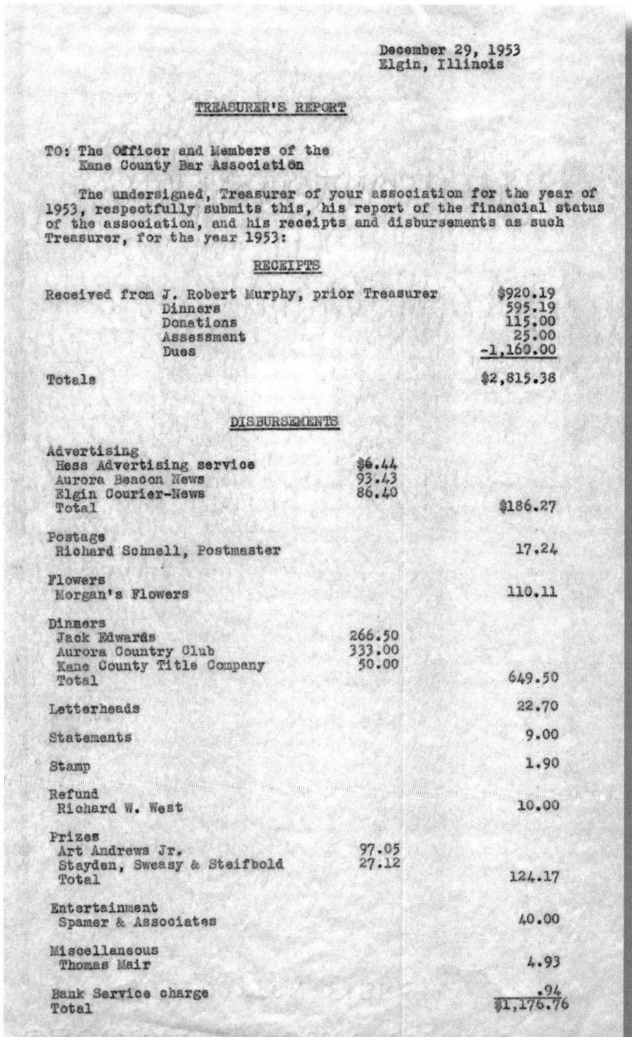

December 29, 1953
Elgin, Illinois

TREASURER'S REPORT

TO: The Officer and Members of the
Kane County Bar Association

The undersigned, Treasurer of your association for the year of 1953, respectfully submits this, his report of the financial status of the association, and his receipts and disbursements as such Treasurer, for the year 1953:

RECEIPTS

Received from J. Robert Murphy, prior Treasurer	$920.19
Dinners	595.19
Donations	115.00
Assessment	25.00
Dues	-1,160.00
Totals	$2,815.38

DISBURSEMENTS

Advertising		
Hess Advertising service	$6.44	
Aurora Beacon News	93.43	
Elgin Courier-News	86.40	
Total		$186.27
Postage		
Richard Schnell, Postmaster		17.24
Flowers		
Morgan's Flowers		110.11
Dinners		
Jack Edwards	266.50	
Aurora Country Club	333.00	
Kane County Title Company	50.00	
Total		649.50
Letterheads		22.70
Statements		9.00
Stamp		1.90
Refund		
Richard W. West		10.00
Prizes		
Art Andrews Jr.	97.05	
Stayden, Sweasy & Steifbold	27.12	
Total		124.17
Entertainment		
Spamer & Associates		40.00
Miscellaneous		
Thomas Mair		4.93
Bank Service charge		.94
Total		$1,176.76

Kane County Bar Association Treasurer's Report dated December 29, 1953, showing receipts of $2,815.38 and disbursements of $1,176.76

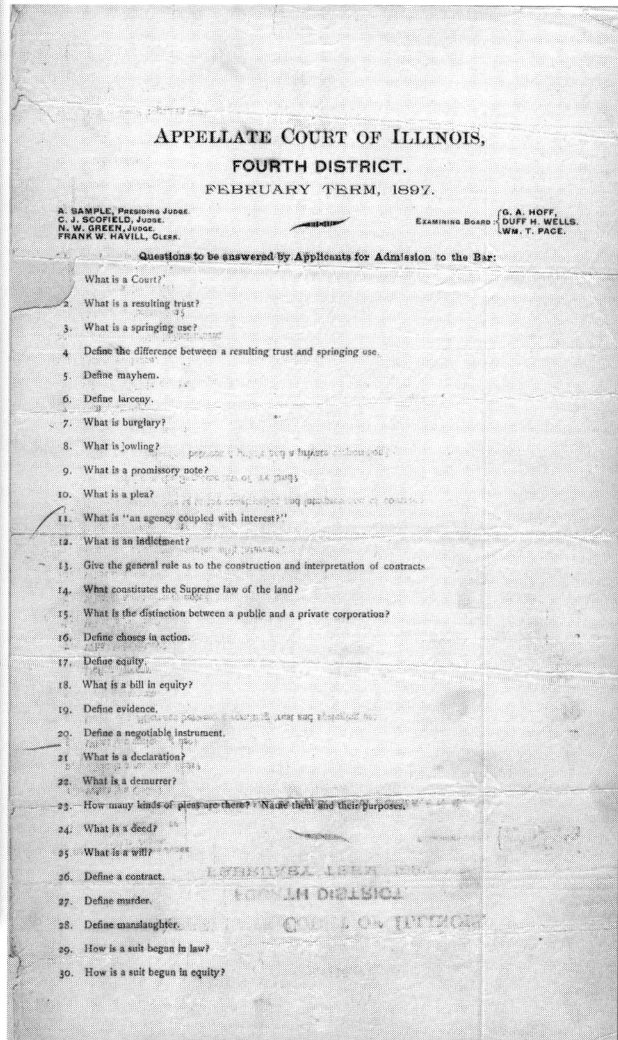

APPELLATE COURT OF ILLINOIS,
FOURTH DISTRICT.
FEBRUARY TERM, 1897.

A. SAMPLE, Presiding Judge.
C. J. SCOFIELD, Judge.
N. W. GREEN, Judge.
FRANK W. HAVILL, Clerk.

Examining Board: G. A. HOFF, DUFF H. WELLS, WM. T. PACE.

Questions to be answered by Applicants for Admission to the Bar:

1. What is a Court?
2. What is a resulting trust?
3. What is a springing use?
4. Define the difference between a resulting trust and springing use.
5. Define mayhem.
6. Define larceny.
7. What is burglary?
8. What is howling?
9. What is a promissory note?
10. What is a plea?
11. What is "an agency coupled with interest?"
12. What is an indictment?
13. Give the general rule as to the construction and interpretation of contracts.
14. What constitutes the Supreme law of the land?
15. What is the distinction between a public and a private corporation?
16. Define choses in action.
17. Define equity.
18. What is a bill in equity?
19. Define evidence.
20. Define a negotiable instrument.
21. What is a declaration?
22. What is a demurrer?
23. How many kinds of pleas are there? Name them and their purposes.
24. What is a deed?
25. What is a will?
26. Define a contract.
27. Define murder.
28. Define manslaughter.
29. How is a suit begun in law?
30. How is a suit begun in equity?

Questions to be answered by applicants for admission to the bar in 1897

Harry Hanson was a prominent attorney, former mayor, and city attorney of Geneva.

Kane County Bench and Bar in 1938

An aerial view of the City of Aurora looking east in 1949. The city court is one block south of the twenty-two-story Leland Hotel, which was the tallest building in Illinois outside of Chicago when it was built in 1921. It was topped by the Sky Club, a popular nightspot for many years. (Aurora Historical Society)

Daniel Schifeling, a sole practitioner in Kane County, was a B-24 pilot during World War II.

The monument in front of the Third Street courthouse was dedicated in 1915 to the soldiers and sailors who fought in the Civil War and the Mexican and Spanish Wars. John F. Kennedy spoke in front of the monument on October 25, 1960, during his presidential campaign.

CHAPTER 4

The Association Reborn: 1959–1965

The Kane County Bar was reborn in the 1950s and early 1960s. In 1953, when Zalmon Goldsmith, Ben Rifken, and Lambert Ochsenschlager were the mainstays of the local bar, the Association's first minute book of the modern era reported annual revenues of $2,815. That was a respectable sum given the sometime penurious state of the finances of many Kane County attorneys at the time. But it was nowhere near enough to fund the operation of a modern, formal bar association. The revenues were sufficient to pay the rent on an office in a clapboard house several blocks from the Geneva Courthouse and little else besides several social functions each year, including a pig roast.

The number of lawyers in the county was little changed from the end of World War II. There were an estimated 300 practicing attorneys in Kane County in 1959, with one hundred each in the Elgin and Aurora areas and the rest practicing in Geneva, St. Charles, Batavia, and the other small towns of the Fox Valley.

The Bar Association itself only had about one hundred members in 1959 and would not reach 200 members until the early 1970s. Most of the attorneys in the county were in sole practice or in practice with a son, father, or other relative. There were only a handful of multi-lawyer firms, and they were all in Aurora or Elgin.

Joe Radovich, the son of Serbian parents from Chicago, practiced in Geneva throughout the 1950s. Radovich, who earned his law degree at the DePaul University College of Law and practiced with the staff judge advocate in the U.S. Army during World War II, settled into a sole practice in Geneva after practicing postwar title and mortgage work.

Throughout the 1950s, Geneva's population of 5,000–6,000 was typical of northern Illinois farm towns. But the postwar boom that was transforming so much of America in the 1950s was rapidly reaching out to the Fox River Valley.

Suburban Growth

With the 1956 launching of the construction of the nation's interstate highway system, Kane County became enmeshed in a web of concrete that bound its fortunes inextricably to the Chicago metropolitan area. In 1960, the completion of Interstate 294, also known as the Tri-State Tollway, opened up suburban growth to the west and north. Although Kane County still retained much of its exurban and rural character in the 1960s, the growth of the automobile culture ensured that it would inevitably be a part of the Chicago metropolitan area.

Honorable Earl R. Shopen, probate judge from 1952 to 1965

In the 1920s and 1930s, attorneys journeyed into Chicago for trials, depositions, hearings, and various other types of legal proceedings at the Cook County Courthouse. These trips, involving the interurban railway system, usually consumed an attorney's entire day. And often, if legal business was concluded on a Friday afternoon, an overnight stay in Chicago and a Saturday afternoon trip on the "L" to Wrigley Field for a Cubs game would bring the workweek to a close.

This suburban isolation continued until the end of World War II, when the country reestablished a peacetime economy and automotive production resumed in 1946. During these early postwar years, the city of Chicago and the suburbs to the west gradually moved toward each other as farmland turned into suburban shopping malls and new housing developments filled in the remaining open spaces. The biggest single event that hastened the urbanization of the region was the opening of O'Hare Airport in 1955.

Howard E. Smith, Sr. and Howard E. Smith, Jr. in 1953

The airport, originally known as Orchard Place Airport/Douglas Field, was constructed between 1942 and 1943 as a manufacturing plant for Douglas C-54's during World War II. When Douglas Aircraft Company's contract ended in 1945, the City of Chicago chose the field as the site for a facility to meet future aviation demands. Though its familiar three-letter IATA code "ORD" still reflects the early identity of the airport, it was renamed in 1949 after Lieutenant Commander Edward O'Hare, a World War II flying ace who gave his life in combat in the Pacific and was awarded the Medal of Honor.[1]

The first commercial domestic flights started in 1955, and an international terminal was built in 1958. When Chicago's first airport, Midway, was deemed too small to handle the first generation of passenger jets in 1962, O'Hare was developed as

February 18, 1963

The Hon. Judge Roy J. Solfisberg, Jr.
122 Downer Place
Aurora, Illinois

Dear Judge:

It is my pleasure to inform you, as Secretary of the Kane County Bar Association, that you have been elected to an Honorary Membership in our Association.

This was done under the by-laws, Article 3, Section 2, Honorary Members.

The Board of Managers at its discretion may elect to honorary membership in the Association, any member of this Association or any member of the profession who does not practice in Kane County, who by reason of his standing in the profession or his contribution to the profession or the public service is wothy of the honor.

This action was taken by unanimous vote of the officers and Board of Managers at their meeting on the 17th day of January, 1963.

I am enclosing your 62-63 refund of dues in the amount of $10.00.

Yours very truly,

HAROLD D. NEALIS, Jr.
Secretary

HDN:jh
Encl.

A February 18, 1963 letter from KCBA Secretary Harold Nealis advised Honorable Roy J. Solfisburg, Jr. that he was elected to an honorary membership in the KCBA.

1962 - 1963 TREASURER REPORT
Kane County Bar Association
Through May 13, 1963

RECEIPTS:				
Balance on hand, May 1, 1962				$2,654.81
Dues: 1961 - 1962			$180.00	
1962 - 1963		$1,950.00		
less refunds: Judges and overpayments		- 55.00	1,895.00	
1963 - 1964		$1,120.00		
less refunds: overpayments		- 10.00	1,110.00	3,185.00
TOTAL UNALLOCATED RECEIPTS				$5,839.81
DISBURSEMENTS:				
1962 Golf Stag - green fees		$136.00		
less allocated receipts		- 81.00	$55.00	
Flower Committee - Reid, Streit, Tobin, O'Malley, Oddsen, and Meyers			185.67	
Postage and Printing: Billings Forms		$17.50		
Letterhead Stationery		23.50		
Postage		55.00	96.00	
Public Relations Committee:				
Public Information Pamphlets			117.00	
Bar Functions:				
6th District Meeting:				
Ladies Luncheon and hospitality	$488.58			
Men's Luncheon, coffee and rolls	439.40	$927.98		
Less allocated receipts		-698.00	229.98	
Valentine Day Meeting			400.00	
Judge Wither's Robe			62.75	
Guest Luncheons - Board Meetings			6.48	
Joint Legal - Medico Dinner:				
Receipts - allocated		$430.00		
Less: Guests Dinners	$15.00			
Cost of Dinners	415.00	-430.00	-0-	1,152.88
BALANCE ON HAND, MAY 13, 1963				$4,686.93

Respectfully submitted,

Treasurer

The 1962–1963 Kane County Bar Association Treasurer Report showing a beginning balance of $2,654.81 and an ending balance of $4,686.93

the main airport of the future. After a planned expansion and a new terminal were completed in 1962, all remaining domestic flights were transferred from Midway to O'Hare. The new airport instantly became the new "World's Busiest Airport."[2]

The Steer Roast in 1963 was hosted by Honorable John S. Petersen on his farm at the intersection of Galena Boulevard and Barnes Road in Aurora.

O'Hare triggered an explosion of growth in Kane County and other counties surrounding Chicago. Hotels, restaurants, warehouses, and new retail malls began to spring up and many people left for the suburbs to take advantage of the jobs that this growth provided. Many attorneys, anxious to expand their client base, now found it easier to travel to other cities thanks to the proximity of the new airport.

In the ensuing years, the cities of the Fox Valley, connected by a modern interstate highway system with Chicago, would experience an increase in population that was undreamed of when the twentieth century began. Kane County's population in 1960 stood at 208,000, and in the next thirty years, the population would grow more than 50 percent to reach almost 320,000 by 1990. And the Kane County Bar Association, with a stagnant membership count of approximately 200 attorneys scattered through Aurora, Elgin, and other communities along the Fox River, would begin to coalesce and expand as the practice of law became more complex and the organization entered the second century of its existence.

Kane County Bar Association members enjoy dinner at the inaugural Steer Roast.

Aerial view of O'Hare Airport in 1976 (Sidwell)

Real Estate Law

The growth of the suburbs in the 1950s and early 1960s meant that many members of the Kane County Bar Association made the bulk of their living practicing real estate law. With large tracts of farmland being turned into suburban shopping malls and housing developments, expertise in real estate law became paramount. In addition, more complex and creative financing packages were constantly being introduced by banks and insurance companies to facilitate such development, so attorneys needed to stay acquainted with the ever-increasing number of debt instruments available in the local marketplace.

Attorneys in the 1950s and 1960s also did not have to deal with the plethora of reports that are now needed for completion of a real estate transaction, including environmental impact studies and various and sundry Environmental Protection Agency (EPA) reports. Joseph Radovich, who began his legal

Control tower at O'Hare Airport in 1955

Control tower at O'Hare Airport in 2008

career working as a title examiner at Chicago Title, remembers how uncomplicated real estate law was in the late 1940s. "There are more tax considerations now in exchanges of real estate. Real estate deals are so much more complex than in the old days. Back then you brought a deed and a simple mortgage to a closing. Today, you need a survey, inspections, and a sheaf of papers that include approvals of the various boards, as well as EPA studies. It has become very, very expensive. The development of real estate is also far more complex."[3]

State Street in Geneva looking east from Third Street during the 1960s (Geneva Historical Society)

During the 1960s, re-zoning became a specialty area in the practice of real estate law as private land holdings became available for commercial use. Zalmon Goldsmith, of Aurora, recalled the growth of his real estate practice in those years. "During the 1960s, we got involved in a lot of real estate work, doing zoning for commercial use. We were changing zoning ordinances up and down the Valley."[4]

Elgin cityscape looking north in 1957 (Elgin Historical Society)

Although Goldsmith's firm enjoyed significant success in its zoning practice, he still remembers one case that he lost almost fifty years ago. "I was responsible for creating Randall Road," he recalled. "A farm that a lady owned had land bordering . . . Randall Road. . . . She hired me to rezone the land from farm use because a veterinarian wanted to buy the land. But the mayors of Batavia, Geneva, and St. Charles were dead set against the rezoning." The battle heated up because the *Batavia Herald*, the local newspaper, also opposed the rezoning. "I lost that case, but had I been successful, the corner of Randall Road and Main in Batavia wouldn't have been developed," he said. "Randall Road just grew busier and busier and became what it is today."[5] Randall Road is currently Kane County's primary retail corridor.

Perhaps the biggest change that attorneys of the Kane County Bar Association have seen in real estate is the increase in the value of land since the 1950s. Joseph Radovich remembers that "Farms were selling for $300 an acre in 1949, and now it can cost almost $100,000 an acre for farmland."[6]

Jacob and Sam Alschuler with their father, Benjamin Alschuler, c. 1960

The Role of the Title Companies

Much of the real estate work performed by members of the Kane County Bar involved transferring, filing, and insuring deeds and land titles. Real estate attorneys in Kane County were helpless to do anything without the historical support of the area's two big title companies, Chicago Title Insurance Company and Kane County Title Company. Both had deep roots in the county.

Chicago Title Insurance Company and its predecessor companies have a history of service to the people of northern Illinois that goes back to 1857. In the twenty-first century, the company is one of the oldest continually operated businesses in Geneva, furnishing abstract and title work for the real estate industry which is then used in nearly all land transactions.

Abstracting is the chronological listing of items affecting real estate and individuals during specific periods of time regarding a particular parcel or parcels of land. In Kane County, abstracts can trace the origin of land titles to the early nineteenth century. Title insurance policies list the present owners and existing encumbrances against the property and individuals involved, as well as state the amount of insurance and name the party insured.[7]

The first local incorporated title company in Kane County was organized in 1902 under the name of Kane County Title & Trust Company. In 1906, by a certificate of change in location, the Chicago Artificial Flower Company became the Kane County Abstract Company. In 1920, the two companies merged under the name of Kane County Abstract Company. And in 1930, the Kane County Abstract Company began issuing title insurance policies as an agent for the Chicago Title & Trust Company, giving Chicago Title its first major presence in Kane County.

In 1937, the Kane County Title Company, a new corporation, was organized to purchase the title plant and assets of the Kane County Abstract Company. Three of the original directors of the Kane County Title Company were Frank Renwick, Sr. of Geneva; Emil Benson, a prominent Kane County attorney, of Batavia; and Chester R. Davis of Wayne, who was a director and senior vice president of Chicago Title & Trust Company.[8]

Kane County Title Company had three presidents during its history as an independent title company in the county. The first was Frank Mitchell, who became president when the company was incorporated in 1937. The late Judge Thomas J. Hoban of Elgin, a vice president of Chicago Title & Trust Company, succeeded Mitchell as president and was a director of Kane County Title Company from 1938 until 1942. A. J. Yates was then elected president in 1942.[9]

Yates served as president until 1960, when Kane County Title Company merged with Chicago Title and the business was continued as the Kane County Division of the Chicago Title & Trust Company.[10] Since Kane County Title had been issuing title insurance policies as a representative of Chicago Title for many years, this merger merely formalized a business relationship that was already successful in its past performance.

Bill Murphy, a former Kane County Bar Association president, recalled in a 2007 interview that "Home Building & Loan was the largest savings and loan in Aurora. In 1948, Kane County Title Company issued abstracts, and some of those abstracts would frequently go back to the time of President Polk. Sometimes we had a stack of abstracts a foot thick."[11]

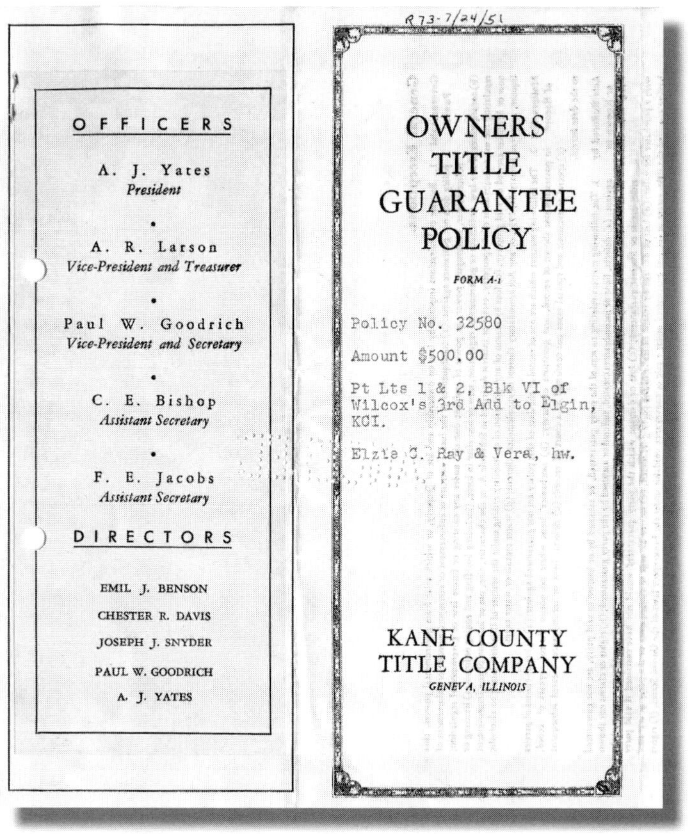

OFFICERS

A. J. Yates
President

A. R. Larson
Vice-President and Treasurer

Paul W. Goodrich
Vice-President and Secretary

C. E. Bishop
Assistant Secretary

F. E. Jacobs
Assistant Secretary

DIRECTORS

EMIL J. BENSON
CHESTER R. DAVIS
JOSEPH J. SNYDER
PAUL W. GOODRICH
A. J. YATES

OWNERS TITLE GUARANTEE POLICY

FORM A-1

Policy No. 32580
Amount $500.00
Pt Lts 1 & 2, Blk VI of Wilcox's 3rd Add to Elgin, KCI.
Elzie C. Ray & Vera, hw.

KANE COUNTY TITLE COMPANY
GENEVA, ILLINOIS

Kane County Title Company owner's title guarantee policy from 1951

Today, Chicago County Title continues to provide critical services in the form of title insurance, searches, and escrow work that drive the real estate business in Kane County. With its connection to Kane County Title, Chicago Title can trace its roots back to the early 1840s, when government land patents were first issued.

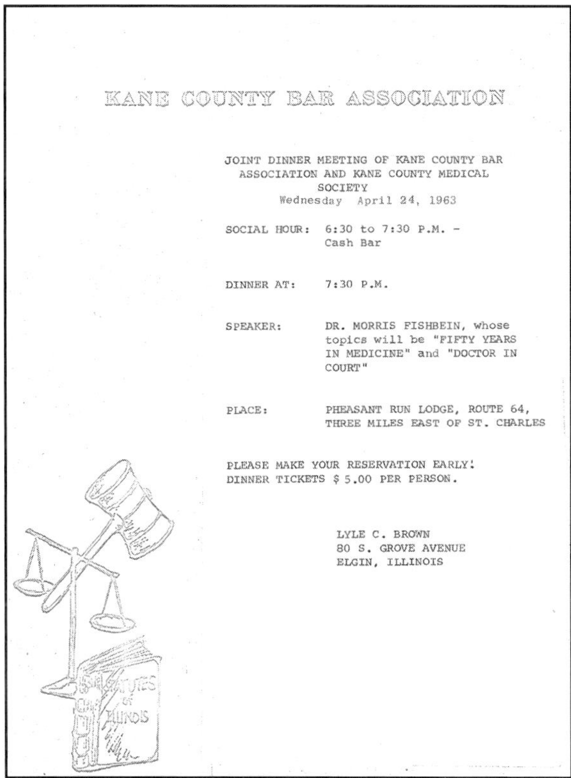

KANE COUNTY BAR ASSOCIATION

JOINT DINNER MEETING OF KANE COUNTY BAR ASSOCIATION AND KANE COUNTY MEDICAL SOCIETY
Wednesday April 24, 1963

SOCIAL HOUR: 6:30 to 7:30 P.M. - Cash Bar

DINNER AT: 7:30 P.M.

SPEAKER: DR. MORRIS FISHBEIN, whose topics will be "FIFTY YEARS IN MEDICINE" and "DOCTOR IN COURT"

PLACE: PHEASANT RUN LODGE, ROUTE 64, THREE MILES EAST OF ST. CHARLES

PLEASE MAKE YOUR RESERVATION EARLY: DINNER TICKETS $ 5.00 PER PERSON.

LYLE C. BROWN
80 S. GROVE AVENUE
ELGIN, ILLINOIS

An announcement of the joint dinner meeting of the Kane County Bar Association and the Kane County Medical Society on April 24, 1963, at Pheasant Run

The Mainstays

Any Kane County attorney who did business with Chicago Title during the 1960s had fond memories of Elmer Pierce. A native of a small farming community in south central Nebraska, Pierce earned his law degree from the University of Nebraska in 1939 and was immediately commissioned a lieutenant in the U.S. Cavalry. An impacted wisdom tooth cut short his army career, but he re-enlisted and was accepted in an army engineering boat battalion following Pearl Harbor. Pierce participated in the Allied invasions of North Africa and Italy during the war and returned to civilian life in 1945.

He joined Chicago Title as a title attorney in Wheaton in 1959 and transferred to Chicago Title's Geneva office in 1962. For the next seventeen years, Pierce was the face of Chicago Title in Kane County. "Elmer became well-known and liked by the members of the Kane County Bar because of his willingness to help clear up title objections and expedite title orders," recalled Joe Radovich.[12] Pierce, a sociable man, was responsible for the annual parties that Chicago Title threw to show its appreciation for the Kane County Bar Association.

One of the better-known members of the Kane County Bar during the 1960s was Alfred Younges Kirkland. The son of a Chicago newspaper editor, Kirkland was captain of the University of Illinois varsity swim team during the 1940–1941 season.[13] Like most of his contemporaries, he served in World War II, where he was an army infantry lieutenant for three years. He helped revive the Kane County Bar Association when he served as the Association's president in 1961–1962 and went on to win a contested statewide election in 1968 to serve as president of the Illinois State Bar Association.[14] In the 1970s, Kirkland was appointed by President Gerald Ford to U.S. District Court for the Northern District of Illinois. Kirkland's daughter, Pamela K. Jensen, also served as a judge on the bench of the Sixteenth Circuit.[15]

Honorable Alfred Y. Kirkland, former Sixteenth Judicial Circuit judge, Federal District judge, KCBA president, and Illinois State Bar Association president

Kirkland, Brady, McQueen & Churchill later became the firm of Brady & McQueen, which continued to be one of the most prominent firms in Kane County during the late twentieth and early twenty-first centuries.

Although most of the attorneys who dabbled in local politics in Kane County were Republicans, a few members of the Kane County Bar Association were good "Yellow Dog Democrats." Richard L. Cooper was active in Kane County Democratic Party politics for fifty years. A native of Carbondale, Cooper worked his way through Georgetown University Law School by taking classes at night during the Great Depression. He shared a passion for politics with one of his classmates at Georgetown, a big-eared Texan by the name of Lyndon Baines Johnson.[16]

Kane County attorneys: (left to right) Richard P. Bartsch, Clarence J. Ruddy, and Charles J. Myler, c. 1961

Cooper served his country as captain of a tank landing ship during the savage fighting in the South Pacific during World War II. He returned to Illinois, first as a government attorney in Chicago and then as a private practitioner in Geneva in the late 1940s. He led a series of successful battles against school tax increases in Geneva during the 1950s and 1960s and would later serve on the Kane County Board of Supervisors. In 1953, Cooper and a group of friends purchased the *Elburn Herald,* a weekly newspaper in the county. Cooper served as publisher of the newspaper, a role he relinquished to his oldest son in 1958.[17]

The Chicago Contingent

Not all members of the Kane County Bar Association practiced in Kane County. By the 1960s, the proximity of Chicago and the northwest suburbs made it attractive for certain members of the Association to live in Kane County and to practice in Chicago, usually in a corporate environment. Theodore G. Schuster was typical. A Wisconsin native, Schuster graduated from high school in 1939 and was a weather observer and forecaster with the U.S. Army Air Corps during World War II.

Election poster for Honorable John S. Petersen, circuit judge of the Sixteenth Judicial Circuit

With the end of the war, Schuster returned to Madison, Wisconsin, and earned his B.S. degree on the G.I. Bill at the University of Wisconsin in 1949 and his law degree from Wisconsin in 1951. From 1951 to 1970, Schuster was a member of the corporate legal staff of the Chicago, Burlington & Quincy Railroad. When the CB&Q merged with the Great Northern and Northern Pacific railways in 1970, Schuster moved into management, operating the BN's commuter railway service between Chicago and Aurora.[18] Throughout his career in corporate law in Chicago, Schuster maintained a residence in Batavia. Schuster was named Batavia's Citizen of the Year in 1988 and served on the Batavia School Board well into his seventies.

Kane County Abstract Office in Geneva during the 1890s (Geneva Historical Society)

*Kane County Bar Association Board in 1953: (left to right) David Givler, Joseph Wiederman, Dan Withers, Jacob Alschuler, and Joseph Radovich. (*Beacon News*)*

Kane County Bench and Bar in 1959

Another longtime member of the Kane County Bar Association who practiced his specialty in the Chicago legal community was James Van Santen of Geneva. Born and raised on the south side of Chicago, Van Santen was a graduate of the Illinois Institute of Technology who picked up a fascination with the law when he was assigned to be a shipboard member of a JAG team during his World War II service in the U.S. Navy. Van Santen used his G.I. Bill credits following the war to earn a law degree at the University of Chicago. He combined his engineering and law background into a distinguished career in intellectual property law in Chicago.[19]

Van Santen was a member of the Geneva School Board from 1964 to 1970, and as a longtime board member of the board of trustees of the Community Hospital in Geneva, Van Santen was instrumental in facilitating the merger of Community Hospital with Delnor Hospital in St. Charles.

By the mid-1960s, the Kane County legal community had assumed the profile it would maintain for much of the remainder of the twentieth century. The major change the bar would undergo in the years to come was substantial, sustained growth.

Ben Rifken

Ben Rifken's love affair with the law spanned three quarters of a century. In an interview conducted in 2000, Rifken, the Kane County Bar Association's president in 1959–1960, noted that he always loved the law.[20] "Most young lawyers that I talk to today tell me that they can't wait to quit," he said. "If that is the case, then there is something wrong with the practice. I love the law. If I had my legs to go into a courtroom today, I would love to argue a case and get in front of a jury and give a closing argument."[21]

The son of Russian immigrants, Rifken grew up in Elgin and graduated from Elgin High School in 1933 in the depths of the Great Depression. When his parents came to the United States, they couldn't speak any English, so his father taught himself to read by reading all the advertising signs on the streetcars in New York City, where they lived before they moved to Elgin. "Our house was always full of books because my father valued education," Rifken recalled.[22] The love of language was transmitted from father to son. Ben Rifken took great pride in serving as a member of the Elgin High debate team when he was a senior in 1933.

Kane County Bar Association member Ben Rifken, KCBA president in 1959–1960

After graduating from high school, he took correspondence courses for college credit in the newly created junior college system that had just been started by the State of Illinois. He received a half-year of credit for the courses he had taken, and in 1934, Rifken started as an undergraduate at the University of Illinois. Economically, he was in the same boat as most of his fellow students, even shipping his laundry home by mail to save money. Rifken also served on the University of Illinois debate team, putting his experience from high school to good use.

Rifken graduated from Illinois in 1938 with a degree in political science and a minor in history. He then attended law school at what is now called the Illinois Institute of Technology, graduating in 1941. As with most young men of his generation, Pearl Harbor would be the defining moment of his youth. "When Pearl Harbor happened, I enlisted in the navy and trained at the Great Lakes Naval Training Center as a yeoman-typist," Rifken explained. "I was in the navy for four years, serving at sea from 1943 through 1945. Toward the end of the war, I became an officer in charge of the Shore Patrol in New Orleans. I was there when V-J Day was declared."[23]

After the war, Rifken returned to Elgin. He opened his first law office, sharing space with Theodore Schnell. His first desk in the office was his mother's card table. Schnell had lost his hearing as a result of the flu pandemic in 1918 after serving in World War I, so Ben would be his ears in the courtroom when they tried cases together. "Ted Schnell was a stickler for looking up the law and making sure what the law was," Rifken recalled.[24]

From 1956 through 1961, Rifken served in the state's attorney's office for which he was paid the grand sum of $3,000 a year, plus $100 a month for a secretary. The job took up two-thirds of his time, but he kept up his law practice while performing his duties in the state's attorney's office. "I was never home for supper because I was always working," Rifken said.[25]

Rifken's two mentors during his legal career were Judge Seidel and George Carbary. Charles Seidel was a product of the University of Michigan Law School, and Carbary was a product of reading the law in a lawyer's office. Rifken considered both men to be tremendous lawyers and great trial attorneys. "My son, Jeffrey, still has all of Judge Seidel's law books and all of his notes from law school," Ben said.[26]

Rifken was involved in many charitable activities during his long legal career. He was continuously active in his synagogue. In addition, he was president of the United Way for two years and active in veterans' affairs and his Masonic lodge. He was also one of the oldest members of the Elgin Turnverein, a German fraternal organization. For many years, Rifken contributed his time to the Illinois Board of Admissions to the Bar by conducting the interviews that new lawyers must undergo with regards to character and moral fitness for a legal career.

Jeff Rifken said his father was a key supporter of Provena St. Joseph Hospital when the Elgin health care facility built the new hospital on the west side of the Fox River. William Brown, the hospital's president and CEO, noted that Rifken "boldly spearheaded the effort to build a new St. Joseph Hospital, our current facility, to fulfill the growing health care needs of the west side of Elgin."[27]

Reflecting on his long and rewarding legal career, Ben Rifken remained awed by the majesty of the law. "The practice of law goes all the way back to the King of England and the birth of common law. You do not have a right to be a lawyer. I considered it a privilege to be an attorney because you are an officer of the court and you must obey its rules. We are the legatees of the King's bench in England."[28]

Ben Rifken died at the age of ninety-one in the spring of 2008 as the history of the Kane County Bar Association was going to press.

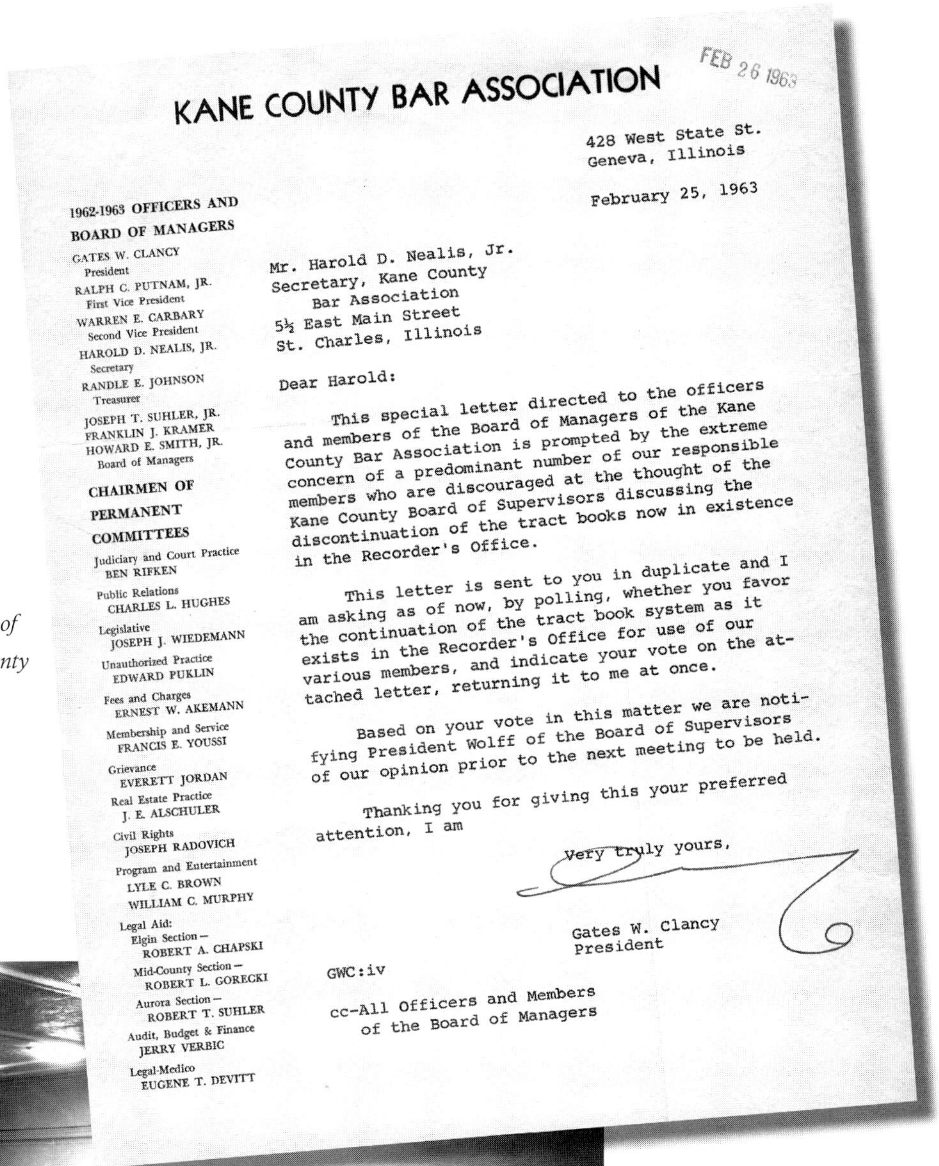

FEB 26 1963

KANE COUNTY BAR ASSOCIATION

428 West State St.
Geneva, Illinois

February 25, 1963

1962-1963 OFFICERS AND BOARD OF MANAGERS

GATES W. CLANCY
President
RALPH C. PUTNAM, JR.
First Vice President
WARREN E. CARBARY
Second Vice President
HAROLD D. NEALIS, JR.
Secretary
RANDLE E. JOHNSON
Treasurer
JOSEPH T. SUHLER, JR.
FRANKLIN J. KRAMER
HOWARD E. SMITH, JR.
Board of Managers

CHAIRMEN OF PERMANENT COMMITTEES

Judiciary and Court Practice
BEN RIFKEN
Public Relations
CHARLES L. HUGHES
Legislative
JOSEPH J. WIEDEMANN
Unauthorized Practice
EDWARD PUKLIN
Fees and Charges
ERNEST W. AKEMANN
Membership and Service
FRANCIS E. YOUSSI
Grievance
EVERETT JORDAN
Real Estate Practice
J. E. ALSCHULER
Civil Rights
JOSEPH RADOVICH
Program and Entertainment
LYLE C. BROWN
WILLIAM C. MURPHY
Legal Aid:
Elgin Section –
ROBERT A. CHAPSKI
Mid-County Section –
ROBERT L. GORECKI
Aurora Section –
ROBERT T. SUHLER
Audit, Budget & Finance
JERRY VERBIC
Legal-Medico
EUGENE T. DEVITT

Mr. Harold D. Nealis, Jr.
Secretary, Kane County
Bar Association
5½ East Main Street
St. Charles, Illinois

Dear Harold:

This special letter directed to the officers and members of the Board of Managers of the Kane County Bar Association is prompted by the extreme concern of a predominant number of our responsible members who are discouraged at the thought of the Kane County Board of Supervisors discussing the discontinuation of the tract books now in existence in the Recorder's Office.

This letter is sent to you in duplicate and I am asking as of now, by polling, whether you favor the continuation of the tract book system as it exists in the Recorder's Office for use of our various members, and indicate your vote on the attached letter, returning it to me at once.

Based on your vote in this matter we are notifying President Wolff of the Board of Supervisors of our opinion prior to the next meeting to be held.

Thanking you for giving this your preferred attention, I am

Very truly yours,

Gates W. Clancy
President

GWC:iv

cc-All Officers and Members
of the Board of Managers

A February 25, 1963 letter from Gates Clancy to the KCBA Board of Managers addressed the continuation of the tract book system at the Kane County recorder's office.

Courtroom in Aurora City Hall and Court of Common Pleas, c. 1950 (Aurora Historical Society)

Aerial view of the City of Aurora looking west in the 1950s (Aurora Historical Society)

Construction of the Fermi National Accelerator Laboratory began in 1968 on 6,800 acres near Batavia. The land was previously occupied by fifty-five farms and the 450-person Village of Weston, which voted to dissolve in order to make room for the laboratory. (Fermilab)

CHAPTER 5

The Growth of the Legal Community: 1965–1970

Kane County landed squarely on America's energy map in 1967 when President Lyndon B. Johnson signed a bill commissioning the National Accelerator Laboratory.[1] The high-energy physics lab was located on 6,800 acres of Kane County farmland just outside of Batavia. It was named in honor of atomic pioneer Enrico Fermi, who developed the first self-sustained nuclear reaction beneath the bleachers of Stagg Field at the University of Chicago in 1942.

Fermi Laboratory would create nearly 2,000 jobs and a payroll of $150 million a year in Kane County as well as nearby DuPage County.[2] In 2003, Batavia Mayor Jeff Schielke noted that Fermilab, as the locals soon called it, created an infrastructure for orderly growth in the middle Fox River Valley during the last third of the twentieth century. The 6,800 acres that Fermilab occupied, Schielke said, might well have been destined to be "ticky-tack" suburban housing developments. Schielke noted that "instead of being a city of 25,000, we would be a city of 50,000. Now we have this 6,800 acres of open space that we can enjoy."[3]

The coming of Fermilab ensured that Kane County's growth during the last quarter of the twentieth century would be controlled, and that the area along the Fox River between Aurora and Elgin would continue to maintain its exurban charm. As Chicago pushed outward toward the north and west in the 1970s, Kane County was an island of tranquility in the metropolitan sea of growth and change. Increasingly, the region was an attractive place to locate for attorneys practicing in Chicago and the western suburbs. And the growing income levels of the county's residents ensured that Kane County's resident attorneys would find plentiful work in real estate and civil law.

Fermi National Accelerator Laboratory in 1999 (Fermilab)

A Nice Place to Work

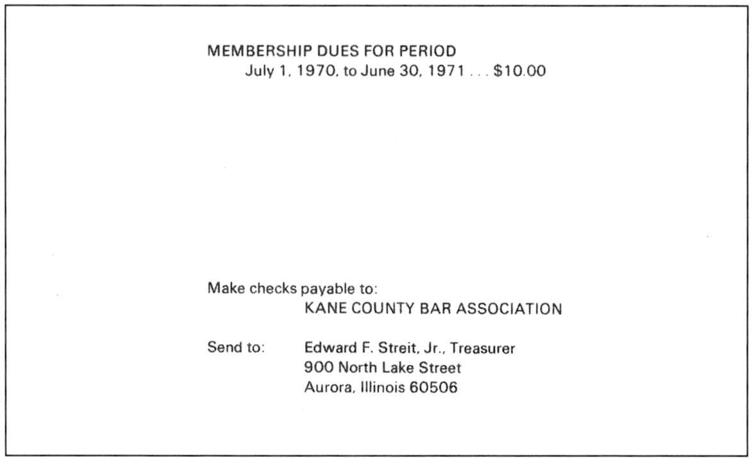

MEMBERSHIP DUES FOR PERIOD
July 1, 1970, to June 30, 1971 . . . $10.00

Make checks payable to:
KANE COUNTY BAR ASSOCIATION

Send to: Edward F. Streit, Jr., Treasurer
900 North Lake Street
Aurora, Illinois 60506

KCBA membership dues statement of ten dollars from 1970–1971

The 1960s were a time of great collegiality in the Kane County legal community. By the end of that decade, many of the practicing attorneys in the county had known each other since returning from duty in World War II nearly a quarter-century before. During the 1950s and 1960s, a small-town atmosphere prevailed in the legal communities of Kane County.

In the 1960s, every lawyer knew practically every other lawyer who was practicing in the county. At the time, very few Chicago firms had yet to establish a presence in the area. According to Joe Radovich, "lawyers from Chicago were considered outlanders."[4]

In the late 1940s and early 1950s, the court system of Kane County was also much smaller, given the lower population in northwest Illinois at the time. "Back in 1949, there were three judges, one on the DuPage Circuit, one in Kane County, and one in DeKalb County," Joe Radovich recalled. "Those three judges would also take care of Kendall County. Today, the Sixteenth Circuit has thirty-five judges, Kane County has twenty-seven judges, and Kendall County has three."[5] DeKalb County has five.

William Murphy also remembered the closeness of the Kane County legal community when he began his practice in 1949. "The legal community in Aurora was very small in 1948, with probably fifty lawyers at most. We almost never went to Elgin. The Circuit Court was in Geneva, and it would take a grave accident to get us to go there."[6]

Judge John S. Petersen, who alternated with Judge Seidel in holding court in Geneva, also did his part in protecting the collegiality of the legal community in Kane County from outsiders. He did not like lawyers from outside of the county, particularly lawyers from Chicago. Wendell Clancy remembered that "Judge Petersen had a local rule that Chicago attorneys had to hire a local attorney when they were in the collar counties. Judge Petersen's head would get red when a Chicago attorney appeared before him."[7]

Kane County
Bar Association
This is to certify that
Peter K. Wilson, Jr.
ATTORNEY AND COUNSELOR AT LAW,
IS A MEMBER OF THIS ASSOCIATION
Dues Paid To
JUNE 30th
1970
Treasurer

A 1970 KCBA membership card

These pleasant, insular times would soon come to an end as the turbulent 1960s approached. The practice of law became ever more complex. The massive revisions

Kane County Bar Association members in 1968

embodied in the Internal Revenue Code of 1954 ensured that attorneys with extensive tax practices and probate work would need to stay current with almost constant training updates and continuing education.

At the end of the 1960s, the Solfisburg Scandal would rock the Kane County legal community. Roy J. Solfisburg of Aurora, chief justice of the Illinois Supreme Court, would be forced to resign in 1969 for concealing his stock ownership in the Civic Center Bank & Trust Company, which had litigation pending before his court. This case would lend impetus to the legal career of John Paul Stevens, who served the state as independent counsel, and set the stage for his eventual rise to the United States Supreme Court.

The case would be a reminder to the Kane County legal community of the growing importance of legal ethics.

The Solfisburg Scandal

Roy J. Solfisburg was one of the Kane County Bar Association's success stories in the 1950s and 1960s.

Solfisburg, who was born and raised in Aurora, graduated from the University of Illinois College of Law in 1940. He served as the City of Aurora's corporation counsel from 1949 until 1953, when he became a commissioner of the Illinois Court of Claims. After serving as master in chancery of the Circuit Court of Kane County, he won a by-election in 1956 to fill a vacancy for the position of circuit judge for the Sixteenth Judicial Circuit. After being re-elected to the same position in 1957, the Illinois Supreme Court appointed Solfisburg to the Appellate Court, Second District, and he served as that court's presiding judge from 1959 to 1960.[8]

*Illinois Supreme Court Chief Justice Roy Solfisburg (left) and his attorney Lambert Ochsenschlager (right) of Aurora during the hearings of the special commission investigating Solfisburg and fellow justice Ray Klingbiel. They were prosecuted by then attorney and now United States Supreme Court Justice John Paul Stevens. (*Chicago Sun-Times*)*

Solfisburg was elected to the Illinois Supreme Court in 1960, serving as chief justice for the 1962–1963 court term. In 1967, his fellow justices elected him to a three-year term as chief justice. In the wake of the resignation of Abe Fortas from the United States Supreme Court over an inappropriate fee arrangement with financier Louis Wolfson, Solfisburg was mentioned as a possible replacement. In fact, both United States senators from Illinois, Everett Dirksen and Charles H. Percy, had encouraged President Richard Nixon to appoint Solfisburg to the Supreme Court. The set of circumstances that caused Abe Fortas' judicial woes in the spring of 1969 would force Solfisburg to resign his position before the year was out. For Solfisburg, the timing of the Percy and Dirksen appeal to the Nixon administration about the Fortas vacancy could not have been worse.

In June 1969, less than a month after Fortas' resignation, a Chicago political gadfly named Sherman Skolnick, the head of the Citizens' Committee to Clean Up the Courts, acted on a tip regarding an Illinois Supreme Court case, *People v. Isaacs.* Skolnick discovered that Theodore J. Isaacs, the general counsel of the Civic Center Bank & Trust Company (CCB) in Chicago, had had charges against him dismissed and that the Illinois Supreme Court had upheld the dismissal.

After examining the stockholder records of the bank, Skolnick discovered that both Roy Solfisburg and Associate Justice Ray Klingbiel owned stock in the bank. He further noted that the two men had acquired the stock shortly before the *Isaacs* decision was rendered. Skolnick decided to go public with his discovery and contacted several members of the media. The story was first published in the Alton *Evening-Telegraph* before being picked up by all the state's major newspapers and media outlets.

In the uproar over this suspected malfeasance, the Illinois House of Representatives voted unanimously to appoint a special committee to investigate the matter. Henry Hyde, a state legislator, was charged with finding an impartial counsel for the Illinois House Committee. Hyde would later get elected to Congress and chair the House Judiciary Committee during the Clinton impeachment hearings.

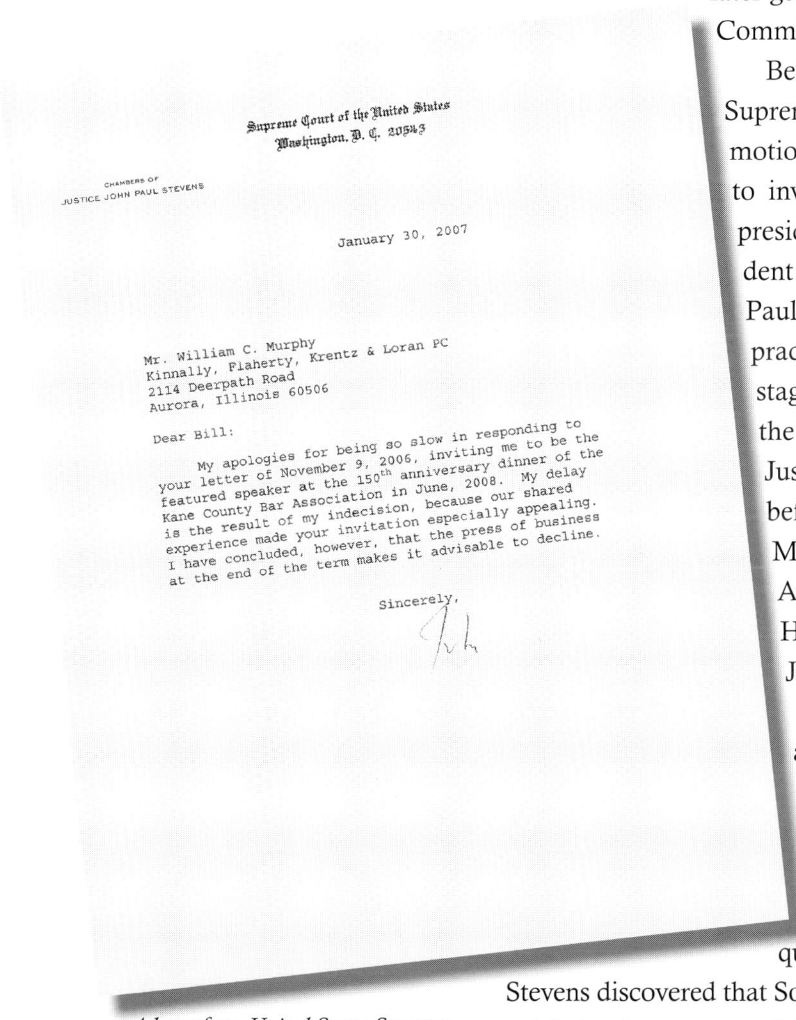
Supreme Court of the United States
Washington, D. C. 20543

CHAMBERS OF
JUSTICE JOHN PAUL STEVENS

January 30, 2007

Mr. William C. Murphy
Kinnally, Flaherty, Krentz & Loran PC
2114 Deerpath Road
Aurora, Illinois 60506

Dear Bill:

My apologies for being so slow in responding to your letter of November 9, 2006, inviting me to be the featured speaker at the 150th anniversary dinner of the Kane County Bar Association in June, 2008. My delay is the result of my indecision, because our shared experience made your invitation especially appealing. I have concluded, however, that the press of business at the end of the term makes it advisable to decline.

Sincerely,

A letter from United States Supreme Court Justice John Paul Stevens to William Murphy regretfully declined an invitation to speak at the KCBA 150th Anniversary Dinner. The first-name basis throughout the letter acknowledges the "shared experiences" they had opposing one another during the Solfisburg-Klingbiel scandal forty years earlier.

Before the Illinois committee could act, however, the Supreme Court, acting on its "inherent powers," granted a motion filed by Skolnick to appoint a special commission to investigate.[9] The commission was co-chaired by the president of the Chicago Bar Association and the president of the Illinois Bar Association. They named John Paul Stevens, a private attorney with a thriving antitrust practice, as their independent counsel, thus setting the stage for Stevens' meteoric rise to the Supreme Court of the United States. Chief Justice Solfisburg and Associate Justice Klingbiel were represented in the public hearing before the commission by KCBA members Lambert M. Ochsenschlager and William C. Murphy of the Aurora law firm of Reid, Ochsenschlager, Murphy & Hupp. Prominent Chicago attorney Albert Jenner of Jenner & Block represented Theodore Isaacs.

Stevens initially questioned Justice Klingbiel and uncovered the fact that the CCB stock had been given to him prior to the *Isaacs* decision by Robert M. Perbohner, an Isaacs associate. The investigation also revealed that Chief Justice Solfisburg himself owned $14,000 worth of CCB stock, which raised further questions regarding the integrity of the *Isaacs* decision.[10] Stevens discovered that Solfisburg had established a trust fund to hold the stock solely for the purpose of concealing his ownership from the public record.

Stevens also learned that Justice Klingbiel was assigned the *Isaacs* case even though it was not his turn in the court's rotation. The plot thickened immensely when Stevens discovered that it was actually Chief Justice Solfisburg who ultimately recommended that CCB officials "do something nice for Judge Klingbiel." It was this testimony that enabled Stevens to paint a conspiratorial link between the two justices and CCB officials.[11]

Based on Stevens' findings, the special commission appointed by the Illinois Supreme Court ultimately recommended that both Justice Klingbiel and Chief Justice Solfisburg resign from the bench, which they reluctantly did

Judges of the Sixteenth Judicial Circuit: (front row, left to right) Dan Withers, Jr., Cassius Poust, Charles Seidel, John S. Petersen, and Robert J. Sears; (back row, left to right) Thomas O'Malley, Neil Mahoney, Ross Millet, Earl Shopen, John Krause, John S. Page, and Carl A. Swanson, Jr.

Francis Youssi, KCBA president in 1968–1969

a short time later. In its decision, the commission stated that "the confidence of the public and the bar in the court is a most essential foundation of our society. It has been severely shaken by the facts disclosed in this record." The commission went on to state that it "believes that such confidence can best be restored by the prompt resignation of the two justices."[12]

Ray Klingbiel remained bitter about the "political push" which took him from the bench. To the end of his career, Klingbiel refused to admit that he had done anything wrong.[13]

After he resigned from the bench, Roy Solfisburg returned to private practice in Aurora, taking on his first case less than a month after his resignation. In 1971, one of his cases actually took Solfisburg back to the Illinois Supreme Court for argument, a case that he won. He argued before the Illinois Supreme Court again in 1984. Solfisburg passed away in April 1991 in Ft. Myers, Florida, at the age of seventy-nine.[14]

Legendary Attorneys

There was no secret as to why Roy Solfisburg wanted Lambert Ochsenschlager and Bill Murphy representing him before the special commission appointed by the Illinois Supreme Court. In the 1960s and 1970s, Ochsenschlager and Murphy were two of the most respected and most accomplished attorneys in Kane County, if not all of northern Illinois.

Lambert Ochsenschlager was born in 1910 in Aurora, where he attended East Aurora High School. He graduated from the University of Illinois and then from the John Marshall School of Law in 1937. For the next fifty-two years, he practiced law in Aurora with the firm of Reid, Ochsenschlager, Murphy & Hupp (ROMH).

Bob Hupp, a former law partner, remembered that "Lambert was totally dedicated to his practice and his clients. When he took a case he was totally

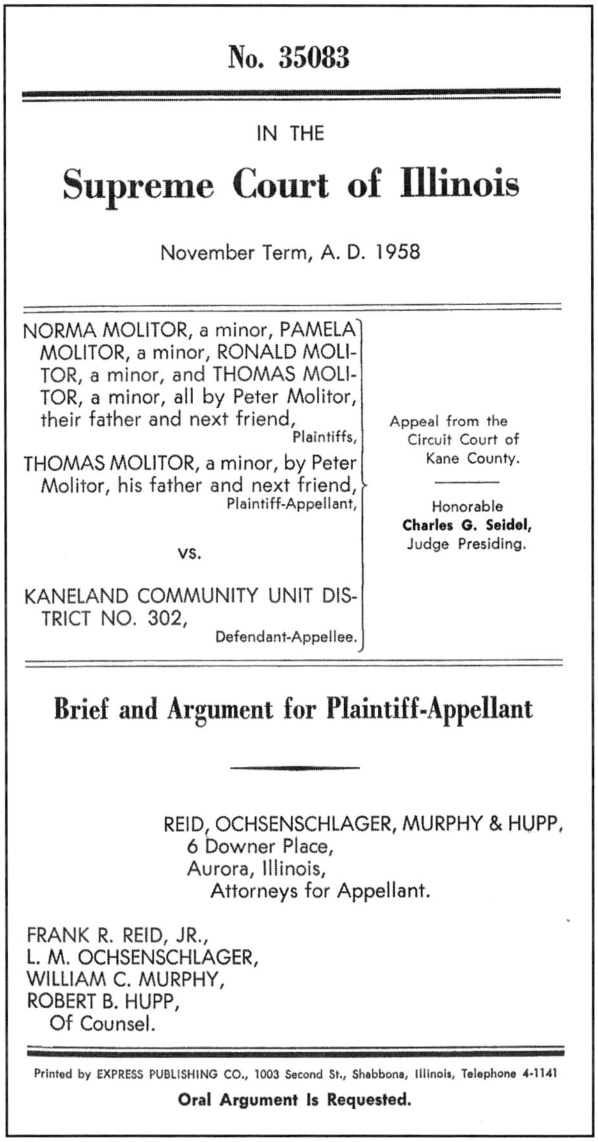

No. 35083

IN THE

Supreme Court of Illinois

November Term, A. D. 1958

NORMA MOLITOR, a minor, PAMELA MOLITOR, a minor, RONALD MOLITOR, a minor, and THOMAS MOLITOR, a minor, all by Peter Molitor, their father and next friend, Plaintiffs,

THOMAS MOLITOR, a minor, by Peter Molitor, his father and next friend, Plaintiff-Appellant,

vs.

KANELAND COMMUNITY UNIT DISTRICT NO. 302, Defendant-Appellee.

Appeal from the Circuit Court of Kane County.

Honorable **Charles G. Seidel,** Judge Presiding.

Brief and Argument for Plaintiff-Appellant

REID, OCHSENSCHLAGER, MURPHY & HUPP,
6 Downer Place,
Aurora, Illinois,
Attorneys for Appellant.

FRANK R. REID, JR.,
L. M. OCHSENSCHLAGER,
WILLIAM C. MURPHY,
ROBERT B. HUPP,
Of Counsel.

Printed by EXPRESS PUBLISHING CO., 1003 Second St., Shabbona, Illinois, Telephone 4-1141

Oral Argument Is Requested.

Brief and argument of the plaintiff-appellant filed with the Illinois Supreme Court in the 1958 landmark case of Molitor v. Kaneland School District. *The plaintiff was represented by Aurora attorneys William Murphy and Lambert Ochsenschlager. The court sided with the plaintiff and abolished sovereign immunity in Illinois.*

committed to it, and he would identify completely with his client."[15] His knowledge of the law was legendary, and he was constantly immersed in its theory and practice. "For years, he had the Smith-Hurd statutes at home so that he could do research when the rest of us were seeking diversion from the daily chores," Hupp recalled.[16]

Ochsenschlager was a large man with a folksy manner and a good sense of humor. Addressing the special commission at the Solfisburg hearings, Ochsenschlager said: ". . . do you have any preference as to how we proceed in cross examination? Shall we go by weight or intelligence?" Albert Jenner responded: "Mr. Ochsenschlager would win on both counts."[17]

In addition to his considerable legal talents, Ochsenschlager was known to wield significant influence within the Republican Party in matters of judicial and political appointments. For a period of four or five years in the early 1960s, Ochsenschlager and his partners at ROMH hosted a two-day overnight outing for justices of the Illinois Supreme Court and selected clients at the Millbrook Hunt Club in Kendall County. All of the justices usually attended except Justice Walter Schaefer. In addition to catered lunch and dinner, a controlled hunt was held with the release of pheasants and ducks. As a young partner, Bill Murphy recalled hoping the guests were all bad shots after learning with great alarm that every bird hit would cost the firm $4.00.

According to Murphy, "the take one year was 237 pheasants, 200 ducks, and one client shot by another, although not seriously." The outings ended with the Solfisburg-Klingbiel scandal. "Lambert was bigger than life and twice as real," said Murphy.[18] Ochsenschlager died at the age of seventy-nine on September 22, 1989, marking the end of a long and productive life.

William C. Murphy was born in Chicago in 1920 and raised in Aurora. He attended West Aurora High School and graduated from Harvard College and Harvard Law School, after being a finalist in the Ames Moot Court Competition in an argument before United States Supreme Court Justice Felix Frankfurter. Murphy joined Ochsenschlager and Frank Reid, Jr. in 1948 and has practiced with the firm or its successors for fifty-one years.

Murphy was regarded as one of the best trial lawyers in Illinois. His skill, creativity, and eloquence have been a model for generations of trial lawyers inspired by his example. James Dooley, former dean of Illinois trial lawyers

A Tale of Two Firms

From the mid-1950s to the mid-1980s, there were firms at each end of Kane County that were notable for their size, concentrated talent, business portfolio, and record of propagation. In Aurora, it was Reid, Ochsenschlager, Murphy & Hupp, and in Elgin, it was Brady & Jensen.

Reid, Ochsenschlager, Murphy & Hupp (ROMH) started in the 1930s as Reid & Ochsenschlager. Frank Reid, Sr. was born in Aurora in 1879 and began practice there in 1901, after graduating from the University of Chicago. He served as state's attorney of Kane County from 1904 to 1908, as a member of the Illinois General Assembly, and as a member of Congress from 1923 to 1935. He joined Lambert Ochsenschlager in practice in 1937. Reid died in 1945 and was succeeded in the firm by his son, Frank Reid, Jr. Bill Murphy joined the firm in 1949, followed by Robert Hupp in 1950. Reid, Jr. was nominated by the Republican Party to run in 1962 for the congressional seat previously held by his father. When Reid died of a heart attack during the campaign, the party selected his widow to replace him on the ballot. Charlotte Reid won and served the district with distinction for five terms.

ROMH grew at one point to twenty lawyers, making it one of the largest firms outside of Chicago. It had a broad general practice that included expertise in corporate and tax work, estate planning, domestic relations, school law, personal injury, and general litigation. Many prominent businesses and citizens in the southern half of the Valley were clients of the firm, and the firm frequently served as local counsel for Chicago and out-of-state firms who had cases pending in the Sixteenth Judicial Circuit. Many notable cases were handled by the firm over the years, including cases that resulted in record verdicts and changed the law in such fields as tort litigation and insurance litigation.

Six members of the firm have served as president of the KCBA (William C. Murphy, Gilbert X. Drendel, Charles F. Thompson, Jr., Robert L. Speers, Patrick M. Flaherty, and Patrick M. Kinnally). A total of thirty-one lawyers got their start and training with the firm, and the firm produced a number of spin-off firms which went on to establish successful and prominent practices. The familiar names of Kane County lawyers who practiced at ROMH are:

Frank R. Reid, Jr.
Lambert M. Ochsenschlager
William C. Murphy
Robert B. Hupp
William J. Foote
Gilbert X. Drendel, Jr.
Charles F. Thompson
George P. Lindner
Stephen Mrkvicka
John M. Lamont
William C. Schanlaber
George W. Brannen
Robert L. Speers
Loren Heuertz
Timothy J. Reuland
Gary G. Piccony
Wayne F. Weiler
P. Scott Courtin
Richard L. Horwitz
David Oakes
Vince C. Metlicki
Robert M. Foote
Craig Mielke
Patrick M. Flaherty
Patrick M. Kinnally
Paul G. Krentz
Joseph C. Loran
Patrick J. Gallagher
William Porter
Phillip Mann
James C. James III

The Reid, Ochsenschlager, Murphy & Hupp firm owned and occupied the Columbia Conservatory of Music and Dramatic Art building at 75 South Stolp Avenue in Aurora from 1960 to 1985. The Conservatory was regarded as one of the best-equipped schools in Illinois and had among its faculty nationally regarded watercolorist Ruth VanSickle Ford.

Brady & Jensen in Elgin has roots dating back to 1907. The modern firm started in 1951 as McQueen, Churchill, Kirkland & Brady. The name changed to Kirkland, Brady, McQueen & Churchill in 1957 and evolved thereafter to the present name of Brady & Jensen.

Alfred Y. Kirkland, Sr. was one of the better-known members of the Kane County Bar during the 1960s and 1970s. He was born in 1917 and was the son of a Chicago newspaper editor. He was captain of the University of Illinois varsity swim team during the 1940–1941 season. He graduated from the University of Illinois Law School in 1943. Like most of his contemporaries, he served in World War II, where he was an army infantry lieutenant for three years.

Kirkland started with the firm in 1946 and practiced there until his appointment to the Circuit Court of Kane County, where he served from 1973 to 1974. He was later appointed to the Federal District Court in Chicago and served there from 1974 to 1979. Kirkland was president of the KCBA in 1961–1962 and president of the Illinois State Bar Association in 1968–1969. Three of his children became lawyers, including Al Kirkland, Jr. and Pamela K. Jensen, both of whom joined the firm led for so many years by their father.[27]

William Brady was born in 1914 and graduated from Northwestern University in 1936 and from Northwestern University Law School in 1940. He then took the C.P.A. exam and, at the age of twenty-one, was the youngest person ever to have passed. After military service in the army and several years practicing in Chicago, he joined Al Kirkland and John McQueen in Elgin. He quickly developed a reputation as an excellent business lawyer. In addition to his professional accomplishments, Brady was committed to community service. An editorial in the *Courier News* after his death in 1989 said that when Elgin residents are asked at the end of the 1990s to select their "Citizen of the Century," Bill Brady "will be high on the list of those considered."[28]

Like ROMH in the southern half of the county, Brady & Jensen represented many prominent businesses and citizens in the northern half. The firm had well-recognized expertise in both transactional matters and litigation. Its many attorneys were active in the community as well as in the Bar Association. Four of its members, or former members, have served as president of the KCBA (Alfred Kirkland, Sr., James Martin, Wiley Edmondson, and Frank Ariano), and three have served as judges in Kane County (Alfred Y. Kirkland, Sr., Pamela K. Jensen, and Wiley Edmondson).

In 1929, McQueen & Churchill moved to the Elgin Tower Building and remained there until 1957, when the firm reorganized as Kirkland, Brady, McQueen & Churchill and moved its offices to 80 South Grove Avenue in Elgin.

Brady & Jensen grew at one point to fourteen lawyers. A total of forty-six lawyers got their start and training at the firm, and Brady & Jensen produced a number of successful spin-off firms. The familiar names of Kane County lawyers who practiced at Brady & Jensen are:

Fred C. Churchill
Alfred Y. Kirkland, Sr.
John W. McQueen
William W. Brady
William R. Ketcham
Randle E. Johnson
Kenneth McGaw, Jr.
James L. Martin
Theodore E. Schnell, Jr.
Van R. Richards, Jr.
Charles E. Sheppard
Lyle C. Brown
Norman Lefstein
John P. Callahan, Jr.
Richard B. Collins
Frederick I. Steffen
Richard I. Marblestone
John Kent
Wayne M. Jensen
Richard L. Heimberg
Bruce R. Johnson
John H. Lewis
Michael C. Deutsch
Fred J. Beer
Marios N. Karayannis
Keith A. Spong
Ralph C. Hardy
Frank V. Ariano
Thomas W. Montgomery
Allen M. Anderson
Roger K. Frandsen
Ronald E. Rasmussen
Alfred Y. Kirkland, Jr.
Glen T. Dobosz
Wiley W. Edmondson
George A. Mueller
Pamela K. Jensen
James R. Cundiff
Diana S. Larson
Charles F. Haverty
Craig J. Randall
Brian L. Heimberg
Patrick J. Crimmins
Roberto Acevedo
Frank E. Kear
A. Frank McAleenan
Bruce R. Johnson

Reid, Ochsenschlager, Murphy & Hupp and Brady & Jensen provided a learning environment rich in experience and tradition that is difficult to replicate in the modern competitive market. Each firm was developed by unique and colorful personalities who have left a legacy in the Fox Valley as rich as the institutions they created.

(preceding Phil Corboy) and former justice of the Illinois Supreme Court, once remarked that Bill Murphy was the only Harvard graduate he knew who could try a case. Following a cross examination by Murphy in a DeKalb County trial, Judge John Countryman whispered to his court reporter: "It doesn't get any better than that." Murphy was president of the KCBA in 1972–1973. In 2008, at the age of eighty-eight, he remains of counsel with Kinnally Flaherty Krentz & Loran, a successor of ROMH.

Philip Ruddy (second from left) and Clarence Ruddy (third from left) in the Illinois Supreme Court dining room on November 26, 1966, with five Illinois Supreme court justices, including Roy T. Solfisburg (fifth from left)

Murphy and Ochsenschlager were co-counsel in a landmark 1958 lawsuit, *Molitor v. Kaneland School District*, the outcome of which abolished the doctrine of sovereign immunity in Illinois and allowed individuals for the first time to sue government entities in tort for negligent conduct. They also obtained a $7-million judgment in 1968 for breach of a non-competition covenant in sales and employment contracts. Murphy later coordinated the national defense of a Kane County manufacturer of asbestos insulation and in a personal injury case obtained the then largest verdict in the history of the Sixteenth Circuit.

KCBA members Allen Landmeier and Peter K. Wilson, Jr. worked with other Valparaiso law students to launch the Valparaiso Law Review.

Gates Clancy, KCBA president in 1962–1963

Gates Clancy

Of course, you could not mention Ochsenschlager or Murphy without discussing the legal acumen of Gates Clancy, another well-regarded Kane County attorney from the period. Clancy, the son of an attorney, was from West Lafayette, Indiana, where he graduated from Purdue University. Clancy attended night school for five years at the John Marshall College of Law and was admitted to the bar in 1933 during the depths of the Great Depression.

His father, John Clancy, who was also an attorney, served as a justice of the peace back in Indiana, handling municipal and traffic cases. It is easy to see that Gates Clancy inherited his take-no-prisoners attitude from his father, as demonstrated by a legendary exchange in Traffic Court in Lafayette. Judge John Clancy was handling a traffic violation hearing, and he told the offender: "Speeding, were you? The fine is ten dollars." When the offender asked, "Can you change a twenty?" Judge Clancy announced, "No. The fine is now twenty dollars."[19]

Clancy's prowess in the courtroom was legendary and it could be an ordeal facing him. "Gates was extremely cantankerous, yelling at witnesses and screaming in the courtroom," remembered Jack Callahan, himself a legendary trial lawyer who tried 147 cases and lost only twenty from 1963 to 1987. "Gates wouldn't talk to you before a trial because he read depositions right up until the gavel came down, and he never wanted to settle before a trial."[20] Clancy also liked to hide witnesses in the courtroom building so he didn't have to list witnesses.

Wendell Clancy gave the memorial address for his father, Gates Clancy, at the KCBA Memorial Service in 2001.

But even Gates Clancy's courtroom strategies would occasionally backfire on him. "One time, he brought the Hamm's brewmaster down from St. Paul, Minnesota, to prove a point about beer bottles exploding, which Gates thought was exceedingly rare," said Jack Callahan. "However, on cross examination, the brewmaster admitted that it happens all the time on the bottling line. This discovery pretty much took the wind out of Gates' case."[21]

Wendell Clancy, Gates' son, began practicing law with his father in 1962 before starting his own firm in 1978. "We would meet every Wednesday night with my dad, and every time during those meetings at least one of us would get fired," he recalled. "I was never named a partner, and I was never allowed to write checks for the firm."[22]

Gates Clancy's knowledge of the law was legendary. "My father never cited a case, but he was never wrong when it came to the law because he knew the law," Wendell Clancy explained.[23] Gates Clancy passed away in 2001, and up to the day he died, he never officially retired. Wendell Clancy remarked that "although I have tried cases in twenty-five counties in the State of Illinois, I'm still considered Gates Clancy's son."[24]

Brochure from the official opening of the Kane County Division of the Chicago Title and Trust Company on August 8, 1969, at 113 South Third Street, Geneva, Illinois

The Social Bar Association

For much of the 1960s, the Kane County Bar Association was still primarily concerned with fostering and encouraging the collegiality that had marked the practice of law in the county for much of the twentieth century. As with other professional associations of the period, the Kane County Bar Association was no different when it came to the social aspects of membership in the organization. As time went on, the KCBA became an early pioneer in providing highly regarded continuing legal education programs for its members well before minimum continuing education was mandatory.

For the last fifty years, the highlight of the social season has been the Association's annual Steer Roast, which was originally held at Judge Petersen's farm in Aurora. In addition, the Kane County Title Company began hosting an annual dinner for the members of the KCBA. These activities allowed attorneys to meet other local attorneys in a non-adversarial setting and enabled them to acquaint each other with different areas of the law that they might not normally encounter.

William Murphy and host Honorable John S. Petersen at the KCBA Steer Roast

Wendell Clancy recalled that making the Kane County Bar Association more than a social club began with the start of continuing legal education (CLE) in the late 1960s. "CLE was responsible for making the KCBA what it is today. There were lots of programs started to make sure young lawyers were fully integrated into the legal community."[25] The KCBA took the lead in establishing substantive law committees to discuss and improve practice in various fields of law.

KCBA Steer Roast at Honorable John S. Petersen's farm

Bill Ketcham and Joe Barnett enjoy the KCBA Steer Roast.

By 1996, there were thirty-five active committees of the KCBA dealing with a wide range of legal topics, from environmental law to alternative dispute resolution.[26]

Attorneys were encouraged to pick an area of the law that they were interested in and that was germane to their practice and join the committee that dealt with that topic. In this way, the members of the KCBA were constantly being encouraged to improve their expertise and demonstrate proficiency in particular areas of the law.

As an annual tribute to a member of the KCBA, the Association each year presents the Community Service Award to someone who has given back to the community his or her time or talent. This recognition demonstrates that the members of the Kane County Bar Association are interested not only in fellowship, but also in how much they can contribute to the communities they serve.

That doesn't mean they can't enjoy the annual Steer Roast and other events each year, but it does indicate that the social function the Association once fulfilled for its members has been eclipsed by a commitment to strengthening the profession and serving society. That became far more evident in the 1970s, when the Kane County Bar Association and its members took the lead in providing legal aid services to those who needed it most.

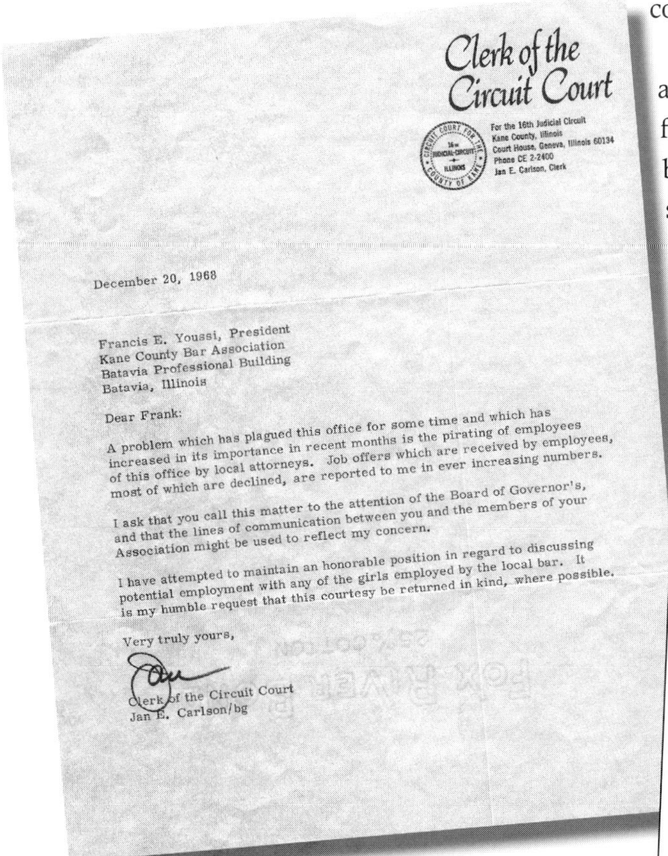

Clerk of the Circuit Court

For the 16th Judicial Circuit
Kane County, Illinois
Court House, Geneva, Illinois 60134
Phone CE 2-2400
Jan E. Carlson, Clerk

December 20, 1968

Francis E. Youssi, President
Kane County Bar Association
Batavia Professional Building
Batavia, Illinois

Dear Frank:

A problem which has plagued this office for some time and which has increased in its importance in recent months is the pirating of employees of this office by local attorneys. Job offers which are received by employees, most of which are declined, are reported to me in ever increasing numbers.

I ask that you call this matter to the attention of the Board of Governor's, and that the lines of communication between you and the members of your Association might be used to reflect my concern.

I have attempted to maintain an honorable position in regard to discussing potential employment with any of the girls employed by the local bar. It is my humble request that this courtesy be returned in kind, where possible.

Very truly yours,

Clerk of the Circuit Court
Jan E. Carlson/bg

A December 20, 1968 letter from Jan Carlson, clerk of the circuit court, to KCBA President Francis Youssi requested an end to the pirating of county employees by local attorneys.

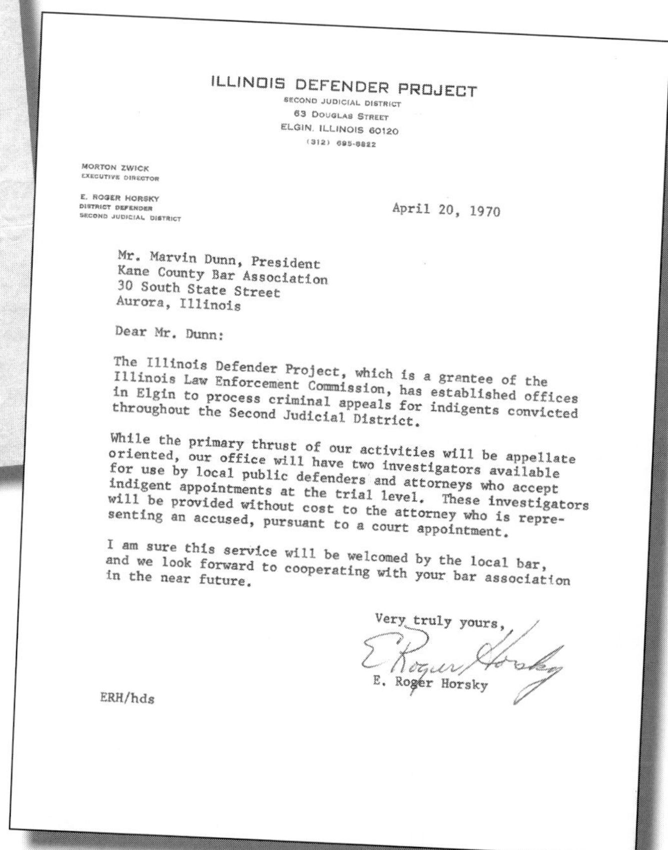

ILLINOIS DEFENDER PROJECT
SECOND JUDICIAL DISTRICT
63 DOUGLAS STREET
ELGIN, ILLINOIS 60120
(312) 695-6822

MORTON ZWICK
EXECUTIVE DIRECTOR

E. ROGER HORSKY
DISTRICT DEFENDER
SECOND JUDICIAL DISTRICT

April 20, 1970

Mr. Marvin Dunn, President
Kane County Bar Association
30 South State Street
Aurora, Illinois

Dear Mr. Dunn:

The Illinois Defender Project, which is a grantee of the Illinois Law Enforcement Commission, has established offices in Elgin to process criminal appeals for indigents convicted throughout the Second Judicial District.

While the primary thrust of our activities will be appellate oriented, our office will have two investigators available for use by local public defenders and attorneys who accept indigent appointments at the trial level. These investigators will be provided without cost to the attorney who is representing an accused, pursuant to a court appointment.

I am sure this service will be welcomed by the local bar, and we look forward to cooperating with your bar association in the near future.

Very truly yours,

E. Roger Horsky

ERH/hds

An April 20, 1970 introductory letter from E. Roger Horsky of the Illinois Defender Project to KCBA President Marvin Dunn

The naval guns on the east lawn of the Third Street courthouse were given to the Kane County government on April 1, 1925, and dedicated on July 4, 1925.

CHAPTER 6

The Bar Association Comes of Age: 1971–1979

Picture the equipment in what might have been a typical Kane County Bar Association member's law office in the early 1970s: The keyboard was built into a bulky typewriting machine manufactured by Remington, Royal, or Smith Corona, or, for the ultramodern office, IBM. Correspondence was conducted by mail or telegraph.[1] The telephone was about the size of one of Dick Butkus' football shoes and rested on a desktop, not in someone's shirt pocket or purse. The lawyer's blackberry was a fruit he enjoyed with his breakfast cereal. On the radio—perhaps one of those new transistor models that made the medium truly portable—effusive Peoria native Jack Brickhouse was still calling the Cubs' games on WGN. And the Cubs haven't won a World Series since 1908.

But change was coming to the Association and its members, and technology was only part of the transformation that would evolve during the 1970s. Most significantly, the Association would lead the way in recognizing a new avenue of service: legal aid for low-income citizens.

The Association first announced its intentions of seeking a legal aid program in February 1968.[2] In mid-1971, the Association's Legal Aid Committee launched a twelve-month study of legal aid in the county, and in June 1972, the Committee reported the results of its study in a recommendation for a three-stage legal aid program.[3] The proposal's authors—Patrick J. Dixon, William C. Schanlaber, Thomas A. Wingader, and Joseph M. McCarthy—wrote that "our proposal proceeds with certain assumptions: a) that the Bar Association should initiate and implement any legal aid program, b) that any program be flexible enough to take advantage of changing circumstances, and c) that there is a need in Kane County for an effective legal aid program."[4]

That there was a "need," the proposal said, "has been documented often enough in the past as to go without saying. Individuals involved in past [le-

Kane County Board of Managers, 1979–1980: (front row, left to right) Wayne Weiler, Larry Crisanti, Gail Erschen, Thomas Prindable, and Michael Colwell; (back row, left to right) Richard Schiller, Ray Strass, and Robert Morrow.

gal aid] volunteer programs have seen only the tip of the iceberg. In 1967–1968, of approximately 78,687 families in Kane County, 7,147 were living on incomes under $3,000 annually. Thus in terms of economic need, legal services are justified."[5] The Committee laid out a clear and bold path, including an eventual move "from purely voluntary legal aid to a permanent full-time legal aid service" that would include a central office, a secretary, and full-time legal aid attorneys. At the same time, the proposal said, the new legal aid service would be a "limited program restricted to civil practice, but not to include contingent fees, which can be served by practicing attorneys."[6]

In presenting its proposal, the Committee let there be no doubt as to its intent. "The Kane County Bar Association will be the prime mover," the report noted, "thus assuring the county of a lawyer-like approach to this area of services. From the moment stage one is initiated, there will be a program that will be respected by the community at large and can be pointed to with pride by all Kane County attorneys."[7]

Action on the Committee's recommendations followed rather swiftly. By January of the next year, the Committee notified the Bar Association that a Board of Directors of the Legal Aid Bureau of Kane County had been named. The members were Harry Schaffner, Norbert Ritt, Thomas C. Rydell, Benjamin P. Alschuler, Kenneth C. Blood, Constantine Konstans, Joseph Radovich, Herbert Hill, and Robert J. O'Connor.[8] Other KCBA attorneys active in establishing a legal aid program were Tim Reuland, Steve Cooper, and Tom Prindable.

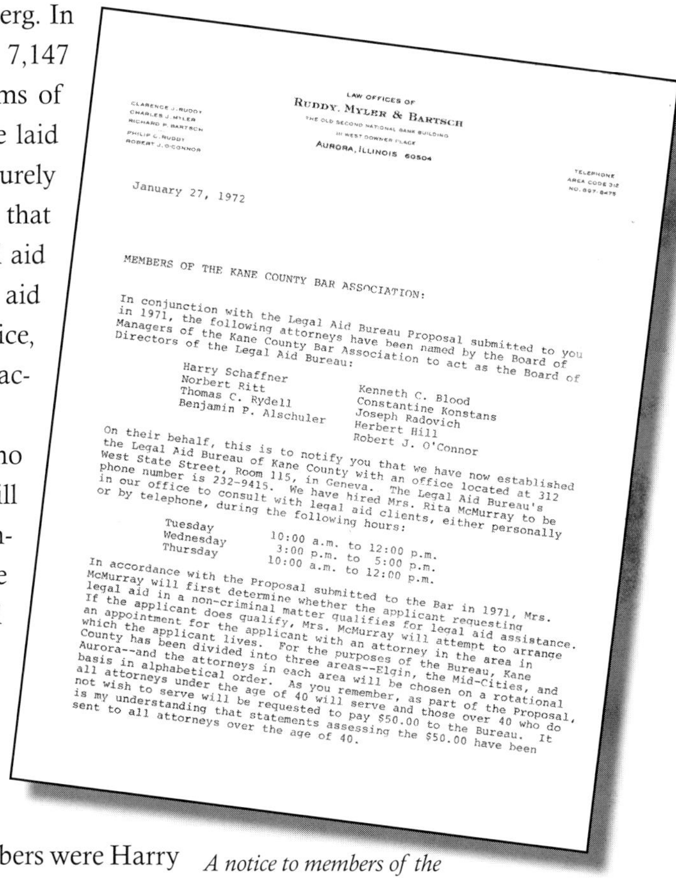

CLARENCE J. RUDDY
CHARLES J. MYLER
RICHARD P. BARTSCH
PHILIP C. RUDDY
ROBERT J. O'CONNOR

LAW OFFICES OF
RUDDY, MYLER & BARTSCH
THE OLD SECOND NATIONAL BANK BUILDING
111 WEST DOWNER PLACE
AURORA, ILLINOIS 60504

TELEPHONE
AREA CODE 312
NO. 897-8475

January 27, 1972

MEMBERS OF THE KANE COUNTY BAR ASSOCIATION:

In conjunction with the Legal Aid Bureau Proposal submitted to you in 1971, the following attorneys have been named by the Board of Managers of the Kane County Bar Association to act as the Board of Directors of the Legal Aid Bureau:

Harry Schaffner
Norbert Ritt
Thomas C. Rydell
Benjamin P. Alschuler
Kenneth C. Blood
Constantine Konstans
Joseph Radovich
Herbert Hill
Robert J. O'Connor

On their behalf, this is to notify you that we have now established the Legal Aid Bureau of Kane County with an office located at 312 West State Street, Room 115, in Geneva. The Legal Aid Bureau's phone number is 232-9415. We have hired Mrs. Rita McMurray to be in our office to consult with legal aid clients, either personally or by telephone, during the following hours:

Tuesday	10:00 a.m. to 12:00 p.m.
Wednesday	3:00 p.m. to 5:00 p.m.
Thursday	10:00 a.m. to 12:00 p.m.

In accordance with the Proposal submitted to the Bar in 1971, Mrs. McMurray will first determine whether the applicant requesting legal aid in a non-criminal matter qualifies for legal aid assistance. If the applicant does qualify, Mrs. McMurray will attempt to arrange an appointment for the applicant with an attorney in the area in which the applicant lives. For the purposes of the Bureau, Kane County has been divided into three areas--Elgin, the Mid-Cities, and Aurora--and the attorneys in each area will be chosen on a rotational basis in alphabetical order. As you remember, as part of the Proposal, all attorneys under the age of 40 will serve and those over 40 who do not wish to serve will be requested to pay $50.00 to the Bureau. It is my understanding that statements assessing the $50.00 have been sent to all attorneys over the age of 40.

A notice to members of the KCBA, dated January 27, 1972, regarding the establishment of the Legal Aid Bureau of Kane County

312 West State Street, Room 115

Board Member Robert J. O'Connor, in a letter, further informed the Association that the Legal Aid Bureau had established an office at 312 West State Street, Room 115, in Geneva, and that the Bureau also had its own local phone number. Most significantly, the Bureau had hired an office staff in the person of Mrs. Rita McMurray.

McMurray was the Bureau's screener, the person who determined whether an applicant requesting legal aid in a non-criminal matter qualified for assistance. If the applicant qualified, McMurray would attempt to arrange an appointment with an attorney in the district in which the applicant lived, since the first stage of the program depended entirely on volunteers. For the Bureau's purposes, the county had been divided into three districts: Elgin, the Mid-Cities, and Aurora. The attorneys in each district would be chosen on a rotating basis in alphabetical order.

The Committee came up with a novel way of funding the Bureau, at least in part. O'Connor's letter reminded Association members that "all attorneys under the age of forty will serve and those over forty who do not wish to serve will be requested to pay $50 to the Bureau. It is my understanding that statements assessing the $50 have been sent to all attorneys over the age of forty."[9]

Near the close of his letter, O'Connor told the Association that the Legal Aid Bureau of Kane County had been operating since January 18, 1972. In 1975, the Bureau secured a state grant that allowed the hiring of the first full-time legal aid staff attorney in the county. David Wolowitz started in February 1976, beginning a career in legal aid that now spans thirty years.

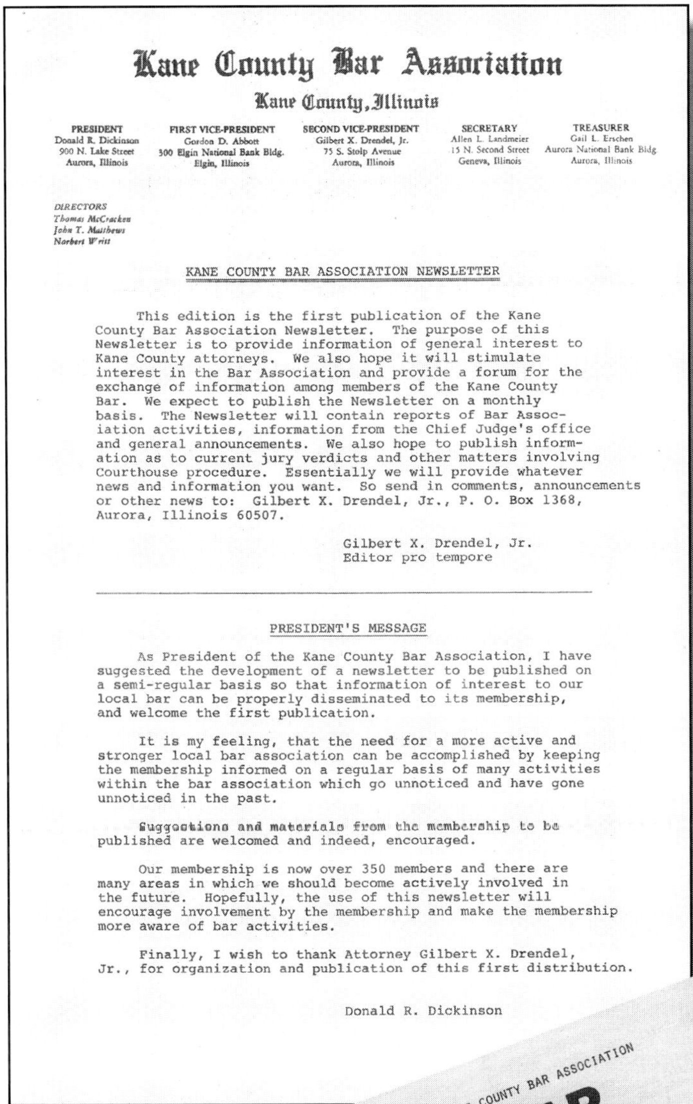

Kane County Bar Association

Kane County, Illinois

PRESIDENT	FIRST VICE-PRESIDENT	SECOND VICE-PRESIDENT	SECRETARY	TREASURER
Donald R. Dickinson	Gordon D. Abbott	Gilbert X. Drendel, Jr.	Allen L. Landmeier	Gail L. Erschen
900 N. Lake Street	500 Elgin National Bank Bldg.	75 S. Stolp Avenue	15 N. Second Street	Aurora National Bank Bldg
Aurora, Illinois	Elgin, Illinois	Aurora, Illinois	Geneva, Illinois	Aurora, Illinois

DIRECTORS
Thomas McCracken
John T. Matthews
Norbert Writt

KANE COUNTY BAR ASSOCIATION NEWSLETTER

This edition is the first publication of the Kane County Bar Association Newsletter. The purpose of this Newsletter is to provide information of general interest to Kane County attorneys. We also hope it will stimulate interest in the Bar Association and provide a forum for the exchange of information among members of the Kane County Bar. We expect to publish the Newsletter on a monthly basis. The Newsletter will contain reports of Bar Association activities, information from the Chief Judge's office and general announcements. We also hope to publish information as to current jury verdicts and other matters involving Courthouse procedure. Essentially we will provide whatever news and information you want. So send in comments, announcements or other news to: Gilbert X. Drendel, Jr., P. O. Box 1368, Aurora, Illinois 60507.

Gilbert X. Drendel, Jr.
Editor pro tempore

PRESIDENT'S MESSAGE

As President of the Kane County Bar Association, I have suggested the development of a newsletter to be published on a semi-regular basis so that information of interest to our local bar can be properly disseminated to its membership, and welcome the first publication.

It is my feeling, that the need for a more active and stronger local bar association can be accomplished by keeping the membership informed on a regular basis of many activities within the bar association which go unnoticed and have gone unnoticed in the past.

Suggestions and materials from the membership to be published are welcomed and indeed, encouraged.

Our membership is now over 350 members and there are many areas in which we should become actively involved in the future. Hopefully, the use of this newsletter will encourage involvement by the membership and make the membership more aware of bar activities.

Finally, I wish to thank Attorney Gilbert X. Drendel, Jr., for organization and publication of this first distribution.

Donald R. Dickinson

The publication of the Kane County Bar Association Newsletter *began in 1974, when Donald Dickinson was KCBA president. Gilbert X. Drendel, Jr. was editor pro tempore.*

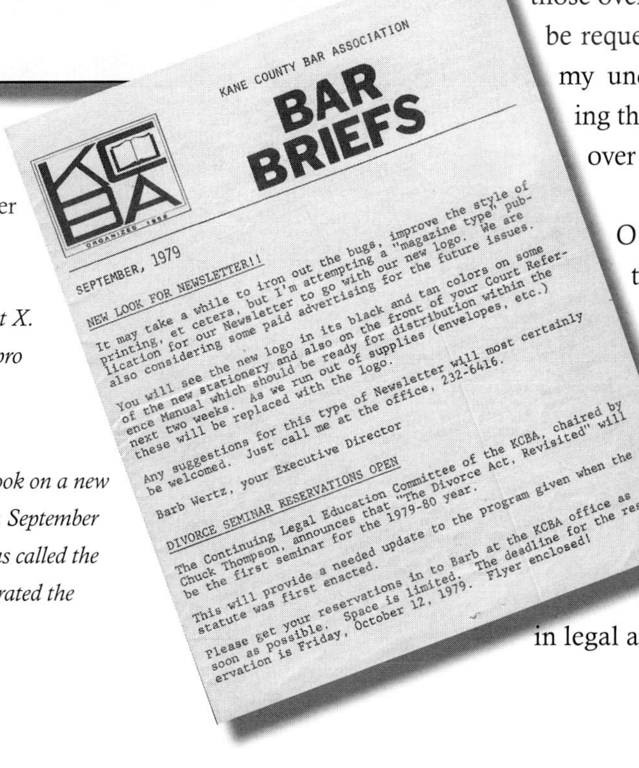

KANE COUNTY BAR ASSOCIATION

BAR BRIEFS

KCBA

SEPTEMBER, 1979

NEW LOOK FOR NEWSLETTER!!

It may take a while to iron out the bugs, improve the style of printing, et cetera, but I'm attempting a "magazine type" publication for our Newsletter to go with our new logo. We are also considering some paid advertising for the future issues.

You will see the new logo in its black and tan colors on some of the new stationery and also on the front of your Court Reference Manual which should be ready for distribution within the next two weeks. As we run out of supplies (envelopes, etc.) these will be replaced with the logo.

Any suggestions for this type of Newsletter will most certainly be welcomed. Just call me at the office, 232-6416.

Barb Wertz, your Executive Director

DIVORCE SEMINAR RESERVATIONS OPEN

The Continuing Legal Education Committee of the KCBA, chaired by Chuck Thompson, announces that "The Divorce Act, Revisited" will be the first seminar for the 1979-80 year.

This will provide a needed update to the program given when the statute was first enacted.

Please get your reservations in to Barb at the KCBA office as soon as possible. Space is limited. The deadline for the reservation is Friday, October 12, 1979. Flyer enclosed!

The KCBA newsletter took on a new look and a new name in September 1979. The newsletter was called the Bar Briefs *and incorporated the KCBA logo.*

Recall the "typical Kane County Bar Association member's law office" that led off this chapter? The Association's Legal Aid Committee proposed an annual budget for the first Legal Aid Bureau office that sheds further historical light on such an office. For instance, the Committee's detailed office equipment list included desks (2), wooden chairs (3), secretarial chairs (1), typewriters (1), wastebaskets (2), file cabinets (1), desk lamps (2), storage cabinets (1), and bookcases (1), all for a total expense of $465. In addition, rent for the 500-square-foot office was budgeted for $1,250 per year, typing paper would cost $13.50 per year, and eligibility forms would add another $35 per year. Also, the Committee was prepared to pay a secretary $5,400 a year plus additional expenses of $259.20 for FICA, $4.86 for worker's compensation, and $100.32 a year for hospitalization. The staff attorney would be paid $10,200 plus FICA, worker's compensation, hospitalization, and ten cents per mile for an estimated 400 miles per month. Malpractice insurance was estimated at $100 per year.[10]

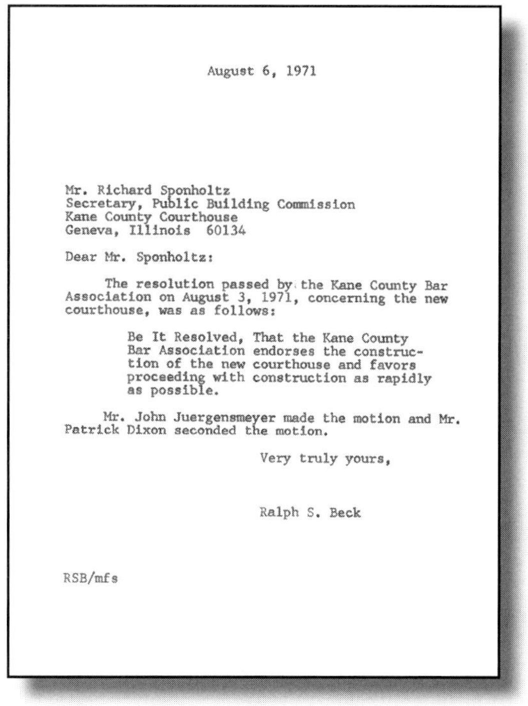

August 6, 1971

Mr. Richard Sponholtz
Secretary, Public Building Commission
Kane County Courthouse
Geneva, Illinois 60134

Dear Mr. Sponholtz:

The resolution passed by the Kane County Bar Association on August 3, 1971, concerning the new courthouse, was as follows:

Be It Resolved, That the Kane County Bar Association endorses the construction of the new courthouse and favors proceeding with construction as rapidly as possible.

Mr. John Juergensmeyer made the motion and Mr. Patrick Dixon seconded the motion.

Very truly yours,

Ralph S. Beck

RSB/mfs

On August 3, 1971, the KCBA passed a resolution endorsing the construction of a new courthouse as rapidly as possible. The Kane County Judicial Center did not open until 1993.

Those simpler, lower-tech days would not last forever. At the March 1972 meeting of the Association, the minutes noted that "Mr. Clapperton of IBM will make a presentation of the various software and hardware that his firm has to offer the legal profession."[11]

Prairie State Legal Services branch office in Geneva. Prairie State began serving low-income residents of Kane County in 1977 and now serves a total of thirty-six counties.

Prairie State Legal Services

In 1974, Congress created the Legal Services Corporation as a quasi-governmental agency responsible for funding legal services throughout the country. The LSC decided to no longer fund legal aid services in individual counties, but to do so on a regional basis. Consequently, the legal aid services in Kane, Lake, McLean, Peoria, and Winnebago counties were merged to form Prairie State Legal Services. Kankakee Attorney Joseph Dailing was named Prairie State's founding director.[12] Dave Wolowitz became the first managing director of the Kane County office and remained in that position until 1984. He is now deputy litigation director for the entire region served by Prairie State.[13]

The Judiciary

From the time John Pearson was assigned to judge the first case in 1837, to the time Kevin Busch was appointed the newest associate judge in 2008, Kane County has had a distinguished and sometimes colorful judicial history.

The shape and structure of the judiciary over the past 150 years has been determined by a succession of state constitutions and state laws. Between 1818 and 1970, there were three constitutions and at least twice as many laws organizing and reorganizing the courts. Whether Supreme Court justices rode the circuit as trial judges or sat only in appellate review changed from time to time. The number and boundaries of circuits and appellate districts, and the number of judges assigned to them, expanded and contracted. Inferior courts, such as county courts, city courts, justices of the peace, and police magistrates, were created and dissolved.[33]

The simplified structure of the judiciary in 2008 is largely due to the Judicial Article of 1964 (an amendment to the 1870 Constitution) and the State Constitution of 1970. The judicial power of Illinois is vested in the Supreme Court elected from the current five districts, the appellate courts sitting in those same five districts, and a circuit court divided into twenty-three circuits presided over by circuit judges and associate judges. All other courts were abolished. The Sixteenth Judicial Circuit was created in 1897 and originally included Kane, DuPage, Kendall, and DeKalb counties. DuPage was carved out into the Eighteenth Circuit in 1957. Cook, DuPage, Will, Lake, and McHenry are the only single-county circuits in Illinois. The remaining circuits have between two and nine counties except the Second Circuit (Mt. Vernon), which encompasses twelve counties.[34]

Interestingly, it was not until 1964 that judges had to be licensed attorneys in order to serve, and that they could not hold other offices or outside jobs while serving. In fact, most judges and state's attorneys before 1964 maintained private practices while in office. William Ketcham of Elgin was the last state's attorney in Kane County to do so when his second term expired in 1972, and he was succeeded by Gerry Dondanville, who became Kane County's first full-time state's attorney.

As is true with the legal profession in general, stories and folklore surrounding the judiciary contribute to the rich history Kane County enjoys, even if some do not meet contemporary standards of political correctness. Judge John S. Petersen, who sat in the 1960s and 1970s, reportedly made known that he kept his own bailiff in the drawer of his bench, alluding to a pistol he reportedly stored in the event proceedings got out of hand.[35]

Lambert Ochsenschlager's father was a grocer on High Street in Aurora, but he also sat as a police magistrate in the 1920s. He was known to listen carefully to the evidence and arguments, but he tended not to look at the litigants standing before him, only to discover on one occasion that he had sentenced his own brother to time in jail. Judge Robert Sears, who presided in the 1960s in Kendall County, was thought, like many of his colleagues at the time, to favor local lawyers. One prominent attorney from a large Chicago firm was outraged when, in less than an hour, he lost his motion, summary judgment was entered against him, and he found his car ticketed in front of the courthouse for parking in Judge Sears' space. He reportedly never returned to Kendall County.

An unfortunate incident that produced significant notoriety occurred in 1975, and resulted in Associate Judge William Vanderwater being removed from office by the Illinois Courts Commission for what the Seventh Circuit Court of Appeals later called "highly irregular conduct." Vanderwater was called in the evening to an apartment building in which he had an interest because an evicted tenant had moved back into one of the apartments. Vanderwater detained the occupant with a handgun and had him arrested and taken to the police station, where Vanderwater completed charging documents, found the defendant guilty, and sentenced him to 240 days in jail, all in one evening and without a prosecutor or a defense attorney being present.[36]

The growth and sophistication of society over the past 150 years has produced an evolving separation between bench and bar. Gone are the days of riding circuit together, sharing lunch after morning hearings, or hosting hunt club weekends. This decline in *ex parte* socialization in Kane County and around the country places greater emphasis on the role of the organized bar. The KCBA has filled that void locally by sponsoring many educational and social events designed to preserve the camaraderie and collegiality among lawyers and judges long valued by the legal profession in the Fox Valley.

During the next three years, Prairie State expanded services to thirty Illinois counties through mergers with other pre-existing legal services programs or by opening new offices. In 2001, Prairie State engineered its largest merger when it merged with the West Central Illinois Legal Aid Society.[14]

Prairie State was established to provide legal help to senior citizens and low-income persons in what would grow to a thirty-six-county area of northern and western Illinois. By 2002, twenty-five years after its founding, Prairie State was providing clients legal advice and representation in areas of basic human need such as medical benefits, housing, and freedom from exploitation. In the twenty-first century, the organization operated from ten local offices across the western and northern third of Illinois.

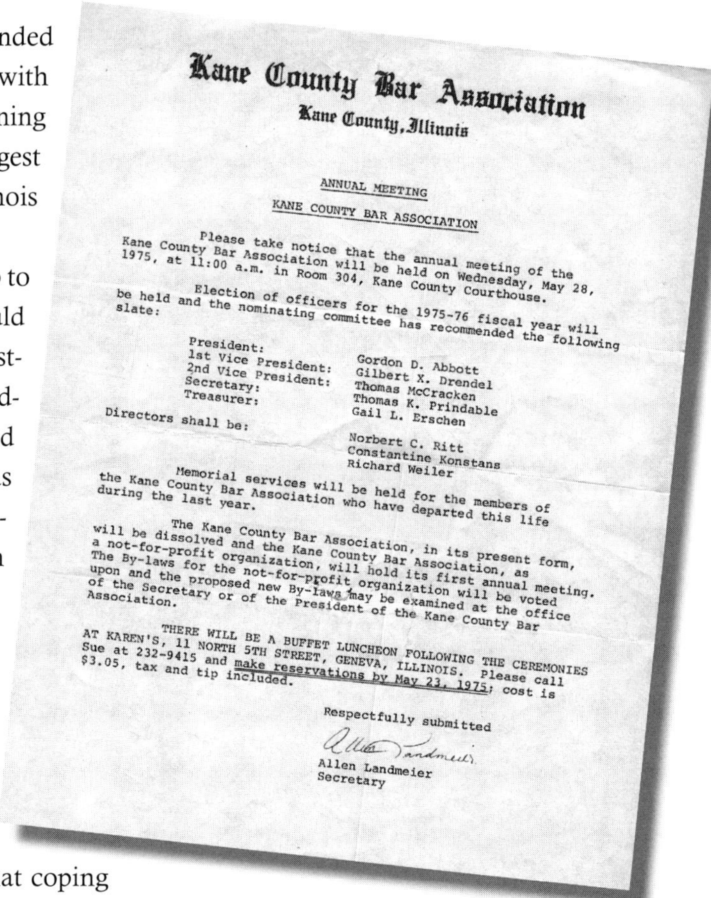

Kane County Bar Association
Kane County, Illinois

ANNUAL MEETING

KANE COUNTY BAR ASSOCIATION

Please take notice that the annual meeting of the Kane County Bar Association will be held on Wednesday, May 28, 1975, at 11:00 a.m. in Room 304, Kane County Courthouse.

Election of officers for the 1975-76 fiscal year will be held and the nominating committee has recommended the following slate:

President: Gordon D. Abbott
1st Vice President: Gilbert X. Drendel
2nd Vice President: Thomas McCracken
Secretary: Thomas K. Prindable
Treasurer: Gail L. Erschen

Directors shall be: Norbert C. Ritt
Constantine Konstans
Richard Weiler

Memorial services will be held for the members of the Kane County Bar Association who have departed this life during the last year.

The Kane County Bar Association, in its present form, will be dissolved and the Kane County Bar Association, as a not-for-profit organization, will hold its first annual meeting. The By-laws for the not-for-profit organization will be voted upon and the proposed new By-laws may be examined at the office of the Secretary or of the President of the Kane County Bar Association.

THERE WILL BE A BUFFET LUNCHEON FOLLOWING THE CEREMONIES AT KAREN'S, 11 NORTH 5TH STREET, GENEVA, ILLINOIS. Please call Sue at 232-9415 and make reservations by May 23, 1975; cost is $3.05, tax and tip included.

Respectfully submitted

Allen Landmeier
Secretary

This notice of the KCBA Annual Meeting to be held on May 28, 1975, announced the restructuring of the KCBA as a not-for-profit organization.

In 2002, Executive Director Joseph Dailing noted that "twenty-five years of access to justice is cause to celebrate. Every year dedicated attorneys, paralegals, volunteers, and support staff change life for the better for thousands of the most vulnerable people in our communities."[15] Dailing also noted that coping with dramatic reductions in federal funding support for legal services was a constant struggle for Prairie State after the administration of President Ronald Reagan slashed federal spending in the early 1980s.

"More time is spent now gathering the financial resources to provide services," Dailing said in 2002, "but the needs of the clients are still the driving force behind our efforts."[16] During the 1980s and 1990s, Prairie State leaned heavily on diversified sources of funding, including the United Way and the Campaign for Legal Services, a fundraising effort focused on the state's attorneys, law firms, and corporations. In 1985, the Kane County Bar Association went on record urging local governmental and charitable entities to help Prairie State eliminate a current deficit of $30,000.[17]

The Illinois Defender Project

During the early 1970s, Kane County attorneys and the KCBA also supported the establishment of the Illinois Defender Project and its successor, the State Appellate Defender. In the late 1960s, the Illinois Public Defender Association conducted a survey to determine the needs of indigent criminal defendants in Illinois. In the 1956 case *Griffin v. Illinois*, the U.S. Supreme Court held that the State of Illinois had the constitutional obligation to provide court transcripts to indigent defendants.[18]

In 1963, the Supreme Court, in *Douglas v. California*, held that indigent defendants had the constitutional right to have an attorney appointed to represent them on appeal. In light of these decisions, the Illinois Law Enforcement Commission funded the Illinois Public Defender Association Survey in the winter of 1968–1969. The result of the survey was the finding that there was a strong need to change the manner in which attorneys for indigent criminal defendants were appointed.

As a result, an Illinois Law Enforcement Commission grant funded the establishment of the Illinois Defender Project effective January 1, 1970. The grant provided for the opening of regional appellate defender offices in the Second, Third, Fourth, and Fifth judicial districts. The Second District office opened in Elgin with Frank Giampoli serving as the first deputy. During the next three years, the Project and its attorneys were appointed legal counsel in some 2,000 criminal appeals.

The success of the Illinois Defender Project resulted in the Illinois Legislature's 1972 decision to create a statewide Appellate Defender Office. Governor Richard Ogilvie signed the legislation into law on August 18, 1972, and the Illinois Supreme Court appointed Theodore A. Gottfried as the state's first appellate defender in December 1972. In December 2007, Gottfried celebrated his thirty-fifth year in the position before retiring. In the fiscal year of 2007, the agency was appointed to 3,253 new cases and it disposed of 3,223 cases.[19]

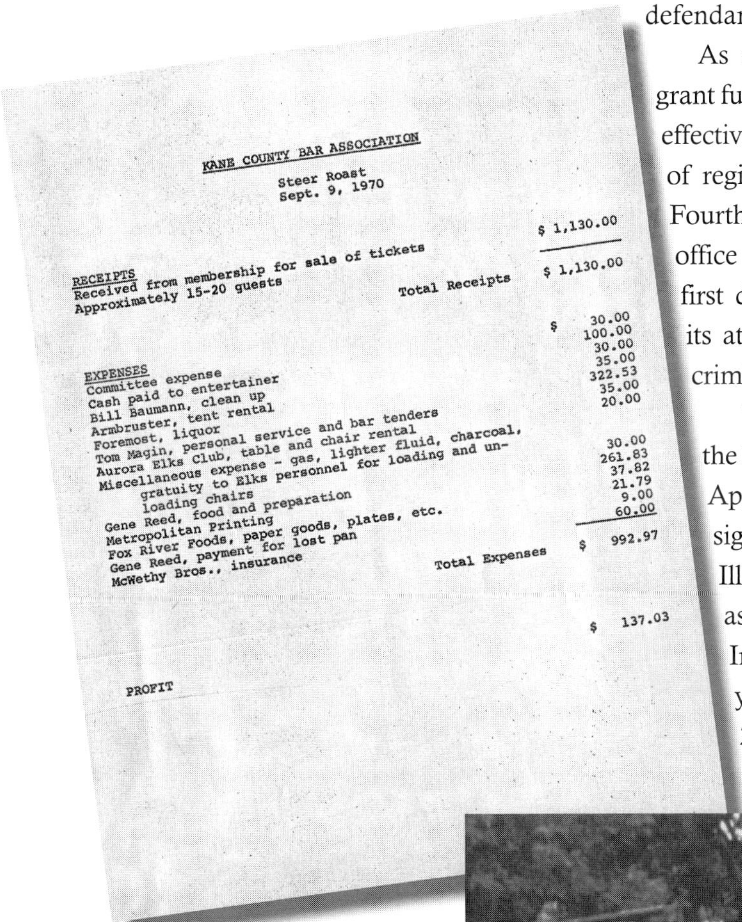

KANE COUNTY BAR ASSOCIATION

Steer Roast
Sept. 9, 1970

RECEIPTS
Received from membership for sale of tickets — $ 1,130.00
Approximately 15-20 guests
Total Receipts — $ 1,130.00

EXPENSES
Committee expense
Cash paid to entertainer
Bill Baumann, clean up
Armbruster, tent rental
Foremost, liquor
Tom Magin, personal service and bar tenders
Aurora Elks Club, table and chair rental
Miscellaneous expense - gas, lighter fluid, charcoal, gratuity to Elks personnel for loading and unloading chairs
Gene Reed, food and preparation
Metropolitan Printing
Fox River Foods, paper goods, plates, etc.
Gene Reed, payment for lost pan
McWethy Bros., insurance

$ 30.00
100.00
30.00
35.00
322.53
35.00
20.00
30.00
261.83
37.82
21.79
9.00
60.00

Total Expenses — $ 992.97

PROFIT — $ 137.03

Budget for the September 9, 1970 Steer Roast

Paul Schnake, Bill Vanderwater, and Roy Laswell were among the Kane County Bar Association members relaxing at the 1972 KCBA Steer Roast.

Addressing the Demise of the Lawyer's Real Estate Practice

Not long after establishing its Legal Aid Bureau, the Kane County Bar Association looked at another gap in its members' array of services. In a special report to the KCBA Board of Managers and Aurora attorneys, the KCBA's Real Estate Practice Committee referred flatly to what it described as "the deteriorating condition of the real estate practice in Aurora."[20]

The problem had been brewing for some time, the report concluded. "From our discussions with title insurers, saving and loan associations, and their lawyers, both inside and outside the county," the Real Estate Practice Committee noted, "it is widely discussed how lawyers have abdicated their responsibilities to both buyer and seller and allowed (or forced) brokers to assume the lawyer's role. It is unfortunate to see the hundreds of real estate closings which occur monthly in Aurora without one or, in most cases, both of the parties having the benefit of being represented by independent counsel."[21]

The report went on to say that "there is no escaping the fact that it is us, the members of the bar, who have created the vacuum into which the broker has moved. In short, it is our fault and ours solely. For too long we have not asserted our proper role in this area."[22]

Kane County Bar Association, 1974–1975

The 1972 KCBA Minimum Suggested Fee Schedule was developed by Charles Myler, David Dyer, Howard Smith, Jr., Jack Callahan, and John Gosselin.

The special report observed that some attorneys and brokers believed that there was no need for lawyers in most real estate transactions, "especially in residential real estate. Also, it is said that such ... transactions are not lucrative enough to justify any firm encouraging this type of business. This Committee feels that these erroneous beliefs have only contributed to the demise of the lawyer's real estate practice in Aurora. The lawyer, if [for] no other reason, plays an important role in the typical real estate transaction by giving his client, whether buyer or seller, undivided loyalty and independent counsel; he is the only person whose sole function is to protect the legal interests of his clients. When the attorney acts as the mere 'hand-maiden' of the broker, it may appear that lawyers' role is of little importance. However, it is submitted that if we, as lawyers, properly and professionally discharge our duties from the time we are retained through closing, we will soon see our importance in our own eyes as well as those of the brokers and our clients increase."[23]

At the heart of the Committee's distress were the "so-called $20 deeds in which the preparation of a deed [by a lawyer] for a broker [rather than the buyer] appears to clearly violate the laws of the State of Illinois, the Illinois Lawyer Broker Accord, and certainly our canon of ethics."[24] The Committee's authors further wrote, "In the opinion of our Committee, the return of the lawyer to his proper role in Aurora real estate transactions will not occur until this unethical conduct on the part of all Aurora-area attorneys is stopped."

The Committee urged the adoption of a resolution that would direct the Aurora Subcommittee of the Real Estate Practice Committee "to investigate and advise the Board of Managers of the names of all lawyers in the Aurora area who continue to engage in this unethical conduct in order that the Board may take such appropriate action as it deems necessary and proper."[25]

A 1971 view of the Kane County jail located immediately west of the Third Street courthouse. The jail was built at the same time as the courthouse in 1892. The jail was demolished when the Kane County Correctional Complex opened on Fabyan Parkway in Geneva in 1975.

The KCBA Reaches Out

I'd like to teach the world to sing in perfect harmony,
I'd like to buy the world a Coke and keep it company.[26]

The spirit of friendship and inclusiveness embodied by an enormously popular commercial for Coca-Cola swept the world in the 1970s, and even reached the Kane County Bar Association, as the Association began to reach out to members who were not fully engaged in the organization and its activities. In part, this might have been a response to the feelings of people like Howard Smith, Jr., who opened an office in Geneva in 1952 and has been there ever since. "In the 1950s and 1960s, you knew every single lawyer in Kane County," Smith said. "But for the past fifteen years that has not been the case."[27]

In an effort to recover at least some of the long-ago feelings of collegiality, the Association in the early 1970s began an informal "reach out" campaign. In 1971, Everett Jordan suggested that the KCBA meet monthly with the bar as a whole "to stimulate fellowship among bar members."[28] Patrick Dixon suggested making two of the monthly Board of Managers meetings open to the entire Association.[29] The outreach efforts continued into the next year. In March 1972, for example, "it was decided that Karen's Tea Room should be the location of the next meeting with the hope that more members from the northern end of the county would attend."[30]

Honorable Joseph McCarthy (right) presents G. William Richards with the KCBA Community Service Award at the 1988 Annual Dinner.

Quick Thinking on Law Day

KCBA President Marvin Dunn and the organizers of the 1970 Law Day Luncheon on May 1 at the Batavia Moose Lodge had to do some quick thinking to avert disaster, as explained in an entry from the budget wrap-up on the event. "Due to mix-up in guest reservations, three dollars each was

Chicago Title Insurance Company office on Third Street across from the courthouse in 1995

Courtroom 310 at the Third Street courthouse. Rooms 310 and 320 were originally one large courtroom when the courthouse was built in 1892.

The installation of the drop ceilings on the third floor of the Third Street courthouse conceals the ornate decor above Courtroom 310.

paid to twelve waitresses so that their food could be used to serve guests and members at the dinner—on-the-spot authorization by President Marv Dunn." The money was posted as a "cash gratuity," the budget report continued. There was no further report on where or what the waitresses might have had to eat later.[31]

Tensions With Chicago

The 1970s were a decade of change for Kane County and its Bar Association. The encroaching suburbanization of Chicago lessened much of the small-town atmosphere of Kane County. During the 1970s, Chicago law firms began opening offices in the county, especially in Geneva, St. Charles, and Batavia.

One thing that didn't change for the Kane County legal community, however, was an innate skepticism about the qualifications and competence of many of their colleagues from the Chicago Bar. Jack Callahan recalled that Judge Seidel, "an old country philosopher," did not like lawyers from outside of the county. "The judge would ask Chicago lawyers if they had their bar license," Callahan said, "and he would suggest that the bailiff check with Springfield to see if they really were lawyers. It is no accident that the two naval guns that are on the courthouse lawn are pointed toward Chicago."[32]

Aerial photograph in 1939 of Route 31 and the future site of Interstate 88. Route 31 runs parallel to the Fox River on the right. The oval shape in the upper left is Aurora Downs, a popular horseracing track from 1891 until the 1970s.

CHAPTER 7

Growth Years: 1980–1989

The 1981 recession delivered a devastating blow to many of the old-line manufacturing companies located in Kane County and northern Illinois. Skyrocketing interest rates, double-digit inflation, and labor upheavals led to the closing of numerous factories in Aurora and Elgin. The disappearance of Barber-Greene Corporation in Aurora was typical of the woes faced by old manufacturing firms in the county during the decade of the 1980s. Barber-Greene, which had manufactured paving equipment for nearly a century, flirted with bankruptcy in the mid-1980s, and was purchased by a Chattanooga venture capital firm in 1986. Soon after, the firm's Aurora and Elgin manufacturing facilities, which dated to early in the twentieth century, were closed and production was moved to more modern factories in nearby DeKalb and in Milwaukee and its suburbs.[1]

Aurora had already experienced the initial decline of its industrial economy in the mid-1960s with the closing of its steel industries and locomotive shops. Elgin had also suffered a manufacturing decline when the Elgin National Watch factory withdrew from the county. But the sting of these closings had been alleviated somewhat when the Fermi National Accelerator Laboratory, constructed east of Batavia in 1968, added numerous well-paying professional jobs during the 1980s.

Another change that evolved through the late 1970s and early 1980s was the decline of the downtown business districts in Aurora and Elgin. The opening of Woodfield Mall in Schaumburg in 1971, Fox Valley Mall in Aurora in 1975, and Spring Hill Mall in West Dundee in 1980 foreshadowed the abandonment of downtown as a retail-shopping district. This migration also affected the legal community in that many law firms began to relocate outside the traditional downtown areas of Aurora and Elgin.

As the traditional manufacturing and downtown service-sector jobs disappeared in Kane County and northern Illinois, they were replaced by white-collar positions that became available as a more service-oriented economy began to develop. For Kane County, the growth and expansion of Fermilab provided additional employment for hundreds of new workers, but not necessarily for those who had been displaced by the woes of the manufacturing sector. And the extension of interstate highways, such as Interstate 88 west to Aurora, created a substantial amount of commercial development at exits across Kane County, as well as increased the exurban sprawl of the metropolitan Chicago area.

Kane County Bar Association 1982 membership roster

Another factor that contributed to the relatively rapid recovery of the Kane County economy was the legalization of riverboat gambling in Illinois. In 1990, the Riverboat Gambling Act legalized gambling "on a riverboat on any water within or on the border of the State of Illinois other than Lake Michigan."[2] Kane County immediately took advantage of this legislation, and gambling boats were quickly allowed on the Fox River at both Elgin and Aurora, bringing in additional revenue to the county's north-south bookend communities.

The increase in real estate development during the 1980s led to an expansion of the practice of real estate law in the region. Since new shopping centers and hotels were now encroaching on many agricultural areas, an increasing number of attorneys in Kane County found themselves with a huge number of real estate transactions to process and handle.

This situation also contributed to a marked increase in title and abstract work as family farms were listed on the market. Since a significant number of the agricultural sales involved land that had been platted when the county was

Kane County Bar Association office at 220 James Street in Geneva

first founded nearly 150 years before, real estate attorneys often dealt with a stack of abstracts, titles, and other ownership papers as much as an inch thick.[3]

The Impact of Female Attorneys

President Ronald Reagan's 1981 nomination of Sandra Day O'Connor to the Supreme Court was affirmation of a trend that had been growing since the first baby boomers entered college in the early and mid-1960s. More and more women were entering the field of law.

By 1980, more than 50,000 women nationwide had been admitted to the bar in the fifty states. They represented about 10 percent of the profession, and that was up from less than 3 percent in 1970. More tellingly, one of three students graduating from law school at the beginning of the 1980s was female.[4]

Susan Tatnall served as the Kane County Bar Association's first female president in 1989–1990.

The number of female attorneys would increase dramatically in the 1980s and 1990s, and by 2000, 27 percent of all attorneys in the United States were female, and nearly half of the nation's law students were women.[5] In Illinois, the numbers were slightly higher. In the mid-1990s, 26 percent of the state's attorneys were women, rising to 30 percent by 2000. Slightly more than 22,000 female attorneys were practicing in Illinois by 1999.[6]

In Kane County, the glass ceiling that Sandra Day O'Connor shattered in 1981 began to crack by the end of the decade. When Susan Tatnall was elected president of the Kane County Bar Association in 1989, she became the first female president of the organization. Tatnall, then a partner in the law firm of Drendel, Schanlaber, Horwitz, Tatnall & McCracken, was emblematic of the change that was sweeping the Illinois legal community in the 1970s and 1980s as thousands of young women entered law school, earned their degrees, and passed the bar exam.

May Simpson was a family law attorney who spent much of her career protecting the rights of the indigent. She eventually began practicing law with her son, John Simpson.

But women pioneers who were practicing law in the county as early as the 1920s helped pave Tatnall's path to the presidency of the KCBA. May R. Simpson, who passed away at the age of ninety in August 1982, was admitted to the bar in 1926. Indicative of women's societal role at the time, notification of her admission to the Illinois Bar was sent via telegram to her husband. As was the custom then, May Simpson read the law and studied for the bar exam on her own, passing it the first time she took it. After interviewing for several positions and being told that she should be home taking care of her children, she opened her own office in Aurora in 1927.

May Simpson's practice primarily involved domestic relations cases, providing representation for those who needed it but for one reason or another could not afford it. This eventually became the bulk of her practice, and throughout her legal career, she protected the rights of the indigent, providing the intellectual framework for what would later become Kane County Legal Aid. May Simpson and her son, John Simpson, eventually practiced law together at the law firm of Simpson & Simpson in Kane County. John Simpson died at the age of ninety-two in 2008.

May Simpson's pioneering efforts at carving out a legal career in Kane County followed in the footsteps of several Illinois women who aspired to the practice of law in the nineteenth century.

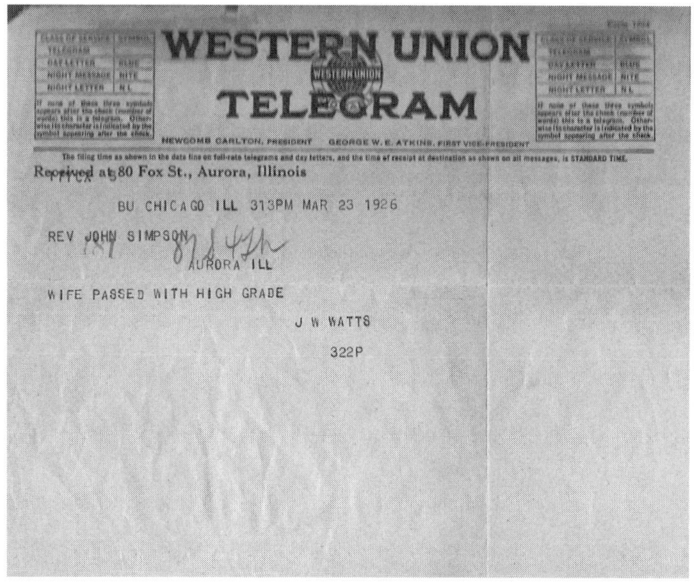
WESTERN UNION
TELEGRAM
NEWCOMB CARLTON, PRESIDENT GEORGE W. E. ATKINS, FIRST VICE-PRESIDENT
Received at 80 Fox St., Aurora, Illinois
BU CHICAGO ILL 313PM MAR 23 1926
REV JOHN SIMPSON
AURORA ILL
WIFE PASSED WITH HIGH GRADE
J W WATTS
322P

The telegram sent to Reverend John Simpson in 1926 informed him that his wife, May Simpson, had passed the Illinois Bar exam with a high grade.

Alta Hulett, who was born in Rockford in 1854, studied law under a family friend, William B. Lathrop. In 1871, she petitioned the Illinois Supreme Court for admission to the bar. Upon her application being refused, she began lobbying the Illinois Legislature, drafting legislation that would prohibit denying access to any occupation because of sex. Her bill was passed into law, making Illinois the first state to enact a law giving women access to the legal profession. It was also the first piece of legislation in the United States that prohibited sex discrimination in employment.[7]

After passing the bar exam in 1873 (and receiving the highest score on the test), Alta Hulett was admitted to the bar on her nineteenth birthday. Hulett was not only the first woman attorney in Illinois, but also the youngest female attorney in the world.[8]

Another pioneer who broke the barriers against women practicing law was Ada Kepley. She enrolled at Evanston's Union College of Law, the predecessor to Northwestern University Law School. Her male classmates no doubt considered her a token woman who would never finish the program. Ada Kepley made history in June 1871, when she became the first woman in the world to receive a law degree.[9]

The female pioneers who led the way for future generations of women attorneys in Illinois and Kane County would have taken immense pride in Susan Tatnall's 1989 election as KCBA president.

Robert Speers introduces Susan Tatnall at the 1989 Annual Dinner as the KCBA's first female president.

Susan Tatnall

Susan B. Tatnall, a graduate of the University of Kentucky Law School, began her legal career after admission to the Illinois Bar in 1980 by opening her own law office. This was a step that not many practitioners took as they began their legal careers, but Tatnall was up to the challenge. She worked diligently to build her practice and her reputation in the Kane County legal community.[10]

The First Female Judges

Honorable Pamela K. Jensen was appointed the first female judge in the Sixteenth Judicial Circuit in 1987.

Even before Susan Tatnall shattered precedent by becoming the first female president of the Kane County Bar Association, Bar Association member Pamela K. Jensen became the first female judge in Illinois' Sixteenth Judicial Circuit.

Pamela Jensen came from proud Kane County legal stock. Her father was Judge Alfred Y. Kirkland (see Chapter 5, "A Tale of Two Firms") and her uncle and two brothers were also lawyers. Jensen married Kane County lawyer Wayne Jensen and raised four children. She had a career as a teacher before joining the legal profession.

Jensen earned her law degree at Northern Illinois University School of Law in 1979. From 1979 to 1983, she served as assistant state's attorney for Kane County.[27] In 1983, she joined her father's firm of Brady, McQueen, Martin, Collins & Jensen, where she became a partner in 1986.

Jensen was appointed associate judge in 1987 and was appointed circuit judge in 1990. She was elected to a circuit seat in 1992, served as presiding judge of the Civil Division, and retired from the bench in 2002.[28]

Jensen was appointed a circuit judge at a time when relatively few females donned the black robes of a judge. Judge Jensen recently remarked, "It is safe to say that during the late 1970s and well into the 1980s, the idea of appointing a woman to the bench in the Sixteenth Circuit was not even remotely on the radar of anyone in a position to move that idea toward reality." It was not until 1986 that members of the KCBA began to support the idea of a female judge. Even during Jensen's campaign for circuit judge in 1991, women constituted only 10.4 percent of Illinois judges. Outside of Cook County, that number dropped to 3.7 percent in 1991.[29]

Sixty years after May Simpson became one of Kane County's first female lawyers, the patronization of women still existed within the profession. Judge Jensen recalled in the 1980s that women were said to practice "hobby law" and were frequently addressed as "honey" or "dear." She characterized the atmosphere for female lawyers then as "too often lacking the same respect that male attorneys would have expected and received under similar circumstances."[30]

Jensen was joined on the Sixteenth Circuit by another Kane County female attorney in 1991.[31] Judith K. Brawka, an Aurora Republican, was appointed associate judge for the Sixteenth Circuit that year and served with Jensen for the next eleven years. In 2002, Brawka successfully sought the circuit seat vacated by Judge Patrick J. Dixon.

Brawka earned her B.A. degree from DePaul University in 1975 and her J.D. degree from Northwestern School of Law–Chicago. After graduation, she served as an assistant public defender. In 1986, she became the first female public defender in Kane County.[32]

Honorable Judith Brawka served as the first female Kane County public defender before her appointment to the bench in 1991.

During her career, Tatnall also believed in networking with other businesswomen and women attorneys. Early in her practice, Susan sought them out and initiated informal gatherings with fellow female lawyers. As these meetings became more popular, male attorneys sometimes joked about a "Kane County Women's Bar Association."[11] The network, which started with very few attendees, had grown to almost one hundred members by the time Tatnall was elected president of the KCBA.[12]

Timothy McNamee

The McNamee Murder

The practice of law is normally a fairly safe profession. Attorneys take depositions, file briefs, and attend court hearings. Occasionally, however, the practice of law can be a very dangerous affair.

The heinous killing of Carpentersville attorney Tim McNamee in 1987 demonstrated that violence has no economic, class, or cultural barriers.

McNamee, a member of the Kane County Bar Association, was killed on the night of June 8, 1987, in the driveway of his Carpentersville law office as he was leaving to attend a softball game. The fatal gunshot was fired by William Nally, Sr., the then boyfriend of Nadine Walter, who was locked in a bitter custody battle with her former husband, Rolando Rodriguez. When Rodriguez, who had legal custody of the one-year-old boy, retrieved his son from Walter's father's home in Tennessee, Walter and her boyfriend drove to Illinois to search for him.

KANE COUNTY BAR ASSOCIATION

BAR BRIEFS

MAY/JUNE, 1987

EXECUTIVE DIRECTOR: Irene T. Van Dyke

TIMOTHY R. McNAMEE

LEAD ARTICLE: "Guidelines to Reduce the Risk of Estate Planning Malpractice" By: Leonard J. Seraphin

The 1987 Bar Briefs *issue paid tribute to the life of Timothy McNamee.*

Their search started in Elgin where Rodriguez lived, and the pair eventually made their way to the law office of Timothy McNamee and Timothy Mahoney in Carpentersville. They had discovered that Nadine Walter's former husband was a client of Timothy Mahoney. On the night in question, Walter waited in the car while Nally, carrying a World War I-era rifle wrapped in a blue blanket, approached McNamee as he exited his law office. There was a shot, and McNamee collapsed bleeding in the driveway. When Nally returned to the car, he announced to Walter, "One down, one to go."

The Kane County Bar Association was profoundly affected at McNamee's untimely death. "Shock, a sense of irreparable loss, and seething rage at the cowardly murder were the reactions felt by most KCBA members upon hearing of the death of Timothy McNamee," said Wiley W. Edmondson, then president of the KCBA.[13] Edmondson, who later became an associate judge of the Sixteenth Judicial Circuit, noted that "a lot of the members had a hard time dealing with this tragedy. Members of our bar have confessed to nightmares, depression, an inability to sleep, and other reactions to our loss and the attack on all of us which it represented. We should not be ashamed of this."[14]

McNamee was only thirty-four at the time of his death. But he left his mark, both as a formidable lawyer in the courtroom and as a good friend to other members of the Kane County Bar Association. In the wake of his death, McNamee was remembered for his tremendous zest for life, his athletic adventures, and his formidable character.

In the wake of the murder, it was speculated that Walter intended for Nally to kill Mahoney, who shot McNamee by mistake since it was dark and both attorneys drove similar cars. But when Walter later testified against Nally at trial, she suggested that Nally might have wanted to kill both lawyers. Walter had developed the insane theory that if both attorneys were killed, it would scare her former husband into returning her son. Both Nally and Walter were considered suspects almost immediately, but remained free for more than a year.

The police caught up with the couple when Walter was questioned in a credit card fraud. Walter received immunity for the murder and the fraud when she agreed to testify against Nally in the case; she was never prosecuted. Nally received a sentence of life in prison for the murder in 1989, serving his time at the Menard Correctional Facility, where he died in 2007 at the age of sixty-four.

A Strange Epilogue

The story does not end there. Nadine Walter was given a new identity and relocated to Florida because she feared retaliation from Nally's family. She attended Florida A&M University and received a law degree from that institution in 2005. The story gained new impetus when Thom McNamee, Tim's twin brother, who is also an attorney, found out that Walter had applied to the Florida Bar for a license to practice law in Florida. He was outraged to learn of her law degree and possible career as an attorney because he always felt that she should have been prosecuted for the murder of his brother.

Nadine Walter's hope for a career in the law was derailed when she had to withdraw her application based on the fact that she had not told the truth regarding her past life.[15] Thom McNamee was satisfied, noting that he hoped that meant that Walter's request to be a lawyer in Florida would be denied.[16]

New Bylaws

By 1980, the Kane County Bar Association was approaching its 125th year of service to the community. A lot had changed in a century-and-a-quarter, and the Association felt that it was high time to amend its bylaws. In actuality, the bylaws, which were amended in 1980 and again in 1981, had stood the test of time very well. Most of the changes dealt with vacancies and terms of Association committees.

The purpose of the Association remained the same: "to maintain the honor and dignity of the profession of law, to facilitate and promote the administration of justice, to encourage continuing legal education, to assist in the delivery of legal services to the public, and to cultivate brotherhood among its members."[17]

Membership was open to Illinois attorneys in good standing. Members who had practiced law in the state for forty years, and had been KCBA members for the previous seven years, were entitled to life membership in the KCBA. The Association waived payment of future membership dues for life members. The bylaws also called for the maintenance of student, honorary, and special membership categories.

The president and two vice presidents were elected for one-year terms, while the secretary and treasurer served for two-year terms. Three directors served three-year rotating terms so that at least one director's seat was up each year. Responsibility for the affairs of the Association was vested in a Board of Managers, which consisted of the five officers and the three directors. An

The 1985 Kane County Board of Managers: (front row left to right) Charles Radovich, Richard Schiller, Wiley Edmonson, and Timothy Sheldon; (back row left to right) Howard Miller, Herb Steinmetz, James Doyle, Susan Tatnall, Pamela Jensen, and Robert Britz.

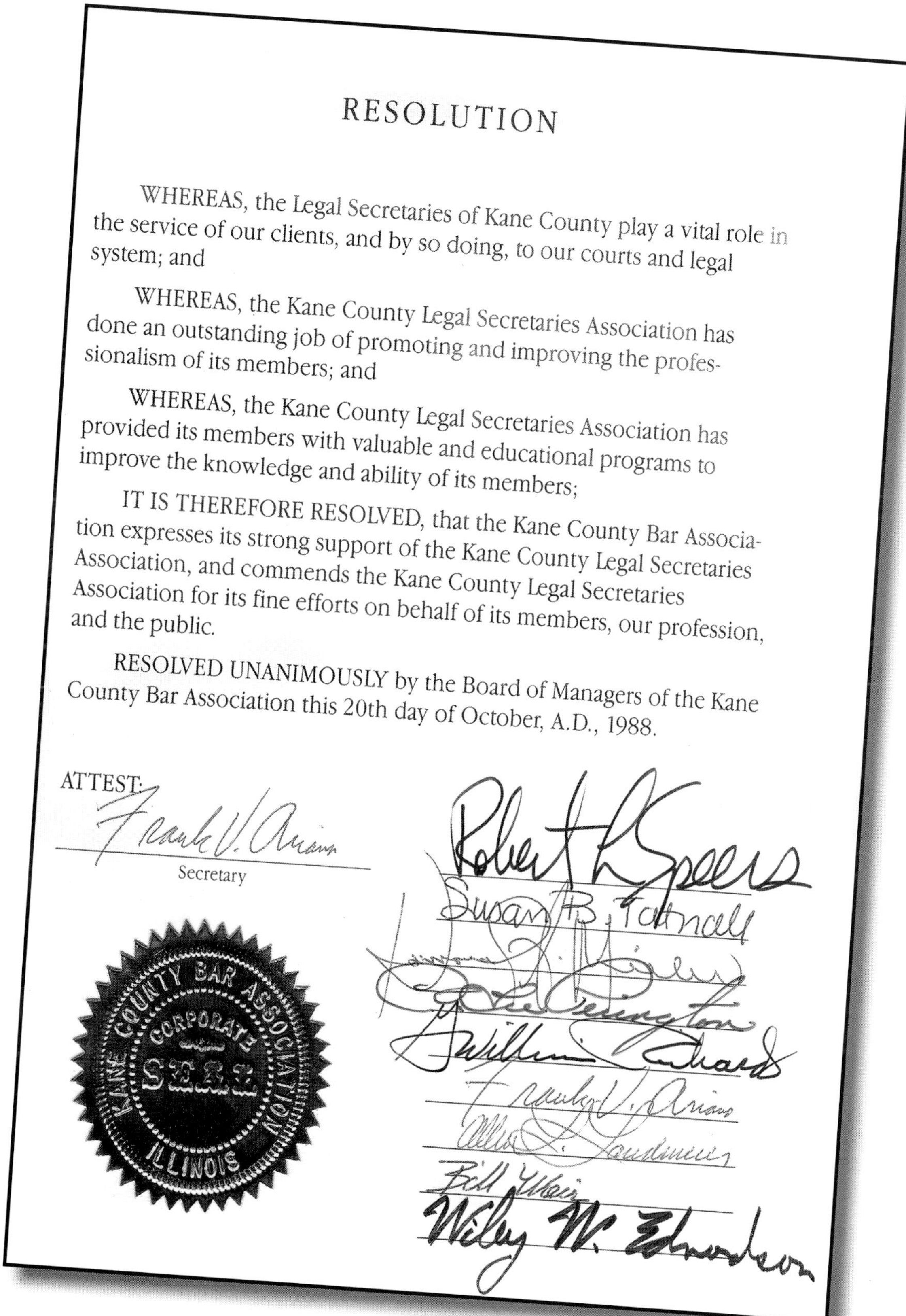

RESOLUTION

WHEREAS, the Legal Secretaries of Kane County play a vital role in the service of our clients, and by so doing, to our courts and legal system; and

WHEREAS, the Kane County Legal Secretaries Association has done an outstanding job of promoting and improving the professionalism of its members; and

WHEREAS, the Kane County Legal Secretaries Association has provided its members with valuable and educational programs to improve the knowledge and ability of its members;

IT IS THEREFORE RESOLVED, that the Kane County Bar Association expresses its strong support of the Kane County Legal Secretaries Association, and commends the Kane County Legal Secretaries Association for its fine efforts on behalf of its members, our profession, and the public.

RESOLVED UNANIMOUSLY by the Board of Managers of the Kane County Bar Association this 20th day of October, A.D., 1988.

ATTEST:

Secretary

KANE COUNTY BAR ASSOCIATION CORPORATE SEAL ILLINOIS

The October 20, 1988 Resolution by the KCBA Board of Managers commended the Kane County Legal Secretaries Association for its efforts.

Kane County Circuit Clerk and County Chairman Jan Carlson and Honorable Melvin Dunn at the 1988 KCBA Steer Roast

executive director was responsible for the day-to-day management of the Association. The Board of Managers also appointed a general counsel to handle the legal affairs of the Association.[18]

The annual meeting was set for a date in the last two weeks of May, and special meetings were called by the president or by a majority of the Board of Managers. Twenty voting members constituted a quorum for any meeting. More than twenty-five years later, the annual meeting continues to be held during the last two weeks of May in conjunction with the KCBA Memorial Service.[19]

Loren Golden plays the piano while Bernard Weiler directs the rehearsal for the 1987 KCBA Bar Show.

A New Home

When the KCBA's Geneva landlord refused to renew the Association's lease at 321 James Street in early 1980, Executive Director Barbara Wertz and the Board of Managers began the process of finding new quarters. When John Nottolini, a cousin of Judge Gene Nottolini, purchased the old Corey House a block down and across Third Street from the Kane County Courthouse, John Nottolini graciously offered to lease part of the downstairs of the century-old residence to the Association for its new office.[20]

Business card given to members of the public for the KCBA Lawyer Referral Service

KANE COUNTY BAR ASSOCIATION

Lawyer Referral Service

708/232-6416

1/2 Hr. Consultation • Nominal Fee

"We are finally moving to larger and better quarters," Wertz informed the members that May. She explained that John Nottolini was restoring the old house and would have two rooms downstairs and a porch facing Third Street ready for occupancy by late May. The new office would also be connected by a concrete walk along the Provincial House to Third Street and the courthouse.

"We wish we could have leased the entire downstairs," Wertz wrote, "but budget-wise, this is impossible."[21] Members helped Wertz move the office one block down James Street on Thursday and Friday, May 29 and 30, 1980.

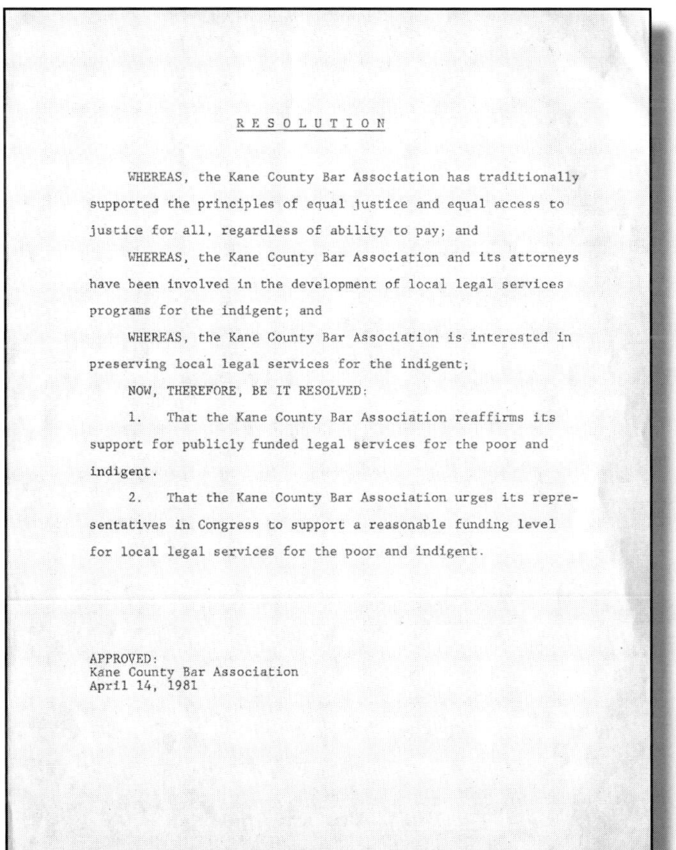

RESOLUTION

WHEREAS, the Kane County Bar Association has traditionally supported the principles of equal justice and equal access to justice for all, regardless of ability to pay; and

WHEREAS, the Kane County Bar Association and its attorneys have been involved in the development of local legal services programs for the indigent; and

WHEREAS, the Kane County Bar Association is interested in preserving local legal services for the indigent;

NOW, THEREFORE, BE IT RESOLVED:

1. That the Kane County Bar Association reaffirms its support for publicly funded legal services for the poor and indigent.

2. That the Kane County Bar Association urges its representatives in Congress to support a reasonable funding level for local legal services for the poor and indigent.

APPROVED:
Kane County Bar Association
April 14, 1981

Resolution of the KCBA reaffirming its support of publicly funded legal services for the poor and indigent approved on April 14, 1981.

Pro Bono

With heavy demand on Prairie State Legal Services, Kane County Bar Association members were asked to volunteer their services in pro bono cases. In 1982, Lawrence Crisanti, president of the Association, reminded members that "the pro bono crisis is upon us."[22] The crisis that Crisanti described concerned the feared demise of the Prairie State Legal Services Corporation in the wake of the Reagan administration budget cuts.

Prairie State survived, but Crisanti noted that "under the Canons of Ethics, the private bar does have an obligation in this area. Additionally, the tradition of the legal profession places a high value on the providing of legal services to all people, regardless of their ability to pay."[23]

Crisanti went on to say that the KCBA could not demand that its members take on pro bono cases. "All it can do," he said, "is request voluntary participation of its members. The Board of Managers is confident that if all of the KCBA members work together to spread the limited number of pro bono cases which qualify under the plan, there will be little or no effect on KCBA members' practices."[24]

By 1984, the KCBA's Board of Managers approved and adopted an agreement between the Association and Prairie State that provided pro bono services by KCBA members. The agreement provided for services in cases involving marriage dissolution, child support, and visitation matters, defense of collection and foreclosure cases, and certain guardianship cases.[25] Prairie State did the initial screening for financial eligibility, and KCBA members provided voluntary pro bono services.

David Wolowitz, managing attorney for Prairie State, noted that "KCBA attorneys have the sincere and continued thanks of the Pro Bono Committee for their willing acceptance of these pro bono assignments and their generous service to the public in the spirit embodied in the Illinois Code of Professional Responsibility."[26]

Pro bono work was a concrete way in which the Kane County Bar Association could serve the needs of the community it called home. Continuing legal education was a way in which the Association increasingly served the needs of its members during the late 1980s and 1990s.

Lawrence Crisanti, KCBA president in 1981–1982

(Left to right) Loren Golden, Greg Slovacek, Timothy O'Neil, Don Hughes, and John Early perform at the KCBA Bar Show.

(Left to right) Patricia Reid Lindner and judges Judith Brawka, Patricia Piper Golden, and Pamela Jensen perform at the KCBA Bar Show.

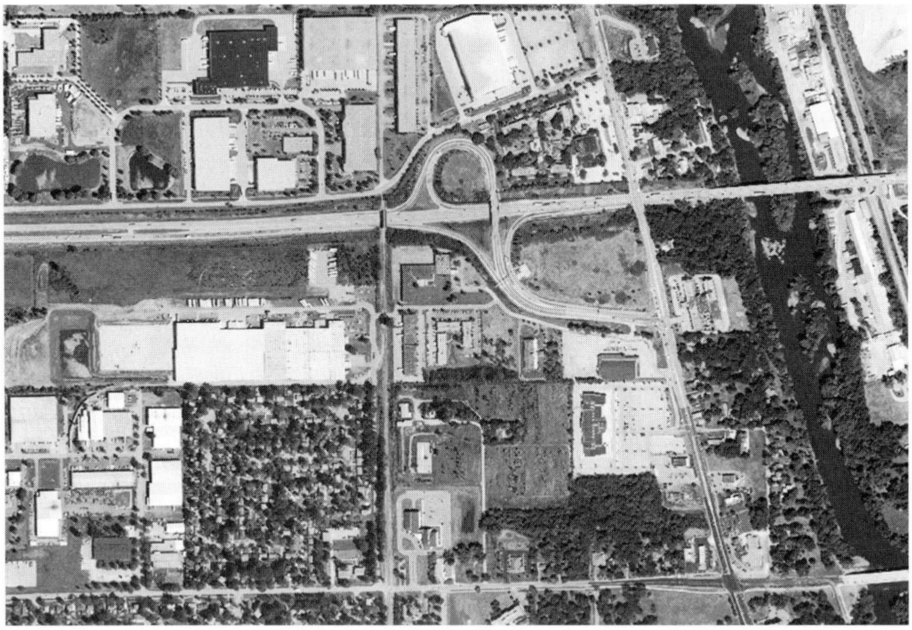

Aerial photograph of Route 31 and Interstate 88 in 2006

Judges Patrick Dixon and Michael Colwell and Justices John Nickels and George Lindberg at the 1988 KCBA Steer Roast. Lindberg, of McHenry County, served on the Second District Appellate Court and later on the United States District Court for the Northern District of Illinois.

Courtroom 340 at the Kane County Courthouse

The Kane County circuit clerk's office was located in the Campana Building at Fabyan Parkway and Route 31 in Batavia from 1988 to 2001. The Campana Building was constructed as a cosmetics factory in 1937, and is a designated landmark because of the art moderne style of architecture.

The Clancy family has produced three generations of Kane County attorneys: (left to right) Michael Clancy, Susan Clancy Boles (now a Sixteenth Circuit associate judge), Wendell Clancy, Tim Clancy, and Gates Clancy.

(Left to right) Judges Don Anderson, John Krause, and Paul Schnake

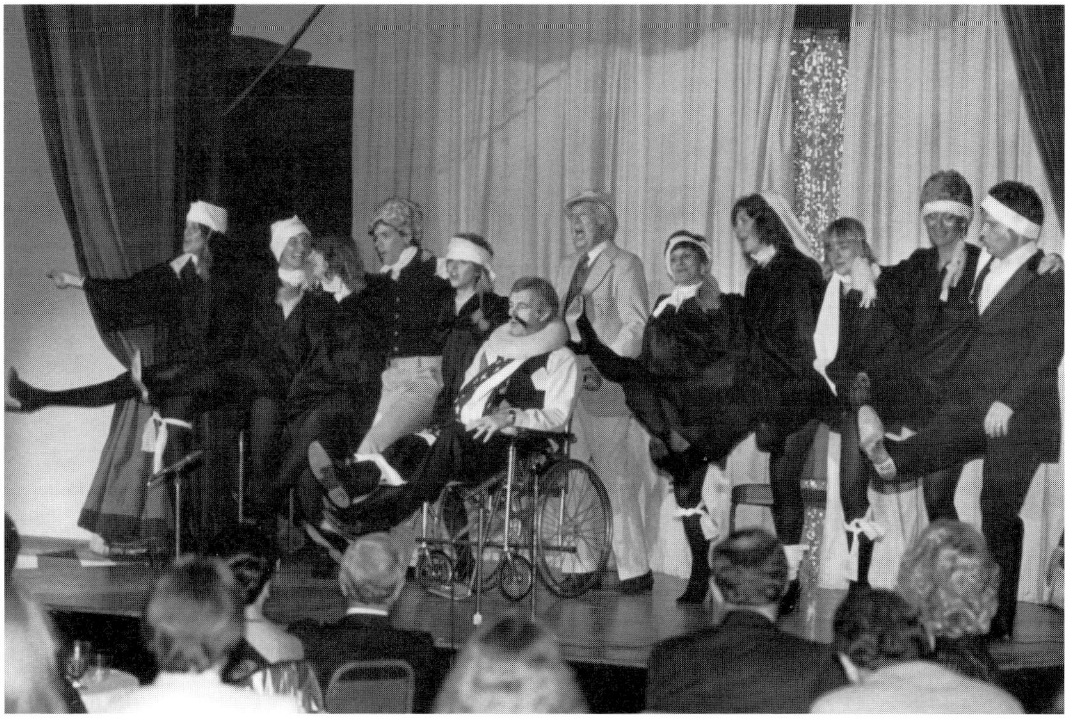

Honorable William Ellsworth and George Lindner (center) with the chorus line during the 1983 KCBA Bar Show

Kane County Bar Association Board of Managers, 1995–1996: (left to right) Carol Larson (executive director), Timothy Reuland, Thomas Streit, Gary Vanek, Steven Peskind, Paul Glaser, Susan Rogaliner, Meg Gorecki, Peter Wilson, Jr., Allen Landmeier, and Leonard Seraphin

CHAPTER 8

A Generation in Transition: 1990–1999

By the late 1980s and early 1990s, the stalwarts who had shepherded the Kane County Bar Association through its growth years since World War II were cutting back their hours or retiring from the practice of law altogether. Several longtime members, including at least four past presidents, were joined in their practices and active KCBA participation by their sons or daughters.

Wendell W. Clancy was elected KCBA president in 1983, twenty years after his father, Gates W. Clancy, finished his term as KCBA president in 1963. Charles A. Radovich became the second member of a father-son team to serve as president of the Association in the modern era in 1986. His father, Joseph Radovich, had served as KCBA president in 1971–1972. Alfred Y. Kirkland, Sr., the Association president in 1961–1962, watched proudly as his daughter, Pamela K. Jensen, took a seat on the Sixteenth Judicial Circuit that he had been appointed to in 1973. Finally, Gilbert Drendel, Jr. served as KCBA president in 1976–1977, a position later occupied by his son, Kevin Drendel, in 2003.[1]

"In 1974, my son joined the practice after graduation from the University of Illinois law school," Joseph Radovich said in a 2007 interview. "The two of us have been in practice since. My son has been Geneva city attorney for thirty years. He's also done a lot of real estate work. I've been becoming gradually more retired for the last several years."[2]

The Passing of the Guard

Another figure who passed from the scene as the 1980s gave way to the last decade of the twentieth century was Irene T. Van Dyke. A longtime legal secretary in Kane County, she had worked in Gates Clancy's office and she was Paul McClennan's secretary. As noted by Wendell Clancy, "We were having trouble dealing with the growth of the Bar Association in the early 1980s, and we needed somebody to take charge as executive secretary. Irene had great organizational skills. She also had personality and knowledge of the legal community. She commanded a great deal of respect from all the attorneys."[3]

Van Dyke, who had planned to retire, agreed to staff the Association's office for a year, and then retire again to spend time with her grandchildren. That one-year commitment turned into a six-year stint with the KCBA. During her tenure as executive director, the KCBA nearly doubled in size, purchased a home on James Street in Geneva for its office, and the KCBA's sponsorship of continuing legal education seminars expanded greatly. The Association's sponsorship of Law Day activities was a well-known annual event, and the *Bar Briefs* had evolved into an effective vehicle for keeping members of the Kane County Bar Association informed about their organization and legal issues affecting the northern Illinois legal community.[4]

In her second retirement, Van Dyke promised to spend more time fishing, her favorite pastime. At the 1989 Board of Managers meeting, the Board made Van Dyke an honorary member of the Association. "It just means more junk mail, Irene," one of the managers joked to Van Dyke.

Van Dyke was replaced by Carol S. Larson, who served the KCBA as executive director until the summer of 1997.

Kane County Bar Association's first executive director, Irene T. Van Dyke (1983–1989), and her successor, Carol S. Larson (1989–1997)

Father and son Joseph Radovich (1971–1972) and Charles Radovich (1986–1987) both served as KCBA president.

In 1991, Judge F. Keith Brown was the first African American judge in the Sixteenth Judicial Circuit.

More Diversity

The Kane County legal community was justly proud when another of its members became a judicial pioneer. In the summer of 1991, F. Keith Brown, a conflict attorney for Kane County who also had his own private practice in Elgin, was appointed as the first African American judge in the Sixteenth Judicial Circuit. As an associate judge, he quickly enjoyed the opportunity to serve as presiding judge of the Traffic Division and the Family Division. Judge Brown presided over numerous matters related to DUIs, mental competency, small claims, domestic violence, paternity, and child support.

After being assigned to the Law Division in Courtroom 340 at the Third Street courthouse, Judge Brown carried on the tradition of each judge in the courtroom writing his or her name in a desk drawer in chambers, a tradition dating back to Judge Solfisburg in 1957.

Born and raised in Elgin, Judge Brown was a 1974 graduate of Larkin High School. He earned his law degree in 1981 from Drake University School of Law, and began his law career as a staff attorney for the Illinois Industrial Commission. He became a hearing referee for the Illinois Department of Labor in 1982, and the next year became a litigation attorney with the firm of Miller, Feda and Barbosa. In 1989, Brown opened a law office in downtown Elgin specializing in personal injury, worker's compensation, and criminal law.[5]

Judge Brown was elected as a circuit judge for the Sixteenth Judicial Circuit in 1996 and reelected in 2002. He was elected chief judge of the circuit in late 2008. He has written extensively on worker's compensation and family law matters, and he served on both the Kane County DUI Task Force and the County's Domestic Violence Task Force. He was instrumental in creating a special county fund to assist in drug and alcohol education, paid for through fines levied against drunk drivers.[6]

Phil Ruddy presents Richard Irvin with the 1997 Kane County Bar Foundation scholarship.

A New Court Facility

After twenty years of leasing office space in Geneva and St. Charles, the Kane County Board voted in the fall of 1991 to build a new Criminal and Domestic Courts Facility on Route 38 at Peck Road west of St. Charles.

The *Bar Briefs* reported that "the new facility will house fourteen courtrooms, including four felony courtrooms, a ceremonial courtroom, and a juvenile hearing room. Each courtroom will have at least two and up to four conference rooms available for use by attorneys and their clients."[7]

The Association's newsletter noted that the new facility would also house the offices of the state's attorney, public defender, court services (probation), and jury commission, as well as a second law library for the county. KCBA members were excited by the fact that the new court facility also would contain a cafeteria serving hot meals during business hours.

Kane County Bar Association office located at 128 James Street, Geneva, Illinois

While construction was underway on the new court facility, the Kane County Bar Association offices on James Street in Geneva underwent a complete remodeling. In April 1992, crews descended on 128 James Street for a complete makeover, including new paint, crown molding, wallpaper, blinds, and carpeting. On April 29, 1992, the KCBA hosted a Funny Run and Cookout at the Association offices, where staff and the Board of Managers took great pride in showing off the new look for the 1990s.[8]

The opening of the Kane County Judicial Center in September 1993 was an occasion for great rejoicing in the Kane County legal community. The Judicial Center, which had been seven years in the planning and construction phases, was the culmination of a tremendous amount of effort on the part of both Kane County's civil government and its legal community. Then KCBA President Frank Ariano paid special tribute to the work of the Courthouse Space Planning Committee that had been appointed by the County Board in 1986 and had worked diligently since to select architectural firms and to coordinate discussion among the bar, court department heads, and elected officials. Ariano singled out the four bar representatives to the Committee—Judge John Nickels, Judge Joseph McCarthy, Judge Patrick Dixon, and Attorney Charles Radovich—for special recognition.[9]

Justice John Nickels

Kane County Bar Association members were justly proud in 1992 when John L. Nickels was elevated to the state's highest court. Nickels, only the second member of the Association to serve as a Justice of the Supreme Court of Illinois, was born in Aurora, the son of a dairy farmer. He attended a one-room country grade school and graduated from Marmion Military Academy in 1948. After graduating from high school, he farmed with his father for five years until 1953, when he was drafted into the U.S. Army just as the Korean War was winding down. He trained as an aircraft engine mechanic at Ft. Leonard Wood, Missouri, and San Marcos, Texas. He then spent the rest of his army career in the aviation section at Ft. Knox, Kentucky.

Illinois Supreme Court Justice John Nickels, who served on the court from 1992 to 1999

Upon leaving the army in January 1956, Nickels enrolled at Northern Illinois University, earning a bachelor's degree in business administration in 1958. He then moved to Chicago to obtain his law degree from DePaul University School of Law and passed the bar exam in mid 1960. Nickels received his license to practice law in 1961.

John Nickels' early law career involved doing insurance work for Gates Clancy in Geneva. He worked with Clancy until 1964, when he left to form a partnership with Louis E. Neuendorf. The two practiced together until 1968 when Nickels branched off to start a general practice in Elburn, Illinois, eight miles west of St. Charles. Nickels noted that "I practiced a little bit of everything in Elburn."[20]

In addition, during his twenty-one years of legal practice with the firm of Nickels & McClowe, he served as a member of the Kane County Zoning Board of Appeals, the Kane County Regional Planning Commission, and as city attorney of Sugar Grove.

In 1982, Nickels was elected as circuit court judge for the Sixteenth Judicial Circuit. He developed a reputation as a fair, hardworking, and scholarly judge.[21]

During his tenure as a circuit judge, Nickels served in Kane County as a felony judge and was presiding judge of the Chancery Division for two years. He then served in DeKalb County for two years as presiding judge until 1988, when he ran for a vacancy on the Appellate Court for the Second District in Elgin.[22] Nickels served on the appellate bench until 1992, when Supreme Court Justice Tom Moran announced his retirement from the Second District seat on the high court. Judge Nickels decided to run for the vacancy.[23]

In the Republican primary held on March 17, 1992, Judge Nickels won an upset victory for his party's nomination, defeating Thomas J. O'Donnell by almost 20,000 votes and another candidate, George Unverzagt, who had the backing of the Republican Committee chairmen in Kane, DuPage, and Kendall counties. Judge Nickels won in the general election in November and was sworn in on December 17, 1992. He spent seven years as a Supreme Court justice in Springfield, retiring in 1999.

Regarding political races, Justice Nickels pointed out that "most elections here were partisan. It was a fairly strong Republican area, so the Republican primary was the big battle. There was very little opposition on the Democratic side. If you won the Republican primary, you were pretty much assured of winning the election."[24]

Reflecting on his particular political races, Justice Nickels said he thought that all of his campaigns were memorable. "I was not politically active until I ran for the position of circuit court judge," he said. "There was a vacancy, and I wanted to give it a try. It was quite a heated race because I was running against Barry Puklin, who was already an associate justice."[25]

The creation of a campaign infrastructure was also very important in "getting out the vote," Justice Nickels said. "My campaign people worked very hard. There was some knocking on doors and handing out handbills at the train stations in Geneva and Elgin. I also had to go to a lot of hog roasts and Lincoln Day dinners. I went to three of them and kind of got Lincoln-dinnered out."[26]

In the course of their marriage, Justice Nickels and his wife, Merita, raised seven children. After his retirement from the Supreme Court in 1999, Justice Nickels and his wife continued to live on a farm in rural Maple Grove, maintaining an interest in farming that he has had since he first farmed with his father after high school. Justice Nickels has remained active in the legal community as well.

In summing up his legal career, Justice Nickels said he became an attorney "because I believed it was an honorable profession. I believed it would provide a livelihood and allow me to support my family. My twenty years in private practice not only allowed me to provide for my family, but to gain the experience necessary to recognize the opportunities presented when I first decided to travel the path to the bench."[27]

In the News

The twenty-four-hour cable news cycle and the rise of the Internet brought increased attention to breaking legal cases during the 1990s. O. J. Simpson's trip down the California freeway system in his white Bronco and the resulting year-long trial made judges and attorneys media superstars. The Kane County legal community found itself in the national spotlight during the decade with a number of intriguing cases.

The 1994 taping of Legal Ease *with host attorney Dick Balog (right) and guests James Guagliardo (left) and Honorable Donald Hudson.* Legal Ease *was a public service television broadcast sponsored by the KCBA.*

The "Home Alone" Case

The strange case of David and Sharon Schoo of St. Charles grabbed the headlines in early 1993. The St. Charles couple had left their two daughters, ages four and nine, alone in their house at Christmas while they went on a nine-day vacation to Acapulco.

Arrested at O'Hare Airport on their return to the United States, the Schoos were briefly lodged in the Kane County Jail before bond was posted by Sharon Schoo's father.[10] The two children were placed in foster care by the Illinois Department of Child and Family Services. According to *The New York Times,* people asked one of the couple's Kane County attorneys, Gerard Kepple, how it felt to represent "the most vilified and hated couple in America."[11]

In February, the Schoos pled not guilty to sixty-four separate counts, including neglect, physical abuse of the two girls, and child abandonment.[12] The case was extensively covered in the national media, including network news,

Kane County Bar Association Board of Managers, 1991–1992: (front row, left to right) Lee Perington, Charles Thompson, and Frank Ariano; (back row, left to right) Carol Larson (executive director), Constantine Konstans, Jane Craddock Ryan, Robert Foote, Herb Steinmetz, Howard Miller, and Stephen Sullivan

Herbert Hill was one of the attorneys appointed to represent Edward Tenney, who was accused of murdering Virginia Johannessen and Mary Jill Oberweis in 1993.

The New York Times, and *Time* magazine. Some considered the case a matter of life imitating art, given its similarity to the 1990 hit movie, *Home Alone,* with actor Macaulay Culkin.

The case was resolved in the summer of 1993, when the Schoos, who had moved from St. Charles to Geneva that spring, quietly gave up their daughters for adoption.[13]

The Tenney Case

Herbert Hill, a member of the Schoos' defense team, figured prominently in a second case that landed Kane County in the legal spotlight. The Edward Tenney case began, ironically enough, on the cold night of January 2, 1993, when David and Sharon Schoo were spending the evening as guests of the Kane County justice system.

In Aurora, Tenney and an accomplice broke into the home of seventy-six-year-old Virginia Johannessen, shot and killed her, and stole jewelry, small appliances, and money. Nine months later, in a similar home invasion, Tenney shot and killed Mary Jill Oberweis, whose family owned and operated the Oberweis Dairy in Aurora.[14]

Kane County attorneys Herbert Hill and William Glisson represented Tenney, who was convicted of both murders in 1998 and sentenced to death. Tenney appealed both convictions. The Oberweis conviction was eventually upheld on appeal by the Second District. Tenney's appeal in the Johannessen case eventually went to the Illinois Supreme Court, and his conviction was overturned in 2002 because of legal error. He was re-tried and convicted in 2007. Tenney was sentenced to life in prison in early 2008, fifteen years after the death of Virginia Johannessen. Tenney is scheduled to be tried later in 2008 for a 1992 murder and robbery he is alleged to have committed in DuPage County.[15]

The inaugural Long Range Planning Retreat was held at the Abbey in 1993: (left to right) Chair Charles Radovich, Ben Schwartz, and Carol Larson. The KCBA continues to conduct annual Long Range Planning retreats in Lake Geneva, Wisconsin.

Planning for the Association's Future

For much of its history during the past half-century, the Kane County Bar Association was more often reactive than proactive. But as the organization grew in membership and stature during the 1980s, it began to realize the value of strategic planning.

Frank V. Ariano, the Association's president in 1993–1994, initiated the KCBA's first strategic planning efforts in the fall of 1993. In October, Ariano proposed that the Board of Managers meet at the Abbey on Lake Geneva, Wisconsin, for a weekend long-range planning retreat. Chairman Charles Radovich, Facilitator Jerry Black, Lee Perington, Pete Wilson, Jr., Leonard Seraphin, Ben Schwartz, Carl Safanda, Tim Reuland, Bill Richards, and Carol Larson spent long hours in front of whiteboards and flip charts, attempting to divine where the organization had been in the past and where it needed to go in the future to meet the growing needs of its members.

Clarence Ruddy and Francis Youssi at the 1995 General Membership Dinner

Ariano noted that "a lot of careful thought, debate, and genuine concern for this bar were used to formulate a long-range plan for the future of this Association and its members, as well as [for] those we serve."[16]

That first strategic plan addressed numerous important issues to the membership, including finances, administration, delivery of legal services, continuing legal education, public relations, relationship with judges, and facilities. Most importantly, it laid the foundation for a continuation of the KCBA's commitment to planning for the Association's future. By the late 1990s, the KCBA was looking at its strategic plan once a year.[17] Many of the issues that Gary M. Vanek and Steve Peskind faced during their presidencies from 1997 to 1999 were similar to or the same as those that Ariano and his planning team had identified in 1993. But the fact that the KCBA could plan confidently for its future spoke volumes about the vision and farsightedness of the Association's leadership during the decade.

Initial construction of the Kane County Judicial Center in 1992

The Association at Mid-Decade

By the mid-1990s, the KCBA was a thriving local bar association that gave its members a voice both in the local community and the state's legal community. With 800 members, KCBA was one of the largest county bar associations in the state, although presidents at mid-decade pointed out that 400 attorneys living or practicing in the Sixteenth Judicial Circuit were not members of the Association.[18]

With a budget approaching $100,000 a year, the KCBA also was one of the better-funded county bar associations in the state. One major result of the 1993–1994 strategic plan was a recommendation that the Board of Managers institute a general dues increase, the first for the organization since the late 1960s. The increase, which created a sliding scale between $115 a year for members in practice more than six years to $35 for brand-new members, students, and affiliates, allowed the Association to fund a growing number of programs and seminars.

In 1994, the KCBA sponsored thirty-six seminars for more than 1,200 attendees and the Association included DeKalb County Bar members in its CLE program. The KCBA formed a Bar Foundation Committee that would bear fruit in 1996 with the establishment

Members of the KCBA tour the interior of the Kane County Judicial Center during construction.

The Kane County Judicial Center opened in 1993.

George Lindner, Honorable Pamela Jensen, Honorable Michael Colwell, Mark Monaco, and Rick Turner are among the participants at the starting line at the 1991 KCBA Funny Run benefiting the KCBA Scholarship Fund.

and initial funding of the Kane County Bar Foundation, a not-for-profit organization formed for the purpose of providing access to the legal system for Kane County citizens through funding of pro bono programs, law student scholarships, and other community-oriented endeavors. The Foundation sponsored a full program of Law Day activities each May, including a Lawyer's Funny Run, mock trials, and the popular "Ask a Lawyer" event. On the social and civic side, the KCBA sponsored a summer golf outing, the annual Steer Roast, Judge's Night, the Holiday Party and Toy Drive, and the Salvation Army Bell Ring.[19]

KCBA Public Relations Committee Chair Paul Glaser and G. William Richards grill for KCBA members after the KCBA Funny Run.

A New Look for *Bar Briefs*

One major change instituted in the mid-1990s was a redesign of *Bar Briefs,* the Association's monthly member magazine. Started in 1980 as a mimeographed legal-size mostly monthly newsletter, *Bar Briefs* was a labor of love for its volunteer editors, including Judge Wiley Edmondson. The newsletter was stapled and produced on an electric typewriter. The 1994 redesign shrank the size of the newsletter to a more standard 8.5-by-11 format with more pages of substantive content for KCBA members to read.

The computer revolution of the 1990s allowed more of the *Bar Briefs* to be set and designed on a dedicated desktop computer, which the Geneva office began using for publishing and administrative tasks in 1994. Four years later, the Kane County Bar Association unveiled its first Web page on the Internet.

Computerization and the Internet propelled Kane County's legal community into the twenty-first century. For the KCBA, the new millennium posed both new challenges and new opportunities.

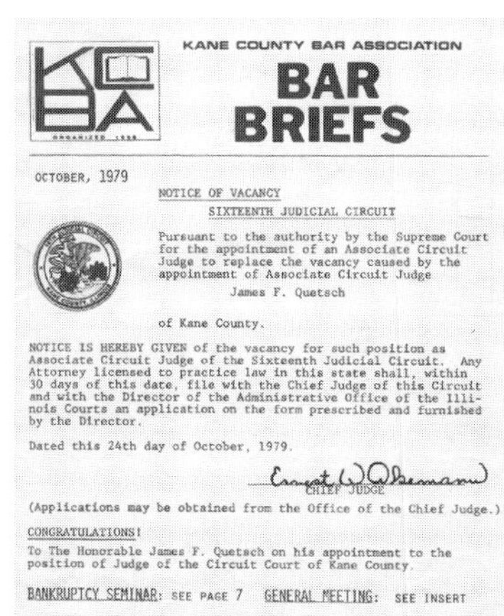

KANE COUNTY BAR ASSOCIATION

BAR BRIEFS

OCTOBER, 1979

NOTICE OF VACANCY

SIXTEENTH JUDICIAL CIRCUIT

Pursuant to the authority by the Supreme Court for the appointment of an Associate Circuit Judge to replace the vacancy caused by the appointment of Associate Circuit Judge

James F. Quetsch

of Kane County.

NOTICE IS HEREBY GIVEN of the vacancy for such position as Associate Circuit Judge of the Sixteenth Judicial Circuit. Any Attorney licensed to practice law in this state shall, within 30 days of this date, file with the Chief Judge of this Circuit and with the Director of the Administrative Office of the Illinois Courts an application on the form prescribed and furnished by the Director.

Dated this 24th day of October, 1979.

CHIEF JUDGE

(Applications may be obtained from the Office of the Chief Judge.)

CONGRATULATIONS!

To The Honorable James F. Quetsch on his appointment to the position of Judge of the Circuit Court of Kane County.

BANKRUPTCY SEMINAR: SEE PAGE 7 GENERAL MEETING: SEE INSERT

Cover of the October 1979 KCBA Bar Briefs

KCBA President Steve Andersson and Executive Director Jan Wade during the 2001 Holiday Party and toy drive

The KCBA hosts an annual Judge's Night to honor the Sixteenth Circuit judiciary. Attendees at the 1995 Judge's Night: (left to right) Mary Ellen Balaguer, Jay Dahl, Honorable Thomas Hogan, Jonathan Carbary, and Bruce David.

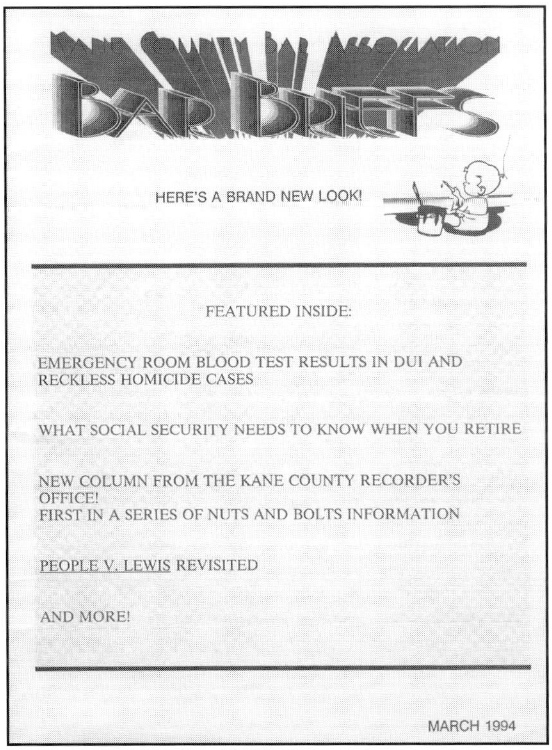

KANE COUNTY BAR ASSOCIATION

BAR BRIEFS

HERE'S A BRAND NEW LOOK!

FEATURED INSIDE:

EMERGENCY ROOM BLOOD TEST RESULTS IN DUI AND RECKLESS HOMICIDE CASES

WHAT SOCIAL SECURITY NEEDS TO KNOW WHEN YOU RETIRE

NEW COLUMN FROM THE KANE COUNTY RECORDER'S OFFICE!
FIRST IN A SERIES OF NUTS AND BOLTS INFORMATION

PEOPLE V. LEWIS REVISITED

AND MORE!

MARCH 1994

Cover of the March 1994 KCBA Bar Briefs

Kevin Drendel (2003–2004) and his father Gilbert Drendel (1976–1977) served as KCBA president.

KCBA members prepare appetizers at the 1994 KCBA Steer Roast: (left to right) Joseph Loran, Mark Pheanis, Tim O'Neil, Paul Krentz, and Thomas Hipp

Judges John Countryman, Patrick Dixon, Patricia Piper Golden, and Thomas Mueller at the 1996 Steer Roast

The desk drawer in Courtroom 340 of the Third Street courthouse bears the name of each judge presiding in the courtroom, dating back to Honorable Roy Solfisburg in the 1950s.

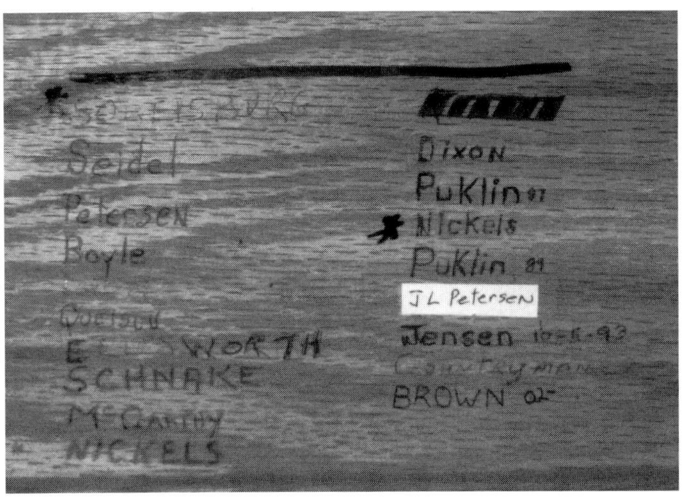

Kim Presbrey and Charles Peterson play tennis at the 1993 KCBA Golf and Tennis Outing.

Rory Weiler, J. Brick Van Der Snick, Stephen Sullivan, and Brad Swearingen enjoy the KCBA Golf Outing in 1998.

(Left to right) David Belshan, Meg Gorecki, and Bill Richards participate in the Salvation Army Bell ringing during the holiday season.

Officers of the 1988–1989 Kane County Legal Secretaries Association

The 2001–2002 KCBA Board of Managers (front row, left to right): John Early, Steve Andersson, and Jan Wade (executive director); (back row, left to right) Kevin Drendel, Mark Wade, Lisa Nyuli, Michael Doyen, Susan Rogaliner, Vince Elders, Honorable Stephen Sullivan, and David Camic.

CHAPTER 9

The Association in the Twenty-first Century: 2000–2008

The dawn of the twenty-first century brought with it societal fears of a Y2K catastrophe, in which computer programs designed and installed in the twentieth century would not recognize the dating system of a new century. As it was, the fears were vastly overblown, and computer technicians easily fixed any problems.

The societal problem that nobody in North America had addressed at the dawn of the new millennium was the rage manifested against the West by Islamic fundamentalist groups. The al-Qaeda attacks against the World Trade Center and the Pentagon in September 2001 was a warning to the United States that the world had irretrievably changed from one century to the next.

In the summer before the horrific attacks in New York and Washington, D.C., the KCBA moved into its newest office at 555 South Randall Road in St. Charles.[1] The Board of Managers had been discussing securing new and more modern offices since moving into the small house at 128 James Street in Geneva in the 1990s. The second-floor Randall Road offices were centrally located near the Kane County Judicial Center on Route 38 and spacious enough to accommodate the organization's near-term growth needs. With interest rates relatively low, the Association was able to purchase the second-floor office suite for $157,000.

The new office also had a new executive director of the Association. In the summer of 2001, Jan Wade joined the KCBA. A Yorkville resident, Wade had extensive experience in the management of not-for-profits. She came to the KCBA from the Fox Valley Family YMCA in Plano, where she had served as the first executive director and spearheaded the local YMCA's capital fund campaign. Prior that that, she had served as the executive director of the Plano Chamber of Commerce.[2]

Wade immediately began strengthening the Bar Association's administrative functions. Driving that effort was the growing volume of continuing legal education seminars sponsored by the Kane County Bar Association. In 2001, the KCBA changed its dues structure and began offering free CLE seminars and programs to its members. Those two decisions helped fuel the KCBA's growth for the next seven years.

The KCBA moved into its new office on the second floor of 555 South Randall Road, St. Charles, in 2001, and acquired adjacent space in 2008.

Continuing Legal Education (CLE)

Wendell Clancy, the KCBA's president in 1983–1984, noted that continuing legal education programs have been the single most important factor behind the growth of the Bar Association during the past quarter-century. When Clancy joined the KCBA in the early 1960s, the Association was essentially a social club.

William Murphy, the KCBA's president in 1972–1973, recalled that in the early days, "the Bar Association was mostly noted for non-activity because we only had one meeting a year. You had to go to Chicago for seminars. There was some continuing legal education, but it was all taught in Chicago. The Bar Association headquarters consisted of a little house in Geneva with an office back in the 1970s."[3]

Executive Director Jan Wade joined the KCBA in 2001.

The Kane County Bar Association Board of Managers formed a Continuing Legal Education Committee in 1979.[4] For much of the 1980s, the KCBA sponsored popular two-hour educational seminars at lunch. Longer seminars began at 3:30 p.m. and typically ran through dinner into the early evening hours.[5]

"It was hard getting away from the social aspects of the bar association," Clancy said. The thing that really did it was the start of continuing legal education. CLE was responsible for making the KCBA what it is today. There were lots of programs started to make sure young lawyers were fully integrated into the legal community. The bar associations of Chicago [and] DuPage and Kane counties have been the leaders in sponsoring CLE programs."[6]

In 2005, the Illinois Supreme Court adopted a program for Minimum Continuing Legal Education (MCLE). The MCLE Board administers the rules established by the Supreme Court mandating that Illinois attorneys complete a certain number of hours of CLE credits, including legal ethics credits.

Paul Glaser leads a meeting of the KCBA Continuing Legal Education Committee to plan seminars for the upcoming year. The CLE Committee consists of the chairs from the KCBA substantive law committees.

KCBA members attend a continuing legal education (CLE) seminar in the multi-purpose room at the Kane County Judicial Center. The KCBA began to offer free seminars to its members in 2001.

The new KCBA became one of the first Accredited CLE Providers in 2006. Recognizing the long tradition of CLE in Kane County, the Supreme Court appointed KCBA member Patrick M. Kinnally to the ten-member MCLE Board, where he was elected vice-chair.

As an Accredited CLE Provider, the KCBA hosts more than a dozen seminars and programs every year. The seminars cover a wide variety of topics, including estate and probate law, real estate law, appellate law, worker's compensation law, employment and labor law, local government law, criminal law, civil law, family law, and ethics.[7] During its second year as an Accredited CLE Provider, attendance at KCBA seminars reached over 2,250, a dramatic increase from the approximately 600 members who attended KCBA seminars in 2001–2002.

MCLE had a perhaps not unforeseen impact on KCBA membership. The Association's aggressive marketing and sponsorship of MCLE seminars turned out to be a highly effective membership recruiting tool. By 2007, membership had exceeded 1,000 members, a 25-percent increase from the membership numbers in the mid-1990s.

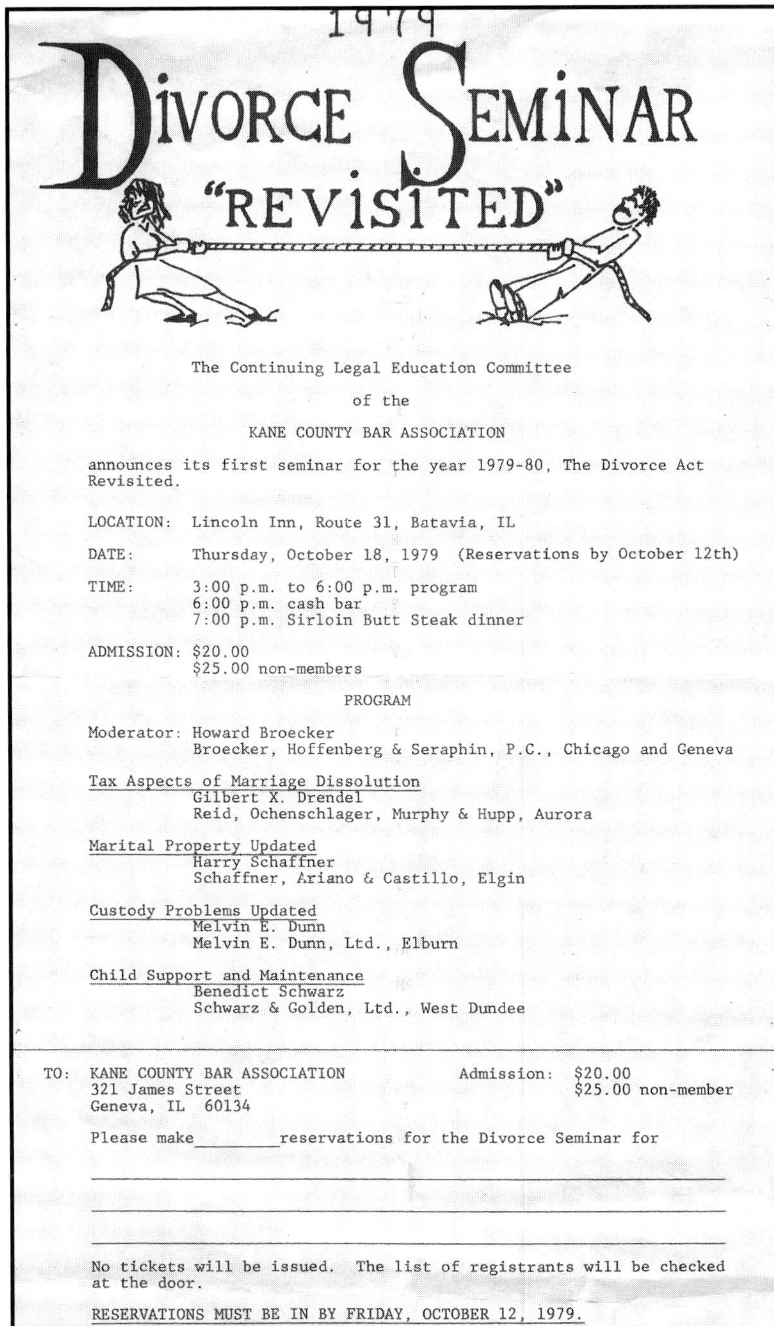

1979

DIVORCE SEMINAR "REVISITED"

The Continuing Legal Education Committee
of the
KANE COUNTY BAR ASSOCIATION

announces its first seminar for the year 1979-80, The Divorce Act Revisited.

LOCATION: Lincoln Inn, Route 31, Batavia, IL

DATE: Thursday, October 18, 1979 (Reservations by October 12th)

TIME: 3:00 p.m. to 6:00 p.m. program
6:00 p.m. cash bar
7:00 p.m. Sirloin Butt Steak dinner

ADMISSION: $20.00
$25.00 non-members

PROGRAM

Moderator: Howard Broecker
Broecker, Hoffenberg & Seraphin, P.C., Chicago and Geneva

Tax Aspects of Marriage Dissolution
Gilbert X. Drendel
Reid, Ochenschlager, Murphy & Hupp, Aurora

Marital Property Updated
Harry Schaffner
Schaffner, Ariano & Castillo, Elgin

Custody Problems Updated
Melvin E. Dunn
Melvin E. Dunn, Ltd., Elburn

Child Support and Maintenance
Benedict Schwarz
Schwarz & Golden, Ltd., West Dundee

TO: KANE COUNTY BAR ASSOCIATION
321 James Street
Geneva, IL 60134

Admission: $20.00
$25.00 non-member

Please make ______ reservations for the Divorce Seminar for

______

______

______

No tickets will be issued. The list of registrants will be checked at the door.

RESERVATIONS MUST BE IN BY FRIDAY, OCTOBER 12, 1979.

Flyer from the 1979 KCBA Divorce Seminar organized by the Continuing Legal Education Committee

The 2004 Supreme Court Trip

Even though the KCBA has sharply increased its involvement with MCLE in recent years, the Association has taken pains not to downplay the social aspects of membership. Encouraging collegiality remains a mission of the organization as much as it did in the heyday of Judge Petersen's annual Steer Roast.

Perhaps the best example of that spirit of collegial fellowship came in the summer of 2004, when the KCBA organized its first U.S. Supreme Court trip. Forty-seven Bar Association members and their families made the trip to Washington, D.C., where the attorneys were admitted to practice before the

Members of the KCBA were admitted to practice before the United States Supreme Court in 2004 during the first trip organized by the KCBA.

nation's highest court. Trip activities during the long weekend included visits to all of the monuments in the nation's capitol, as well as a trip across the Potomac River to the Pentagon, one of the targets of the 9/11 terrorists.[8]

The Kane County contingent made their headquarters at the Hotel George on E Street near Capitol Hill. They sampled the local beer at the Capital Square Brewing Company, as well as such local Washington, D.C. eating establishments as Clyde's, the District Chophouse, 1789, Blackie's

Steakhouse, and the Dancing Crab.[9] The group enjoyed a Potomac River cruise at Old Town Alexandria on one of its evenings in the nation's capitol, and many of the members took in the Smithsonian's Museum of American History. A number of members also saw Barry Bonds hit a long home run as his San Francisco Giants played the Baltimore Orioles in Camden Yards.[10]

The interior of the courtroom where the KCBA members were admitted to practice before the United States Supreme Court

The members of the United States Supreme Court granted the motion of Honorable Gene Nottolini to admit the KCBA attorneys.

The high point of the trip came on June 14, when the KCBA members passed through security at the North Entrance of the Supreme Court Building and were directed to a conference room just down the corridor from the Great Hall. At 10 a.m., seven of the nine justices took the bench, read several opinions, and then entertained a motion from Judge Gene Nottolini to admit the group of attorneys from Kane County. Judge Nottolini read the names of the candidates, including eight current and retired judges. When all had been announced,

Illinois Supreme Court Chief Justice Robert Thomas

then Chief Justice Rehnquist granted the motion and asked all the candidates to stand and recite the oath of office.[11]

"Truly," explained Judge Gene Nottolini of the Sixteenth Judicial Circuit, "this experience was a once-in-a-lifetime occasion. Everyone expressed their total happiness and satisfaction with the bar event."[12]

A Twenty-first-Century Media Storm

If the Kane County legal community was in the national spotlight for the Home Alone and Tenney cases in the 1990s, then the Robert Thomas libel case of 2004 landed Kane County squarely back in the eye of a twenty-first-century media storm.

The case, one of the biggest libel suits tried in Kane County, involved two well-known attorneys in the area. Justice Thomas, the chief justice of the Supreme Court of Illinois, had played football at the University of Notre Dame and was the placekicker for the Chicago Bears for ten seasons. During his twelve-year NFL career, Thomas earned his law degree at Loyola University Chicago School of Law. During the off-season, he practiced law in Kane County with several firms, including John Callahan's in Geneva. After ending his professional football career with the New York Giants in 1986, Thomas returned to Illinois, where he practiced in DuPage County. He was elected circuit judge in DuPage County in 1988, served as acting chief judge in the circuit from 1989 to 1994, and was elected to the Appellate Court Second District in 1994. In 2000, Thomas was elected to the Supreme Court of Illinois as a justice for the Second District.[13] He was named chief justice in 2006.

The other attorney was Mary Elizabeth "Meg" Gorecki, Kane County's first female state's attorney. In 2000, Gorecki won the election for Kane County state's attorney, having previously upset incumbent David Akemann in the Republican primary. Three weeks before the primary, it was revealed that Gorecki had left a message two years before on a friend's answering machine implying that campaign contributions could result in the awarding of political jobs. Although Gorecki won the primary and the general election in November, the Illinois Attorney Registration and Disciplinary Commission charged Gorecki with ethical violations and subsequently recommended that her law license be suspended for two months.[14]

A columnist for the *Kane County Chronicle* wrote in a 2003 series of commentaries that Justice Thomas had worked behind the scenes for a much stiffer sanction against Gorecki, even including disbarment. The columnist implied that Justice Thomas was an ally of the Republican incumbent Gorecki had unseated in the primary, and that a severe penalty would prevent her from holding on to the office. The columnist also wrote that Justice Thomas had agreed to a four-month suspension for Gorecki if her political supporters endorsed a political candidate he favored. When the newspaper refused to print a retraction, noting that the columns were clearly labeled opinions, Justice Thomas sued for libel.[15]

Allen Landmeier (left), Meg Gorecki, and her father Robert Gorecki. In 2000, Meg Gorecki was elected the first female Kane County state's attorney.

The case was heard in Kane County and a jury awarded Justice Thomas $7 million in 2006. Cook County Judge Donald O'Brien presided over the case in Kane County and sliced the award to $4 million in the spring of 2007. The columnist and the *Chronicle* countersued in federal court, charging that the chief justice was violating their civil rights by making an impartial appellate review of the verdict seemingly impossible. In the end, however, Shaw Media Group, the owner of the *Chronicle,* agreed to apologize to the chief justice and pay an out-of-court settlement.[16]

Information at the Speed of Light

It is perhaps instructive that much of the information about the libel case filed by Chief Justice Thomas is easily accessed by anyone with a laptop or desktop computer. The growth of the Internet during the twenty-first century is little short of phenomenal, and information that would have taken hours to retrieve in a library is available at the click of a mouse.

The electronic information revolution has been particularly valuable to the nation's attorneys. Law books that had taken up entire walls of bookshelves are now housed on the Internet. Documents are now often scanned into a PDF file and e-mailed to other counsel. Dictation is increasingly done digitally, and depositions are taken by teleconference and transmitted electronically.

Computerization is one of the big changes William Murphy has experienced in nearly sixty years of practice. "In real estate," he said, "you used to get a letter from the attorney with a draft of the contract. You would correct it and mail it back. With faxes and PDF files, it now moves so much more rapidly. You have the ability to make changes much more rapidly. There is an increased pace with the ability to do more work."[17]

Joe Radovich, KCBA president in 1971–1972, appreciates what technology has done for the practice of law. "The computer now generates reams of paper," he said. "We now have copy machines and combination printers. In the old days, we made carbon copies and typed on onionskin paper. The first

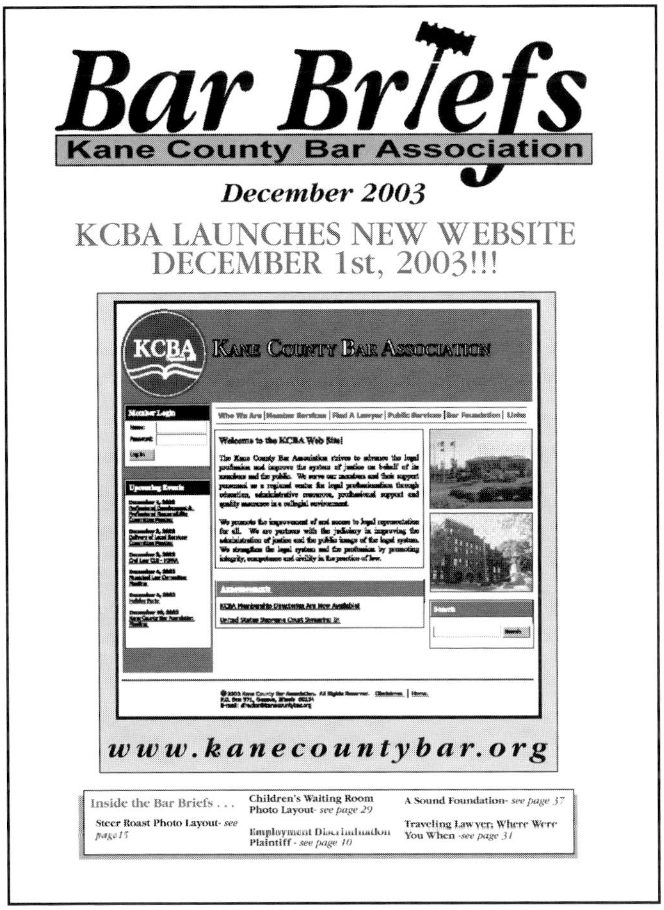

Bar Briefs

Kane County Bar Association

December 2003

KCBA LAUNCHES NEW WEBSITE DECEMBER 1st, 2003!!!

KCBA Kane County Bar Association

www.kanecountybar.org

Inside the Bar Briefs . . .

Steer Roast Photo Layout- *see page15*

Children's Waiting Room Photo Layout- *see page 29*

Employment Discrimination Plaintiff - *see page 10*

A Sound Foundation- *see page 37*

Traveling Lawyer; Where Were You When -*see page 31*

The cover of the December 2003 Bar Briefs *announces the new website.*

copy machine we had was a Verifax machine, and four lawyers contributed to its maintenance. You would squeeze the fluid out to make the copies, and you could literally spend the entire night making copies. More and more, lawyers are now doing their own typing because it saves dictation time. I once bought the wrong software for the computer. Today, you just use the Westlaw on the computer for your briefs."[18]

The KCBA was quick to adapt to the new technology. In the early years of the twenty-first century, *www.kanecountybar.org*, the Association's website, has become an innovative way to keep Bar Association members informed of everything the KCBA is doing. Prospective new members can apply online and members can make referrals to other members. Members can post a résumé online and sign up for MCLE seminars. A discussion forum allows members to post comments or responses to Board of Managers deliberations and decisions. A blast e-mail feature allows the Association to communicate with its members nearly instantaneously. The website also allows the public to search for Kane County lawyers by practice areas and other criteria.[19]

Acknowledging Contributions

Since 1986, in an annual tribute, the Association presents the Community Service Award to a member of the KCBA who has given back to the community. Peers nominate recipients for their broad-based community involvement, impeccable character, and strong sense of family. This recognition demonstrates that the members of the Kane County Bar Association are interested not only in fellowship, but also in how much they can contribute to the communities they serve.

The KCBA also presents the nationally recognized Liberty Bell Award to non-attorney individuals or community organizations. The tradition of bestowing the Liberty Bell Award

The Kane County Bar Association received the 2003 Luminary Award presented by the National Association of Bar Executives for excellence in Web site design.

The Children's Waiting Room
2000–2008

Kane County Bar Foundation Presidents Lisa Nyuli (2002–2003) and Paul Glaser (2003–2004) visit the Children's Waiting Room during construction at the Kane County Judicial Center.

One of the most successful community programs supported by Kane County lawyers and spearheaded by the Kane County Bar Foundation is the Children's Waiting Room at the Kane County Judicial Center.

Envisioned by the fledgling Bar Foundation soon after the Kane County Judicial Center opened in 1993, the Children's Waiting Room was designed to help Kane County's families. It became apparent that there was a need for space in the Judicial Center for children who found themselves in the new courthouse for the day, whether their parent or guardian was a party in litigation or was a witness in a trial.

Lisa Nyuli of the Kane County Bar Foundation reasoned that a courthouse was no place for a child, especially one who was full of energy. Children can sometimes disrupt court proceedings, and the matter under discussion in the courtroom often concerns matters that are not meant for young ears, especially since cases often involve either domestic disputes or criminal matters. *Bar Briefs* proposed that "a children's waiting room will provide a safe and fun haven for children. It will assist the court in conducting business in an orderly fashion."[21]

Nyuli, president of the Kane County Bar Association in 2004–2005, previously served as the president of the Kane County Bar Foundation from 2001 to 2003. She and other attorneys worked with the Bar Foundation to identify a place in the Judicial Center that could serve as a Children's Waiting Room, similar to facilities in other Illinois courthouses. The Sixteenth Judicial Circuit and the Kane County Board cooperated to set aside space on the ground floor of the new Judicial Center to serve as a waiting room for children.

The Kane County Bar Foundation began a formal fundraising drive in 2002 to raise the money for construction of the Waiting Room, furnishings, and other start-up costs. Local law firms, attorneys, and community groups contributed $70,000 by the summer of 2003, more than enough to pay the construction costs. In order to pay for operating costs of the Waiting Room, the Kane County Board approved a five-dollar-per-case filing fee assessed against civil cases.

The Children's Waiting Room at the Kane County Judicial Center opened in January 2004, with room for as many as twenty children, from infants to the age of twelve. During its first year, the Waiting Room staff cared for more than 1,300 children. By 2006, that number had increased to nearly 3,000 children. The facility provides free, short-term, drop-off supervised care for families from 8:15 a.m. to 4:15 p.m., Monday through Friday, with extended hours on Wednesday evening for night court.

Guests admire the completed Children's Waiting Room after the ribbon-cutting ceremony on December 18, 2003.

The 2005 Liberty Bell Award winner, Halle Cox, Kane County law librarian (left), stands with Honorable Judith Brawka, winner of the Community Service Award (center), and Julie Cibulskis, winner of the Outstanding New Lawyer Award (right).

began in 2000 at the KCBA's annual general membership dinner. Honorees are recognized for promoting a better understanding of the rule of law, encouraging a greater respect for the law and courts, stimulating a sense of civic responsibility, and contributing to good government within the community.

More recently, the KCBA established the Outstanding New Lawyer Award. Beginning in 2005, the award has been presented annually to lawyers in their first eight years of practice. Recipients must show a commitment and dedication to the legal profession through committee and community involvement, integrity, professional responsibility, and a high level of professional development at an early stage of their careers.

One of the proudest traditions of the Kane County Bar Association, dating back to at least 1892, is the annual Memorial Service. Each year, the judiciary of the Sixteenth Judicial Circuit, members of the KCBA, and the family and friends of those attorneys being recognized gather together in the ceremonial courtroom to commemorate the lives and careers of the KCBA members who passed away during the previous year. Eulogies by KCBA members pay tribute to the professional and community contributions of their deceased colleagues. The chief judge of the Sixteenth Circuit presides over the Memorial Service, and a transcript of the proceeding is prepared so the remarks made during the service become a permanent part of the court record.

KCBA members are honored for fifty years of service at the 2007 General Membership Dinner: (left to right) Justice Marvin Dunn, Honorable Roger Eichmeier, William Richards, James Martin, and Eugene Ruark

Encouraging Civility

Many longtime members have noted that the fast pace and competitive nature of law in twenty-first-century Kane County has resulted in a loss of the civility that formerly characterized the practice of law. Wendell Clancy agrees that "[a] change that worries me and some of the old-timers is the lack of civility. It's easy to be mean and nasty over the little things in a lawsuit. The Supreme Court of Illinois has started to deal with that problem by disciplining lawyers."[20]

Honorable John Petersen presented a portable defibrillator to Sheriff Kenneth R. Ramsey in memory of Honorable Barry Puklin during the 2001 KCBA Memorial Service.

The Kane County Bar Association has long encouraged a collegial environment among its members. In 2006, the Illinois Supreme Court created the Commission on Professionalism whose goals included promoting integrity, professionalism, and civility in the legal profession. Again recognizing the strong traditions of Kane County, the Supreme Court appointed KCBA member Patrick M. Kinnally to the seventeen-member commission. The KCBA has taken a strong supporting stance for the Supreme Court's initiative by facilitating discussions among its members about the erosion of civility in the legal profession during the past twenty years.

The Association in the twenty-first century carries on a tradition of professionalism that stretches back into a storied past. How well the Association has managed that task is evidenced by its multitude of activities in the sesquicentennial year of 2008.

KCBA member Krista Carls moderates the Law Talk *radio program organized by the Public Relations Committee in 2006.*

Golfers prepare for the shotgun start at the 2006 KCBA Golf and Tennis Outing at Orchard Valley Golf Course in Aurora, Illinois.

Participants anxiously await their turn during the putting contest at the 2004 KCBA Golf and Tennis Outing at Orchard Valley Golf Course.

In 2005, the KCBA worked with Habitat for Humanity to build a home in Elgin: (front row, left to right) Kevin Thomas, Sean Fergus, Sandra Lundgren, Tait Lundgren, Gail Anstett-Patrick, Andrew Nickel, Hannah Cherney, and Bill Cherney; (back row) Wally Wolff.

Local high school students confer during the twenty-second annual Kane County Bar Foundation Law Day Mock Trials at the Kane County Judicial Center.

Mat Perrone fields a telephone call from the public as part of Ask A Lawyer Day, sponsored by the Kane County Bar Association and Illinois State Bar Association.

Melody Davoust and her secretary Mary Najdzron at the KCBA Secretary's Day luncheon in 2000

(Left to right) Honorable Timothy Sheldon, Jack Callahan, and Patrick Rice enjoy the KCBA Steer Roast at the Batavia VFW.

During the 2004 fall social event, the KCBA celebrated diversity by recognizing Judges Keith Brown, Pamela Jensen, and Manuel Barbosa: (left to right) Melissa Barbosa Guzman watches as KCBA President Lisa Nyuli presents Barbosa, judge of the Bankrupcty Court of the Northern District of Illinois, with a plaque.

Sherri Bertane, Honorable Patrick Dixon, and his son Liam Dixon at the 2000 KCBA Judges' Night gathering at the Mill Race Inn, Geneva, Illinois

Honorable Wiley Edmondson reads The True Story of the 3 Pigs *during the 2005 Family Reading Night at the Kane County Judicial Center. (*Daily Herald*)*

KCBA members enjoy the 2006 Kane County Bar Foundation Gala held at the Hotel Baker in St. Charles: (left to right) Karrsten Goettel, Frank Ariano, Lisa Nyuli, Jane Craddock Ryan, and Scott Richmond.

The 2008 KCBA Past President's Dinner: (front row, left to right) Howard Smith, Jr., William Murphy, Steve Andersson, Susan Rogaliner, Zalmon Goldsmith, Susan Tatnall, Frank Ariano, Francis Youssi, and Joe Radovich; (back row, left to right) Lisa Nyuli, Lee Perington, Len Seraphin, Chuck Radovich, Allen Landmeier, Norbert Ritt, Donald Dickinson, Patrick Flaherty, Gary Vanek, Bob Britz, Bob Speers, and Julie Cibulskis

CHAPTER 10

The Association Today and Tomorrow: 2008

A century and a half after its founding in Aurora, the Kane County Bar Association faces the challenges of a new century and a new millennium, just as pioneer attorneys on the Illinois frontier dealt with the problems of mid-nineteenth-century America.

Back then, Abraham Lincoln and Stephen A. Douglas were debating an issue across northern Illinois that would sunder a great nation during the Civil War. From 1861 to 1865, the rule of law would be replaced by marching armies and riverboat navies, all over the question of whether Washington, D.C., had the right to tell the states that they could no longer sanction the evil of slavery. Kane County's legal community flocked to the colors during the Civil War, and those who returned to the county following the war dominated the affairs of the Kane County Bar for the next half-century.

Today's KCBA is a far cry from the small, tightly-knit organization that was formed to allow lawyers in the frontier communities of Kane County to share experiences and solutions to problems facing North America's cities. The Kane County Bar Association evolved through a great Civil War and the industrialization of Illinois, through two world wars and the Great Depression in the twentieth century, an intellectual explosion in North American law, and a late twentieth- and early twenty-first-century technological revolution into the organization that it is today.

The KCBA has emerged after 150 years as a strong voice of northern Illinois legal affairs that allows Kane County's legal community to gather together in a neutral forum to discuss, debate, and solve the legal issues of the day. Through innovative information exchange, professional development, networking opportunities, continuing legal education, and outreach, the KCBA serves more than 1,100 legal professionals in Kane and its surrounding counties. The Association promotes a collegial environment for its members and provides

The 2007–2008 Kane County Board of Managers: (front row, left to right) Kelly Kramer, Robert Britz, Doug Warlick, and William Engerman; (back row, left to right) Patrick Kinnally, Diana Law, Patrick Flaherty, David Camic, Julie Cibulskis, and Steven Titiner

a needed community service that benefits all of the residents of Kane County.

The Bar Association continues its mission to advance the legal profession as well as to improve the system of justice on behalf of its members and the public. The KCBA serves its members and their support personnel as a regional center for legal professionalism through education, administrative resources, professional support, and quality assurance in a collegial environment.

Kane County Bar Association staff members: (front row, left to right) Tami McLaughlin, Jan Wade, and Lynda Fillipp; (back row, left to right) Carolyn Jones and Deb Cook

The Association promotes the improvement of and access to legal representation for all. The KCBA partners with the judiciary in improving the administration of justice and the public image of the legal system. The Association works tirelessly to strengthen the legal system and the profession by promoting integrity, competence, and civility in the practice of law. The Association makes concerted efforts to reach out to the public by providing educational opportunities and information to the community.

In 1858, there were just thirty-two lawyers and four law students listed in the county. Fifty years later, in 1908, there were 122 lawyers. As of June 2008, Attorney's Registration lists more than 1,500 lawyers in Kane County; some of these commute to Chicago and other areas to practice law, but the Kane County Bar membership is more than 1,100.

1,100 Members

Those 1,100 members range in age from their twenties to their nineties. The KCBA's membership of legal professionals from Kane, DuPage, McHenry, Will, Lake, and Cook counties includes judges, attorneys, paralegals, and students. The Association's membership year runs from July 1 to June 30, and the KCBA's dues structure is based on the number of years of practice, or on specialty categories such as government or not-for-profit organization attorneys (who must practice full-time in that field to qualify for this membership rate), judges, paralegals, and students.

Patrick Flaherty, KCBA president in 2007–2008

David Camic, KCBA president in 2008–2009

Julie Cibulskis, KCBA first vice president in 2008–2009

Patrick Kinnally, KCBA second vice president in 2008–2009

Diana Law, KCBA secretary/treasurer in 2008–2009

Governance of the Association is the responsibility of an elected Board of Managers, consisting of the president, past-president, first and second vice presidents, four directors, and a general counsel. Patrick M. Flaherty was president in the first half of the Bar Association's sesquicentennial anniversary year of 2008. David E. Camic is president during the second half of the anniversary year. The remaining members of the 2008–2009 Board of Managers are: Julie L. Cibulskis, first vice president; Patrick M. Kinnally, second vice president; Diana M. Law, secretary/treasurer; William Engerman, Kelly Kramer, Nydia Molina, and Steven D. Titiner, directors; and Dean M. Frieders, general counsel.

The day-to-day affairs of the Association in its 150th year are in the hands of a capable professional staff of five, including Executive Director Jan Wade; Deb Cook, the publications coordinator; Lynda Fillipp, publications assistant; Carolyn Jones, membership services coordinator and CLE coordinator; and Tami McLaughlin, administrative assistant.

The office of the Association remains on the second floor of 555 South Randall Road in St. Charles, where it has been since the summer of 2001. In the summer of 2008, the Kane County Bar Association purchased an adjacent second-floor suite at 555 South Randall Road to accommodate the Association's tremendous growth in recent years.

Illinois Appellate Court, Second District, in Elgin was first occupied in 1966, two years after the Second District was created by the Judicial Article of 1964. Previous to that, appeals from Kane County were heard in Ottawa. A vestige of the "riding the circuit" days is found in the four bedrooms that occupy each corner of the second floor.

The Association's Committee Structure

Like many similar associations, the business of the Kane County Bar Association is conducted in a committee structure that includes both operational and substantive law groups. The operational committees help administer various aspects of the Association and the substantive law committees sponsor educational forums and programs for professional development. More than thirty committees have evolved over the years, including Admissions and Membership, Alternative Dispute Resolution, Appellate, Bar Briefs, Commercial Banking and Bankruptcy, Commercial Real Estate, Civil Court Practice, Criminal Court Practice, Continuing Legal Education, Delivery of Legal Services, Diversity, Employment and Labor Law, Estate and Probate, Family Court Practice, Finance, Intellectual Property, Judicial Evaluation, Local Government Law, Long Range Planning, New Lawyers Division, Paralegals, Past Presidents, Professional Development, Professional Responsibility, Public Relations, Residential Real Estate, Social, Solo and Small Firm Practice, Video Communications, and Worker's Compensation.

The Association is governed by a full set of bylaws, which were last amended in 2007.

KCBA members enjoy Judge's Night in 2008: (left to right) Edward Petti, judges Timothy Sheldon and Keith Brown, Halle Cox, and Matthew Robinson.

Social and Other Benefits

The KCBA sponsors social events throughout the year. These events have included

the Steer Roast, Holiday Party, Golf Outing, Judge's Night, and much more. Social events provide opportunities to make and enhance professional contacts and friendships within the legal community. The Association also reaches out to the community in many ways. Members participate through blood drives, the annual toy drive, providing education for the public through the "People's Law School," and many other beneficial programs. The KCBA has also produced public service television and radio programs, such as *Legal Ease* and *Law Talk*, to address relevant and timely legal topics.

The 2008 Kane County Bar Foundation Gala: (left to right) Philip Lengle, John Locallo, and Dan Weiler

KCBA members can take advantage of many other benefits. The Association staff takes photos for courthouse security passes for both Kane and DuPage counties for easy access to the courthouses in each county. Members can purchase the "Attorney's Diary," which is a calendar with federal and state information, and also mailing labels for the KCBA membership. Conference room space in the Association's office facility on South Randall Road in St. Charles is available for depositions and meetings at no charge for members.

Patrick M. Kinnally and his daughter and son-in-law, Rorry Bonifas and Nick Bonifas, enjoy the 2007 Holiday Party. The KCBA has a long history of multi-generational members practicing law in the Fox Valley.

Information Vehicles

Kane County Bar Association members have access to a number of vehicles that can keep them informed on the state of the legal community in Kane County, including the *Bar Briefs,* the *Annual Membership Directory*, the Find-A-Lawyer Service, and the Association's website.

The *Bar Briefs*, which was first published in 1979, is the monthly magazine of the KCBA and the only legal publication in Kane County. It includes articles on substantive areas of the law and court policies as well as information on bar-sponsored events, happenings in the legal community, and membership profiles. In addition to receiving a free subscription, members can place one free classified ad per month.

Members of the KCBA Continuing Legal Education Committee meet in the KCBA conference room to plan seminars for 2008–2009.

The *Annual Membership Directory* is updated annually to provide vital information for KCBA members. It provides a complete listing of names, addresses, phone, fax, and e-mail information for KCBA members, as well as important KCBA, court, and government information. The directory also provides lawyer referral information for specific areas of practice. This publication is provided free of charge to KCBA members thanks to the generous support of sponsors and advertisers.

The free Find-A-Lawyer Service allows site visitors to select options from several criteria (area of practice, languages spoken, location, years of practice, etc.) to produce a list of attorneys who meet their specifications. The public can also call the Find-A-Lawyer phone line to listen to a recorded message, which contains agency referral numbers and information about accessing the online Find-A-Lawyer Service.

The KCBA website, *www.kanecountybar.org*, is the electronic means of obtaining information on KCBA activities and upcoming events. This site provides a link for both the KCBA membership and the public on legal issues.

The Kane County Bar Foundation

The Kane County Bar Foundation was established in 1996 to facilitate the unrestricted access of all members of the public to the legal programs and services available and necessary for the protection of individual rights and the overall preservation of justice and safety for all residents of Kane County. The Foundation is administered by a sixteen-member Board of Directors and is charged with improving and facilitating the administration of justice, promoting an understanding of the law and assisting in legal education, helping provide equal access to the law for the indigent and needy, and other such tasks as spelled out in the articles of incorporation. Foundation projects have included the Children's Waiting Room at the Kane County Judicial Center, the Lawyer in the Classroom Program, the high school mock trial program, and the annual Pro Bono Award. The Foundation annually awards at least two $1,000 scholarships to deserving Kane County resident law students. The Kane County Bar Foundation offers grants to local non-profit agencies to help them meet the legal needs of Kane County residents. In both 2007 and 2008, $10,000 in grants was awarded.

Two of the more popular programs underwritten each year by the Foundation are the Lawyer in the Classroom and the High School Mock Trial programs. The Lawyer in the Classroom Program pairs a local attorney to every public and private middle and high school serving Kane County students. Nearly fifty attorneys and schools are included.

Volunteering their time, the local attorneys are available to help educators plan and present lessons on the national and local legal system and other issues with law-related themes. Kane County attorneys have regularly spoken on topics such as the Constitution and Bill of Rights, search and seizure, patents and trademarks, the death penalty, contracts, family law, and legal careers. Members of the Foundation have helped organize and serve as judges for mock trials and debates. Members of the Association have even made presentations on the legal issues presented in *To Kill a Mockingbird*.

The Kane County Bar Foundation celebrated the fiftieth anniversary of Law Day by sponsoring its annual high school mock trials.

To provide local high school students with the opportunity to see how our justice system really works, the Kane County Bar Foundation sponsors the Annual High School Mock Trial Program. The mock trials are held around Law Day (May 1) each year. Each school is assigned a part in a hypothetical criminal or civil trial. Students from one school serve as the "attorneys" and witnesses against a team from another school before a jury comprised of students from still other schools. Teachers from the schools coach the teams and local attorneys are available to provide expert assistance along the way.

Thanks to the continued cooperation of the local judiciary, the mock trials are held in actual Kane County courtrooms either at the Third Street courthouse or at the Kane County Judicial Center. In many cases, the trials are presided over by actual Kane County judges.

Members of the KCBA re-enacted an 1858 trial to commemorate the 150th anniversary of the Kane County Bar Association: (front row, left to right) Chief Judge Donald Hudson, Renee Robinson, Linda Santiago, Katherine Motley, and Christine Falls; (back row, left to right) Michael Clancy, Richard Balog, Paul Glaser, Timothy Loats, John Early, and Wendell Clancy.

Since its inception more than twenty years ago, the High School Mock Trial Program has involved thousands of students from local high schools as well as high schools from Cook and DuPage counties. Students participating in the program learn that to be successful, attorneys must prepare long and hard. Excellent research, thinking skills, and good public speaking ability are essential to the presentation of a winning case. They also learn that as in real life, sometimes the best-presented case might end in a less-than-favorable

Daniel Parsons rehearses for the 2008 "Sesqui-sensational" Bar Show.

KCBA members perform in the 2008 "Sesqui-sensational" Bar Show.

outcome. But the skills learned by participation in the program serve the students well in later life. More than a few of the students participating in the program have gone on to legal careers themselves.

As part of the KCBA's 150th anniversary celebration in 2008, in addition to commissioning this book, the Association staged an 1858 mock trial, complete with participants in period dress. It reinstated the Bar Show, an evening of music, comedy, and satire, written, produced, directed, and performed by KCBA members. The KCBA also sponsored a production of *Inherit the Wind* in the rotunda of the historic Third Street courthouse in conjunction with a local theater group, the Geneva Underground Playhouse.

The More Things Change

The Kane County Bar Association and its members will no doubt face unprecedented challenges in the years ahead. They will be on the front lines of a host of emerging legal and regulatory issues, including product liability, global warming and the environment, foreclosure and the economy, civil discourse, elder law, and sweeping political change.

Jack Callahan (pictured) and William Murphy shared their memories regarding the practice of law in Kane County at the 2008 KCBA General Membership and 150th Anniversary Dinner.

The Association and its members will have at their disposal exciting new computer software and electronic technology to do their jobs. The Association will contend with increasingly more complex legislation and regulatory rules as society relies more on lawyers and the judicial system.

The reality is that the future challenges and opportunities faced by the KCBA and its members will be different, but perhaps no more difficult than the challenges and opportunities faced by KCBA members and staff during the past century and a half.

Those who read the law in Aurora or Elgin in 1908 would likely be intrigued by the continuing legal education of the twenty-first century. The Association members who attended Judge Petersen's steer roasts in the 1960s would be astounded by the range of KCBA programs and activities a half-century later. The members who bought typewriters and ordered telephones for their offices early in the twentieth century would immediately see the application of electronic communication one hundred years later.

But Association members from the past—from 1858, 1908, or 1958—would immediately recognize the role that the KCBA and its members play in the ordering of a just and equitable society.

The Kane County Bar Association is a vibrant, ever-changing, dynamic organism that has demonstrated its critical usefulness to Kane County for 150 years now. That essential fact is not likely to change in the years ahead.

The Courthouses of the Sixteenth Judicial Circuit in 2008

The DeKalb County Courthouse in Sycamore was built in 1905 for $100,000. (Daniel Flaherty)

133 WEST STATE
ERECTED
1896
DEKALB COUNTY

The Kendall County Courthouse in Yorkville was built in 1998 and replaced the previous courthouse constructed in 1887. (Daniel Flaherty)

Kane County Courthouse on Third Street in Geneva

Kane County Judicial Center on Route 38 in St. Charles

Kane County Juvenile Justice Center in St. Charles

The interior of the Third Street courthouse in Geneva (Daniel Flaherty)

The new Adult Justice Center is under construction on the campus of the Kane County Judicial Center in St. Charles. The new jail will hold 768 inmates and replaces the 1975 jail on Fabyan Parkway, which has a capacity of 450 inmates.

The 2008 KCBA Past President's Dinner: (left to right) Patrick Flaherty (2007–2008), Zalmon Goldsmith (1947–1948), and William Murphy (1972–1973).

(Left to right) Honorable Gene Nottolini, Len Seraphin, Herb Steinmetz, and John Banbury are recognized at the 2008 KBCA General Membership Dinner for their forty years of service to the legal community.

Thank You to Our Associate Sponsors:

Frank Ariano
Ariano, Hardy, Nyuli, Johnson, Richmond & Goettel, P.C.
Bennett Law Offices
Honorable Judith M. Brawka
Howard Broecker (in Memoriam by Tina Miller)
John P. Chapski
Michael A. Chapski
Michael Childress
Chilton, Yambert, Porter & Young
Vincent S. Cook
Michael C. Doyen
Janet Ellingson
Paul J. Glaser
Loren Golden
Thomas W. Grant
Chief Judge Donald C. Hudson
Kane County Bar Association Paralegal Committee
Daniel J. Kramer
J. Brian McDonnell
Fred Morelli
Robert E. Nelson
Law Office of Daniel Parsons
Mathew R. P. Perrone, Jr.
John F. Philipchuck
Thomas K. Prindable
Joseph & Charles Radovich
Richard Robinson
Susan W. Rogaliner
Schiller, DuCanto & Fleck, LLP
Honorable Paul W. Schnake
Shearer & Agrella
John P. Simpson
Sullivan, Taylor & Gumina
Susan B. Tatnall
Colleen Thomas
Rita Thomas
Truemper & Titiner, Ltd.
Gary M. Vanek
Daniel E. Venuti
Dorothy A. Voigt
Matthew B. Walker
Douglas B. Warlick
Youssi, Youssi & Bina, Ltd.

The Illinois State Bar Association

Thank You to Our Partner Sponsors:

Camic Johnson, Ltd.

Clancy Law Offices

Dreyer, Foote, Streit, Furgason & Slocum, P.A.

Kinnally Flaherty Krentz & Loran, P.C.

Konicek & Dillon, P.C.

Law ElderLaw

Linda Soreff Siegel

Speers, Reuland & Cibulskis, P.C.

Vinkler Law Offices, Ltd.

APPENDIX

Chronology of Kane County Judiciary

1818: Illinois established as twenty-first state
First Constitution adopted
Territory of Kane in Crawford County and in Fifth Circuit

1818–1824: Supreme Court justices sat in circuit courts

1824–1827: Judiciary reorganized
Circuit judges appointed
Judge James O. Wattles presided over Fifth Circuit

1827–1835: Judiciary reorganized
Supreme Court justices sat in circuit courts
Territory of Kane in Fourth Circuit
Supreme Court Justice James Wilson presided

1831: Territory of Kane in La Salle County

1831–1835: Supreme Court Justice Thomas M. Young presided

1835: Judiciary reorganized
Circuit judges appointed
Judge Thomas Ford presided 1835–1837
Judge Daniel Stone presided 1837
Territory of Kane in Sixth Circuit

1836: Kane County established

1837: Kane in Seventh Circuit
Judge John Pearson presided 1837–1839

1839: Kane in Ninth Circuit
Judge Thomas Ford presided 1839

1841–1848: Judiciary reorganized
Supreme Court justices sat in circuit again
Justice Thomas Ford presided

1843: Justice John M. Robinson presided followed by Justice John D. Caton

1848: Second constitution adopted
Judiciary reorganized
Circuit judges appointed
Judge T. Lyle Dickey presided 1848–1852
Judge Edwin S. Leland presided 1852–1855
Judge Madison E. Hollister presided 1855–1866
Judge Edwin S. Leland presided 1866

1851: Kane County in Thirteenth Circuit
Judge Isaac J. Wilson presided 1851–1867
Judge Allen C. Fuller presided 1861–1962
Judge Theodore D. Murphy presided 1862

1870: Third constitution adopted

1872: Kane County in Twenty-eighth Circuit

1873: Kane County in Fourth Circuit
Judge Sylvanus Wilcox presided 1873
Judge Hiram H. Cody presided

1877: Kane County in Twelfth Circuit
Judge Isaac G. Wilson presided 1879–1891
Judge Henry B. Willis presided 1891–1897

1897: Kane County in Sixteenth Circuit

1897–2008: The following served as circuit judge:

C. F. Irwin 1897–1913
John K. Newhall 1924
Frank W. Shepard 1927–1942
Charles A. O'Connor 1942–1952
Harry C. Daniels 1951–1952
Roy J. Solfisburg, Jr. 1955–1960
Charles G. Seidel 1957–1972
John S. Petersen 1961–1976

*John S. Page 1969–1978
*John A. Krause 1971–1984
Ernest W. Akemann 1971–1980
Alfred Y. Kirkland 1973–1974
Paul W. Schnake 1973–1986
James E. Boyle 1975–1976
*Neil E. Mahoney 1975–1984
Joseph M. McCarthy 1975–1988
*Marvin D. Dunn 1977–1988
*James F. Quetsch 1979–1992
*William H. Ellsworth 1981–1982
*Richard Weiler 1983–1986
*Patrick J. Dixon 1985–2002
John L. Nickels 1985–1990
*Michael F. O'Brien 1985–1996
*Melvin E. Dunn 1987–1998
*Barry E. Puklin 1987–2000
*Michael J. Colwell 1989–1992, 2001–
*Philip L. DiMarzio 1989–
*Gene Nottolini 1989–2005; 2007–2008
*Pamela K. Jensen 1991–2002
*James T. Doyle 1993–2006
*Robert P. Grometer 1993–2000
*Kurt P. Klein 1995–
*F. Keith Brown 1997–
*Thomas E. Hogan 1997–2002
*Timothy Q. Sheldon 1997–
*Donald J. Fabian 1999–
Grant S. Wegner 1999–
*Donald C. Hudson 2001–
*Robbin J. Stuckert 2003–
*Judith M. Brawka 2003–
Joseph M. Grady 2003–
Robert B. Spence 2003–
John J. Nelligan 2005–2006
*Thomas E. Mueller 2006–
*Richard J. Larson 2006–
*Patricia P. Golden 2006–
*Susan Clancy Boles 2009–

(*denotes those who previously served as associate judge)

1964: Judiciary reorganized
Judicial officers limited to circuit judge and newly created position of associate judge

1964–2008: The following have served as associate judge since 1964:

Ross E. Millet
Thomas P. O'Malley
Robert J. Sears
Earl R. Shopen
Carl A. Swanson, Jr.
Dan B. Withers, Jr.
John Chivari
Thomas Burke
Donald T. Anderson
James W. Cadwell
Fred M. Morelli, Jr.
James K. Marshall
John L. Petersen
Roger W. Eichmeier
Peter K. Wilson, Jr.
Wiley W. Edmondson
James C. Hallock
Franklin D. Brewe
James Donnelly
Robert L. Janes
James R. Edwards
Mary Karen Simpson
Allen M. Anderson
Leonard J. Wojtecki
Stephen Sullivan
William H. Weir
Alan W. Cargerman
Timothy J. McCann
Linda Abrahamson
William P. Brady
Edward C. Schreiber
Marmarie J. Kostelny
Robert J. Morrow
Thomas J. Stanfa
Jordan Gallagher
Kevin T. Busch

Every effort was made to be complete and accurate in creating this chronology, but historical records are not complete and some errors or omissions may exist. The chronology does not include people who served only as justices of the peace, police magistrates, private judges, or county judges.

ENDNOTES

Chapter 1

1 Vernon Derry. *Aurora in the Beginning*, pp. 6–9; Maps, Indian Settlement Patterns. *Encyclopedia of Chicago*, www.encyclopedia.chicagohistory.org

2 Maps, Indian Settlement Patterns. *Encyclopedia of Chicago*, www.encyclopedia.chicagohistory.org

3 Ibid.

4 James Lewis, Ph.D. "The Black Hawk War of 1832," www.lincolnl.lib.niu.edu/blackhawk/

5 Kane County. *Encyclopedia of Chicago*, www.encyclopedia.chicagohistory.org

6 R. Waite Joslyn and Frank W. Joslyn. *History of Kane County, Illinois*. (Chicago: The Pioneer Publishing Co., 1908), Vol. 1, pp. 132–138

7 Ibid., p. 147; Milo M. Quaife. *Chicago's Highways Old and New*, (Chicago: D.F. Keller and Company, 1923) pp. 96–100; Roger Matile. *By Trace and Trail: The Stagecoach Era in Northern Illinois*, (Oswego, Illinois: Oswegoland Heritage Association, 2001) pp. 16–20

8 History of Kane County, Illinois. "The Government is Established," www.co.il.us/history/section04.htm

9 History of Kane County and the Kane County Bar Association, www.kanecountybar.org/about/history.html

10 History of Kane County, Illinois. "The Courthouses are Built," www.co.il.us/history/section05.htm

11 "History of Kane County's Five Courthouses." *Aurora Beacon News,* March 12, 1961

12 "The Government is Established," p. 1

13 *History of Kane County, Illinois*, p. 456

14 Ibid., p. 474

15 Ibid., p. 460

16 Ibid., p. 141

17 Ibid., pp. 462–463

18 Ibid., p. 457

19 Six-Year Depression, 1837–1843, www.thehistorybox.com

20 Marilyn Robinson. "Joseph Whelpley Churchill, First Attorney to Live in Batavia." Batavia Historical Society Paper, n.d., p. 1

21 Ibid.

22 Ibid.

23 John M. Van Osdel, www.en.wikipedia.org/wiki/John_M._Van_Osdel

24 "Moving Kane County Seat Was Talk of 1852." *Aurora Beacon News,* March 21, 1968

25 John A. Lupton. "The Law Practice of Abraham Lincoln: A Narrative Overview," www.papersofabrahamlincoln.org/narrative_overview.htm

26 Ibid.

27 Robert Barclay. *Aurora: 1837–1987.* (Aurora, Illinois: *Aurora Beacon News,* 1987) p. 14

28 Ibid., p. 15

29 Letter, Abraham Lincoln, Chicago, to Charles Hoyt, Aurora, July 10, 1855

30 History of Kane County and the Kane County Bar Association, www.kanecountybar.org/about/history.html

Chapter 1 Sidebar

31 *History of Kane County, Illinois*, p. 446

32 Ibid., pp. 446–447; www.st-charles.il.us/early

33 *History of Kane County, Illinois*, pp. 446–447

34 Ibid., pp. 129–130

35 www.st-charles.il.us/early; Glennette Tilly Turner. *Underground Railroad in DuPage County*, (Glen Ellyn, Illinois: Newman Education Publishing Company, 1978) pp. 19, 34–39, 47

36 Ibid., p. 1

37 Ibid., p. 4

38 David Herbert Donald. *Lincoln*. (New York: Simon & Schuster, 1995), as printed in *Bar Briefs*, February 1999, p. 8

Chapter 2

1 *History of Kane County, Illinois*, p. 480–481

2 Ibid.

3 Ibid.

4 Ibid.

5 Pamphlet, Kane County History, Geneva Historical Society, n.d.

6 Drew Gilpin Faust. "Introduction." *This Republic of Suffering: Death and the American Civil War.* (New York: Alfred A. Knopf, 2008)

7 Elgin, Illinois. *Encyclopedia of Chicago*, www.encyclopedia.chicagohistory.org/pages/420

8 Kane Co., IL: History of Kane County. The economy and population grows, www.co.kane,.il.us/history/section06

9 Ibid.

10 Ibid.

11 Unidentified newspaper clipping. *Aurora Beacon News*, March 15, 1890

12 Pamphlet, Kane County History

13 "History of Kane County's Five Court Houses," *Aurora Beacon News,* March 12, 1967

14 Edbrooke and Burhnam, Architects, www.apps.atlantaga.gov

15 Pamphlet, Kane County History

16 Kane County. *Encyclopedia of Chicago,* www.encyclopedia.com

Chapter 2 Sidebar

17 *History of Kane County, Illinois*, p. 486

18 Ibid.

19 Ibid.

20 Ibid., p. 592

21 Ibid., pp. 229–230

22 Ibid., p. 233

Chapter 3

1 www.las.uiuc.edu/about/history/index.html

2 DVD-recorded interview with Clarence J. Ruddy, Geneva, Illinois, May 23, 2000

3 *Elgin: An American History*. Chapter VII, "The Whirling Twenties," www.elginhistory.com/eaah/eaah-ch07, p. 19

4 Ibid.

5 Clarence Ruddy interview

6 "Fatal Zeal," *Time* Magazine, April 8, 1929, www.time.com/time/printout

7 Ibid.

8 *Elgin: An American History*, p. 20

9 Telephone interview with Jonathan Carbary, Elgin, Illinois, March 6, 2008

10 Ibid.

11 Tape-recorded interview with Wendell Clancy, St. Charles, Illinois, September 21, 2007, p. 4

12 DVD-recorded interview with Ben Rifken, Elgin, Illinois, July 31, 2000

13 Ibid.

14 Ibid.

15 Ibid.

16 Ibid.

17 Tape-recorded interview with Joseph Radovich, St. Charles, Illinois, June 21, 2007, p. 2

18 Ibid., p. 1

19 Ibid.

20 Ben Rifken interview

21 Tape-recorded interview with William Murphy, St. Charles, Illinois, September 20, 2007, p. 2

22 Digitally-recorded oral history interview with Howard Smith, St. Charles, Illinois, September 21, 2007, p. 3

23 Ibid.

24 Clarence Ruddy interview

25 Ibid.

26 Tape-recorded interview with Zalmon Goldsmith, St. Charles, Illinois, June 21, 2007, p. 1

27 Ibid.

Chapter 3 Sidebar

28 DVD-recorded interview with Sam Alschuler, Aurora, Illinois, August 3, 2000

29 Ibid.

30 *History of Kane County, Illinois*, p. 610

31 Steve Lord. "Aurora Icon Alschuler Dies At 93," *Aurora Beacon News,* June 25, 2006

32 Ibid.

33 Zalmon Goldsmith interview

34 Joseph Radovich interview, p. 5

Chapter 4

1 "O'Hare International Airport," www.en.wikipedia.org/wiki/O'Hare_International_Airport#History

2 Ibid.

3 Joseph Radovich interview, p. 3

4 Zalmon Goldsmith interview, p. 2

5 Ibid.

6 Joseph Radovich interview, p. 5

7 "Richard E. Zollers, Chicago Title Insurance Company," Geneva Historical Society, *The Geneva Fluter*, Autumn 1995, p. 2

8 Brochure, Official Opening Kane County Division, Chicago Title and Trust Company, August 1969

9 Ibid.

10 Ibid.

11 William Murphy Interview, p. 3

12 Joseph Radovich Memoriam to Elmer Pierce, Geneva, Illinois, May 25, 2006, p. 2

13 "Alfred Kirkland: Bar president, judge, writer, athlete," *ISBA Bar News and Illinois Courts Bulletin*, April 2004, p. 33

14 Ibid.

15 Ibid.

16 Obituary, Richard L. Cooper. *The Geneva Republican,* May 19, 2005

17 Ibid.

18 Obituary, Theodore G. Schuster. *Aurora Beacon News,* February 7, 2003

19 Obituary, James Van Santen. n.d.

Chapter 4 Sidebar

20 Kane County Bar Association Past Presidents

21 DVD-recorded interview with Ben Rifken, Elgin, Illinois, July 31, 2000, p. 5

22 Ibid., p. 1

23 Ibid., p. 2

24 Ibid.

25 Ibid., p. 3

26 Ibid.

27 "Veteran lawyer, Elgin 'pillar' remembered for civic efforts," *Elgin Daily Herald*, April 26, 2008

28 Ben Rifken Interview, p. 4

Chapter 5

1 Elizabeth Clements. "Historic Turns in the Windmill City," *Fermi News*, Vol. 26, No. 3, February 14, 2003, p. 1

2 Fermilab. Economic Impacts, www.fnal.gov/pub/presspass/factsheets/

3 "Historic Turns in the Windmill City."

4 Joseph Radovich interview, p. 2

5 Ibid, p. 3

6 Tape-recorded interview with William Murphy, St. Charles, Illinois, September 20, 2007, p. 2

7 Tape-recorded interview with Wendell Clancy, St. Charles, Illinois, September 21, 2007, p. 4

8 Roy Solfisburg, www.en.wikipedia.org/wiki/Roy_Solfisburg

9 Ibid.

10 Joseph N. Patten, Ph.D. Review of "Illinois Justice: The Scandal of 1969 and the Rise of John Paul Stevens," *Journal of Criminal Justice and Popular Culture, 10(3)*, p. 234

11 Ibid.

12 Report of the Special Commission of the Supreme Court of Illinois, July 31, 1969, www.press-pubs.uchicago.edu/manaster/commissionreport.html

13 Ray Klingbiel, www.en.wikipedia.org/wiki/Ray_Klingbiel

14 Roy Solfisburg, www.en.wikipedia.org/wiki/Roy_Solfisburg

15 Robert Hupp Memoriam to Lambert Ochsenschlager, Geneva, Illinois, May 31, 1990, p.14

16 Ibid., p. 14

17 Kenneth A. Manchester. *Illinois Justice: The Scandal of 1969 and the Rise of John Paul Stevens.*

(Chicago: The University of Chicago Press), p. 93

18 Digitally-recorded interview with William Murphy, St. Charles, Illinois, September 20, 2007, p. 1

19 Kelly Scotti. "Family Tree Project Links DuPage, Kane Lawyers," *ISBA Bar News 4*, August 15, 2000, www.isba.org/Association/008-15d

20 Digitally-recorded interview with Jack Callahan, St. Charles, Illinois, September 21, 2007, p. 2

21 Ibid.

22 Wendell Clancy interview, p. 2

23 Ibid, p. 3

24 Ibid., p. 2

25 Ibid., p. 5

26 Leonard J. Seraphin. "What Is the Kane County Bar Association?" *Bar Briefs*, May 1996, p. 4

Chapter 5 Sidebar

27 KCBA Memorial Service, May 1990

28 Unidentified newspaper clipping. *Elgin Courier News*, November 9, 1989

Chapter 6

1 The by-laws of the Legal Aid Bureau of Kane County (Article V, Section 5), as submitted to the Illinois secretary of state in 1971, provided that any notice of any special meeting of the board be issued at least three days in advance and be "delivered personally or sent by mail or telegraphed..." The provision added that, "If notice be given by telegram, such notice shall be deemed to be delivered when the telegram is delivered to the telegraph company."

2 *Illinois Bar Journal*, Vol. 56, No. 11, June 1968, pg. 834, as cited in the Kane County Bar Association Legal Aid Committee report, June 1971

3 Legal Aid Committee proposal, June 1971

4 Ibid.

5 Ibid.

6 Ibid.

7 Ibid.

8 Letter from Robert J. O'Connor, law offices of Ruddy, Myler & Bartsch, January 27, 1972

9 Ibid.

10 Sample Budget, Stage 3, Appendix F, Legal Aid Committee proposal, June 1971

11 KCBA Minutes, March 1972

12 "Kankakee lawyer is named Prairie State's new exec," www.isba.org/association/feb06bn/33.htm

13 Ibid.

14 Press Release, "Celebrating the 25th Anniversary of Prairie State Legal Services," October 8, 2002

15 Ibid.

16 Ibid.

17 Resolution, Kane County Bar Association, March 12, 1985

18 Office of the State Appellate Defender, Annual Report, Fiscal Year 2007

19 Ibid.

20 Special Report from the Real Estate Practice Committee, September 1974

21 Ibid.

22 Ibid.

23 Ibid.

24 Ibid.

25 Ibid.

26 The "Hilltop" Ad: The Story of a Commercial. "Fifty Years of Coca-Cola Television Advertisements: Highlights from the Motion Picture Archives at the Library of Congress," http://memory.loc.gov/ammem/ccmphtml/index.html

27 Howard Smith interview, p. 4

28 Minutes of the regular meeting of the Board of Managers meeting, Lincoln Inn, Batavia, Illinois, December 16, 1971

29 Ibid.

30 Minutes of the Kane County Bar Association, March 23, 1972

31 Minutes of the Annual Meeting of the Kane County Bar Association, May 29, 1970

32 Jack Callahan interview, p. 4

Chapter 6 Sidebar

33 A History of the Illinois Judicial System, http://www.state.il.us/court/SupremeCourt/Historical/judicialsystem.asp

34 Ibid.

35 Digitally-recorded interview with William C. Murphy, St. Charles, Illinois, September 20, 2007, June 2008

36 *Lopez v. Vanderwater*, 620 F2d 1229, 1980

Chapter 7

1 William Beck. *Telsmith: Yesterday, Today and Tomorrow*. (Mequon, Wisconsin: Telsmith Inc., 2006), p. 62

2 Top Chicago Area Gambling Casinos, www.chicagotraveler.com/chicago-casinos.htm

3 William Murphy interview, p. 5

4 "Foot Soldiers of the Law," *Time* Magazine, July 20, 1981

5 American Bar Association. Lawyer Demographics, 2006, www.abanet.org/legaled/statistics/stats.html

6 "Lower enrollments, bar exam pass rates affect percent of women, young lawyers," *Bar News*, September 15, 2000, p. 1

7 Meg Gorecki. "Legal Pioneers: Four of Illinois' First Women Lawyers," *Illinois Bar Journal,* October 1990, p. 512

8 Ibid.

9 Ibid.

10 News Item. *Bar Briefs,* September/October 1989

11 Ibid.

12 Ibid.

13 Wiley W. Edmondson. "Our Murdered Brother," *Bar Briefs,* May/June 1987

14 Ibid.

15 "Getaway Driver in 1987 Murder Pursues Law License," www.abc7chicago.com, June 2, 2006

16 Ibid.

17 Proposed Amended Bylaws for the Kane County Bar Association, *Bar Briefs,* May 1980, p. 2

18 Ibid., pp. 3–5

19 Wiley W. Edmondson. Proposed Committee on Professional Courtesy, *Bar Briefs,* February 1987, p. 2

20 "Kane County Bar Association To Have New Home!!!" *Bar Briefs,* May 1980, p. 12

21 Ibid.

22 "President's Letter In Re Pro Bono," *Bar Briefs,* May 1982, p. 1

23 Ibid.

24 Ibid., p. 2

25 "Pro Bono Program – Explanation of financial guidelines," *Bar Briefs*, February 1984, p. 8

26 Ibid., p. 11

Chapter 7 Sidebar

27 Northern Illinois University Law School, Graduates in the Judiciary, 2006, http://www.niu.edu/about/alumni/law.shtml

28 Ibid.

29 "An Unscholarly Look Back," *Bar Briefs*, March 2008

30 Ibid.

31 Swearing-In Ceremony, February 22, 1991; Cover, *Bar Briefs*, March 1991

32 16th Circuit, *The Catalyst*, Vol. 7, No. 3, March 2002; www.isba.org/sections/catalyst/3-02a.htm

Chapter 8

1 Kane County Bar Association Past Presidents, www.kanecountybar.org

2 Joseph Radovich interview, p. 4

3 Wendell Clancy interview, p. 5

4 "Dear Friends," *Bar Briefs,* July 1989, p. 1

5 In the News, Judge F. Keith Brown, www.nic-noble.org/black-history

6 Ibid.

7 Cover Story, *Bar Briefs*, October 1991

8 "Please Excuse Our Dust…" *Bar Briefs*, April 1992

9 Cover Story, *Bar Briefs*, September 1993

10 "Pair Who Left Children Home Alone Are Freed," *The New York Times*, January 1, 1993

11 Ibid.

12 "Parents in 'Home Alone' Case Plead Not Guilty to 64 Counts," *The New York Times*, February 12, 1993

13 "Girls Left Home Alone Will Get New Home," *The New York Times*, July 11, 1993

14 "Murderer's jail breakout unsuccessful," *Bloomington Daily Pantagraph*, January 5, 2008

15 "Man Convicted in Murder Tried to Dig Out of Jail," January 5, 2008, www.cbs2.com

16 Frank Ariano. "President's Perspective," *Bar Briefs*, October 1993, p. 1

17 Minutes of KCBA Long Range Planning Meeting, Geneva, Illinois, August 1, 1998

18 Frank Ariano. "President's Perspective," *Bar Briefs*, April/May 1994, p. 1

19 Ibid., June 1994, p. 2

Chapter 8 Sidebar

20 Tape-recorded interview with John L. Nickels, St. Charles, Illinois, September 19, 2007, p. 2

21 "Nickels wins on own merits," *The Elburn Herald*, March 28, 1992

22 Cover Story, *Bar Briefs*, December 1992, p. 1

23 John Nickels interview, p. 2

24 Ibid., p. 3

25 Ibid.

26 Ibid.

27 Cover Story, *Bar Briefs*, December 1992, p. 3

Chapter 9

1 Kane County Bar, *ISBA News*, September 4, 2001

2 Telephone interview with Jan Wade, St. Charles, Illinois, May 2, 2008

3 William Murphy Interview, p. 3

4 Committee Report – Continuing Legal Aid Committee, *Bar Briefs*, September 1985, p. 23

5 Ibid.

6 Wendell Clancy Interview, p. 4

7 KCBA Registration/Order Form, *Bar Briefs*, February 2007, p. 26

8 "A Weekend in Washington, D.C. with the KCBA," *Bar Briefs*, August 2004, p. 27

9 Ibid.

10 "A Funny Thing Happened on the Way to the Supreme Court," *Bar Briefs*, August 2004, p. 7

11 KCBA Supreme Court Admission Ceremony, *Bar Briefs*, August 2004, p. 36

12 Ibid., p. 8

13 Robert R. Thomas, Supreme Court Chief Justice, Second District, www.state.il.us/court/SupremeCourt/justices/Bio_Thomas.asp

14 James C. Goodale. "Can Judges Judge Judges?" *New York Law Journal*, June 1, 2007

15 Michael Miner. "Court of No Resort," *Chicago Reader*, February 10, 2006, www.ilcampaign.org

16 "Kane County paper settles libel suit with Illinois chief justice," *Topix Newspapers*, October 11, 2007

17 William Murphy interview, p. 5

18 Joe Radovich interview, p. 3

19 www.kanecountybar.org

20 Wendell Clancy interview, p. 2

Chapter 9 Sidebar

21 "KCBF-Children's Waiting Room – A Myth or Reality," *Bar Briefs*, May 2002, p. 34

Index

A

Acevedo, Roberto, 91
Ackemann, David, 145
Adult Justice Center, 174
Allen, Ethan, 26
Alms House and the Poor Farm, 52
Alschuler, Albert, 60
Alschuler, Benjamin, 39, 60, 71
Alschuler, Benjamin P., 60, 98
Alschuler, George, 60
Alschuler, Jacob, 60, 71, 75
Alschuler, J. E., 27
Alschuler, Norman, 60
Alschuler, Sam, 60, 71
Alschuler, Samuel, 39, 44, 60
Alschuler, Funkey, Loats & Pilmer, 60
Alschuler, Simantz and Hem, 60
American Bar Association, 27
Anderson, Allen M., 91
Anderson, Don, 7, 123
Andersson, Steve, 135, 138, 156
Anstett-Patrick, Gail, 152
Ariano, Frank, 91, 128, 130, 131, 132, 155, 156
Aurora Branch Railroad, 32
Aurora City Hall and Court of Common Pleas, 42, 43, 78
Aurora Cotton Mills, 48
Aurora Downs, 108
Aurora Silver Plate Manufacturing Company, 33, 46

B

Babcock, A. S., 21
Balaguer, Mary Ellen, 135
Balog, Richard, 130, 164
Banbury, John, 175
Barber-Greene Corporation, 109
Barbosa, Manuel, 154
Barnett, Joe, 95
Barr, James G., 18, 21
Barry, Alonzo H., 18, 20
Barry, William D., 18, 31
Bartsch, Richard P., 74
Bates, O. M., 18
Beer, Fred J., 91
Bellevue Institute, 23
Belshan, David, 137
Benson, Emil, 58, 72
Bertane, Sherri, 155
Black, Jerry, 132
Blackhawk, 12
Black Hawk Flour Mill, 26
Blackhawk War of 1832, 12, 14
Blaime, James, 33
Blood, Kenneth C., 98
Bonifas, Nick, 161
Bonifas, Rorry, 161
Booth, Greg, 7
Borden, Gail, 35
Botsford, Richard, 31
Botsford, R. N., 20
Brady, William, 91
Brady & Jensen, 90, 91
Brady & McQueen, 73
Brady, McQueen, Martin, Collins & Jensen, 113
Brannen, George, 90
Brawka, Judith K., 113, 120, 149
Britz, Robert, 116, 156, 158
Brown, F. Keith, 127, 154, 160
Brown, Lyle C., 91
Brown, S. W., 18
Brown, William, 77
Brown, William J., 18
Buckingham, Caleb A., 17
Burlington Northern Santa Fe, 32
Burnham, Franklin, 38
Busch, Kevin, 101

C

Callahan, Jack, 7, 91, 93, 105, 107, 145, 154, 165
Calvert, John, 18
Camic, David E., 9, 138, 158, 159
Capone, Al, 53
Carbary, George, 50, 51, 52, 53, 54, 55, 57, 77
Carbary, Jonathan, 54, 135
Carbary, Warren, 54
Carbary & Carbary, 54
Carls, Krista, 150
Carlson, Jan, 95, 118
Caton, John Dean, 15
Chapman, H. N., 17
Cherney, Bill, 152
Cherney, Hannah, 152
Chicago Artificial Flower Company, 72
Chicago, Aurora & Elgin Railroad, 58, 60
Chicago & Aurora Smelting & Refining Company, 33
Chicago Bar Association, 87
Chicago, Burlington & Quincy Railroad, 12, 32, 33, 34, 48, 74
Chicago Great Western Railway, 32
Chicago Telephone Company, 42
Chicago Title Insurance Company, 70, 71, 106
Chicago Title & Trust Company, 72, 73, 94
Chief Shabbona, 11, 12, 25
Chief Waubonsie, 11, 12
Children's Waiting Room, 148, 163
Churchill, Fred, 91
Churchill, Joseph Whelpley, 22, 23, 26
Cibulskis, Julie, 7, 149, 156, 158, 159
City of Aurora v. Rice Thompson, 60
Civic Center Bank & Trust Company, 85, 86
Clancy Boles, Susan, 123
Clancy, Gates, 54, 78, 93, 94, 123, 125, 129
Clancy, John, 93
Clancy, Michael, 123, 164
Clancy, Tim, 123

Clancy, Wendell, 54, 84, 93, 94, 123, 125, 140, 150, 164
Clark, Colonel George Rogers, 12
Cleveland, Grover, 33
Colby, F., 18
Coleman, James, 21
Collins, John, 19, 22
Collins, Richard B., 91
Colwell, Michael, 98, 121, 134
Community Hospital, 76
Compromise of 1850, 24
Cook, Deb, 7, 158, 159
Cooper, Richard L., 74
Cooper, Steve, 98
Corboy, Phil, 92
Countryman, John, 92, 136
Courtin, P. Scott, 90
Cox, Halle, 149, 160
Crimmins, Patrick J., 91
Crisanti, Lawrence, 98, 119, 120
Cundiff, James R., 91

D

Dahl, Jay, 135
Dailing, Joseph, 100, 102
Damisch, Sheriff M. W., 57
Daniels, Harry, 57
David, Bruce, 135
Davoust, Melody, 153
Day, O. D., 21
Dearborn, Luther, 21
DeKing, Lillian, 52
Delnor Hospital, 76
Deutsch, Michael C., 91
Dickinson, Donald, 99, 156
Dickinson, S. N., 18
Dirksen, Everett, 86
Distribution Preemption Act of 1837, 22
Dixon, Liam, 155
Dixon, Patrick, 97, 106, 113, 121, 128, 136, 155
Dobosz, Glen T., 91
Dodge, A. R., 17
Dondanville, Gerry, 101
Dooley, James, 89
Douglas, Stephen A., 24, 157
Douglass, Frederick, 24
Douglas v. California, 103
Doyen, Michael, 138
Doyle, James, 116
Dred Scott, 25
Drendel, Gilbert, Jr., 90, 99, 125, 135
Drendel, Kevin, 125, 135, 138
Drendel, Schanlaber, Horwitz, Tatnall & McCracken, 111
Dunlop, Winifred, 57
Dunn, Marvin, 95, 106, 149
Dunn, Melvin, 118
Durant House, 25
Dyer, David, 105

E

Early, John, 120, 138, 164
Eastman, D. L., 18
Edbrooke, Willoughby, 38
Edmondson, Wiley W., 91, 115, 116, 155
Eichmeier, Roger, 149
Elders, Vince, 138
Elgin City Court, 42, 45
Elgin National Watch Company, 33, 34, 109
Elgin State Hospital, 35, 44
Ellsworth, William, 123
Emancipation Proclamation, 25
Engerman, William, 158, 159
Erschen, Gail, 98

F

Fabyan, Colonel George, 39
Falls, Christine, 164
Farnsworth, John F., 18, 20, 24, 28, 29
Fergus, Sean, 152
Ferguson, J. H., 18
Fermi, Enrico, 81
Fermi Laboratory, 80, 81, 82, 83, 109, 110
Fillipp, Lynda, 158, 159
First Congregational Church, 24
Flaherty, Patrick, 7, 9, 90, 156, 158, 159, 175
Foote, Robert, 90, 130
Foote, William J., 90
Ford, President Gerald, 73
Ford, Thomas, 18
Fortas, Abe, 86
Fox Valley Center, 60
Fox Valley Mall, 109
Frandsen, Roger K., 91
Frankfurter, Felix, 89
Franklin Medical School, 13
Fridley, Benjamin F., 17, 18, 20
Frieders, Dean, 159
Fugitive Slave Act, 24

G

Galena and Chicago Union Railway, 32
Gallagher, Patrick J., 90
Gallraith, Bert, 57
Garfield, F. G., 20
Giampoli, Frank, 103
Gibson, A. C., 18
Gifford, Edmund, 18
Givler, David, 75
Glaser, Paul, 124, 134, 141, 148, 164
Glisson, William, 131
Goettel, Karrsten, 155
Golden, Loren, 118, 120
Golden, Patricia Piper, 120, 136
Goldsmith, Zalmon, 59, 60, 65, 70, 71, 156, 175
Goldsmith, Thielen, Schiller and Dickson, 59
Gorecki, Meg, 124, 137, 145, 146
Gorecki, Robert, 146
Gosselin, John, 105
Gottfried, Theodore A., 103
Grant, General Ulysses, 29, 30
Great Northern Railway, 74
Griffin v. Illinois, 102
Guagliardo, James, 130
Guzman, Melissa Barbosa, 154

H

Hale, Norman, 60
Hanson, Harry, 57, 58, 61
Hardy, Ralph C., 91
Haverty, Charles F., 91
Heimberg, Brian L., 91
Heimberg, Richard L., 91
Herndon, William H., 26
Herrington, Augustus M., 18, 20, 30
Herrington, James, 15
Herrington's Tavern, 15, 16
Heuertz, Loren, 90
Hill, Herbert, 98, 131
Hipp, Thomas, 136
Hoban, Thomas J., 72
Hogan, Thomas, 135
Holcomb, O. A., 39
Horsky, E. Roger, 95
Horwitz, Richard, 90
Hoyt, Charles, 26, 27
Hudson, Donald, 130, 164
Hughes, Don, 120
Hulett, Alta, 112
Hupp, Robert B., 88, 89, 90
Hyde, Henry, 87

I

Illinois Defender Project, 95, 102, 103
Illinois Law Enforcement Commission, 103
Illinois State Bar Association, 87, 91
Indian Creek Massacre, 12
Insull, Samuel, 49
Ireland, R. M., 21
Irvin, Richard, 127
Irwin, Judge, 50
Isaacs, Theodore J., 86, 87

J

James, James C., III, 90
Jenner, Albert, 87, 89
Jensen, Pamela K., 73, 91, 113, 116, 120, 125, 134, 154
Jensen, Wayne, 91, 113
Johannessen, Virginia, 131
Johnson, Bruce R., 91
Johnson, President Lyndon Baines, 74, 81
Johnson, Randle E., 91
Joliet, Louis, 11
Jones, Carolyn, 7, 158, 159
Jones, S. S., 17, 18, 21
Jordan, Everett, 106
Joslyn, Edward S., 20, 39
Joslyn, Frank W., 39, 59
Joslyn, R. Waite, 39

K

Kane, Elias Kent, 13
Kane County Abstract Company, 72
Kane County Abstract Office, 75
Kane County Anti-Slavery Society, 24
Kane County Bar Foundation, 127, 134, 148, 152, 155, 162, 163
Kane County Board of Supervisors, 38, 53, 74
Kane County Home and Farm, 52
Kane County Judicial Center, 100, 128, 132, 133, 139, 141, 148, 152, 155, 164, 171
Kane County Juvenile Justice Center, 171
Kane County Title Company, 71, 72, 94
Karayannis, Marios N., 91
Kear, Frank E., 91
Kennedy, President John F., 64
Kent, John, 91
Kepley, Ada, 112
Kepple, Gerard, 130
Ketcham, William, 91, 95, 101
Kinnally, Patrick M., 90, 142, 150, 158, 159, 161
Kinnally Flaherty Krentz & Loran, 92
Kirkland, Alfred Y., Jr., 91
Kirkland, Alfred Y., Sr., 73, 91, 125
Kirkland, Brady, McQueen & Churchill, 73, 91
Klingbiel, Ray, 86, 87, 88, 89
Klink Wagon Shop, 22
Konstans, Constantine, 98, 130
Kramer, Kelly, 158, 159
Kraus, Alschuler & Holden, 39, 60
Krause, John, 88, 123
Krentz, Paul, 90, 136
Kruse, William, 57

L

Lamont, John M., 90
Landmeier, Allen, 92, 124, 146, 156
Landry, Isabelle, 26
Larson, Carol, 124, 126, 130, 131, 132
Larson, Diana S., 91
LaSalle, Robert, 11
Laswell, Roy, 103
Lathrop, William B., 112
Law, Diana, 158, 159
Law Talk, 150, 161
Lefstein, Norman, 91
Legal Aid Bureau of Kane County, 98, 99, 100, 104
Legal Ease, 130
Legal Services Corporation, 100, 119
Lengle, Philip, 161
Lewis, John H., 91
Lincoln, President Abraham, 18, 23, 24, 25, 26, 27, 29, 157
Lincoln, Mary Todd, 23
Lincoln-Douglas debates, 24
Lindberg, George, 121
Lindner, George P., 90, 123, 134
Lindner, Patricia Reid, 120
Little, Alexander C., 29, 31, 60
Little, John, 18
Loats, Timothy, 164
Locallo, John, 161
Lockwood, Samuel D., 18, 21
Logan, Stephen T., 26
Loran, Joseph, 136
Lord, Maurice, 59
Lord & Parker, 59
Love Brothers Foundry, 33, 45
Lovell, E. C., 21
Lundgren, Sandra, 152
Lundgren, Tait, 152
Lynch, W. F., 21

M

Mahoney, Neil, 88
Mahoney, Timothy, 114
Mangan, E. M., 57
Mann, Phillip, 90
Marblestone, Richard I., 91
Marquette, Father Jacques, 11
Martin, James, 91, 149
Mayborne, J. H., 18, 20
Mayer, Maggie, 7
McAleenan, A. Frank, 91
McCarthy, Joseph M., 97, 106, 128
McCarty, Joseph, 14
McClennan, Paul, 125
McGaw, Kenneth, Jr., 91
McLaughlin, Tami, 158, 159
McMurray, Rita, 99
McNamee, Thom, 115, 116
McNamee, Tim, 114, 115
McQueen, John, 91
M'Dole, A. G., 21
Mercer, William Moffett, 39
Metlicki, Vince C., 90
Metzner, Charles J., 18
Mexican-American War of 1846–1848, 24
Midway, 67, 68
Mielke, Craig, 90
Miller, Howard, 116, 130
Miller, Feda and Barbosa, 127
Millet, Ross, 88
Mitchell, Frank, 72
Molina, Nydia, 159
Molitor v. Kaneland School District, 89, 92
Monaco, Mark, 134
Montgomery, Thomas W., 91
Montony, R. G., 18, 20
Moore, Thomas C., 18
Moran, Tom, 129
Morrow, Robert, 98
Motley, Katherine, 164
Mrkvicka, Stephen, 90
Mueller, George A., 91
Mueller, Thomas, 136
Murphy, John C., 39
Murphy, William, 7, 9, 58, 72, 84, 87, 88, 89, 90, 92, 94, 140, 146, 156, 165, 175
Murphy and Alschuler, 60
Myler, Charles, 74, 105

N

Najdzron, Mary, 153
Nally, William, Sr., 114, 115
Nealis, Harold, 67
Neuendorf, Louis E., 129
Nickel, Andrew, 152
Nickels, John, 121, 128, 129, 185
Nickels & McClowe, 129
Nixon, President Richard, 86
Norris Funeral Home, 25
Northern Illinois Hospital for the Insane, 35, 44
Nottolini, Gene, 118, 144, 145, 175
Nottolini, John, 118, 119
Nyuli, Lisa, 138, 148, 154, 155, 156

O

Oakes, David, 90
Oberweis, Mary Jill, 131
O'Brien, Donald, 146
Ochsenschlager, Lambert M., 65, 86, 87, 88, 89, 90, 91, 92, 93, 101
O'Connor, Charles, 55
O'Connor, Robert J., 98, 99, 183
O'Connor, Sandra Day, 111
O'Donnell, Thomas J., 129
Ogilvie, Governor Richard, 103
O'Hare, Lieutenant Commander Edward, 67
O'Hare Airport, 66, 67, 68, 69, 130
O'Malley, Thomas, 88
O'Neil, Timothy, 120, 136

P

Page, John S., 88
Panic of 1837, 22
Panic of 1893, 40
Parker, Hugh, 59
Parker, Samuel, 18
Parker, William R., 18
Parks, B. F., 18, 20
Parsons, Daniel, 164
Patten, George, 38
Payne, Christopher, 13
Pearson, John, 15, 101
People v. Isaacs, 86
Perbohner, Robert M., 87
Percy, Charles H., 86
Perington, Lee, 130, 132, 156
Perrone, Mathew, 153
Peskind, Steven, 124, 132
Petersen, John S., 59, 68, 74, 88, 94, 101, 142, 150, 165
Peterson, Charles, 136
Petti, Edward, 160
Pheanis, Mark, 136
Phiney, A. B., 18
Piccony, Gary G., 90
Pierce, Elmer, 73
Pinney, Columbus, 26
Plato, W. B., 18
Porter, William, 90
Potawatomi,11, 12, 25
Poust, Cassius, 88
Prairie State Legal Services, 100, 102, 119, 120
Presbrey, Kim, 136
Preston, Issac, 24
Prichard, E. A., 18
Prindable, Thomas, 98
Puklin, Barry, 129, 150

R

Radovich, Charles, 116, 125, 126, 128, 131, 132, 156
Radovich, Joseph, 57, 60, 65, 69, 71, 73, 75, 84, 98, 125, 126, 146, 156
Ramsey, Sheriff Kenneth R., 150
Randall, Craig J., 91
Ranstead, J. W., 21
Rasmussen, Ronald E., 91
Reagan, President Ronald, 102, 111
Rehnquist, Chief Justice William, 145
Reid, Charlotte, 90
Reid, Frank, Jr., 89, 90

Reid, Frank, Sr., 90
Reid, Ochsenschlager, Murphy & Hupp, 87, 88, 89, 90, 91
Renwick, Frank, Sr., 72
Reuland, Timothy, 90, 98, 124, 132
Revolutionary War, 12, 26
Reynolds, John, 12
Rice, Patrick, 154
Richards, G. William, 106, 132, 134, 137, 149
Richards, Van R., Jr., 91
Richmond, Scott, 7, 143, 155
Rifken, Ben, 55, 56, 58, 65, 77
Rifken, Jeff, 77
Ritt, Norbert, 98, 156
Riverboat Gambling Act, 110
Robinson, Matthew, 160
Robinson, Renee, 164
Rodriguez, Rolando, 114
Rogaliner, Susan, 124, 138, 156
Roosevelt, President Franklin D., 60
Roosevelt, President Theodore, 39
Ruark, Eugene, 149
Ruddy, Clarence J., 51, 52, 58, 61, 74, 92, 132
Ruddy, Philip, 60, 92, 127
Ryan, Jane Craddock, 130, 155
Ryan, Terence E., 21, 31
Rydell, Thomas C., 98

S

Safanda, Carl, 132
Santiago, Linda, 164
Schaefer, Walter, 89
Schaffner, Harry, 98
Schanlaber, William C., 90, 97
Schielke, Mayor Jeff, 81
Schifeling, Daniel, 57, 63
Schiller, Richard, 98, 116
Schnake, Paul, 103, 123
Schnell, Theodore, 77
Schnell, Theodore E., Jr., 91
Schoo, David, 130, 131
Schoo, Sharon, 130, 131
Schuster, Theodore G., 74
Schwartz, Ben, 131, 132
Scott, General Winfield, 14
Searles, A. E., 18
Sears, Robert, 88, 101
Second District Appellate Court, 18, 121
Seidel, Charles G., 57, 59, 77, 84, 88, 107
Seraphin, Leonard, 124, 132, 156, 175
Sheldon, Timothy, 116, 154, 160
Shepherd, Frank W., 59
Sheppard, Charles E., 91
Sherman, General William Tecumseh, 29, 30
Shopen, Earl R., 66, 88
Simpson, John, 111, 112
Simpson, May, 111, 112, 113
Simpson & Simpson, 112
Skolnick, Sherman, 86, 87
Slovacek, Greg, 120
Smith, Howard, Jr., 66, 105, 106, 156
Smith, Howard, Sr., 57, 66
Smith, Howard M., 58
Smith, N. J., 18
Solfisburg, Roy J., 67, 85, 86, 87, 88, 89, 92, 127, 136
Southworth, M. O., 39
Speers, Robert, 90, 112, 156
Spong, Keith A., 91
Spring Hill Mall, 109
St. Charles Patriot, 13
State Appellate Defender, 102
Steffen, Frederick I., 91
Steinmetz, Herb, 116, 130, 175
Stevens, Justice John Paul, 85, 86, 87
Stolp Island, 12, 27, 60
Strass, Ray, 98
Streit, Thomas, 124
Strong, Deacon William, 24
Stuart, John Todd, 23, 26
Sullivan, Stephen, 130, 137, 138
Swanson, Carl A., Jr., 88
Swearingen, Brad, 137

T

Tatnall, Susan, 111, 112, 113, 114, 116, 156
Tazewell, Rose, 57
Tenney, Edward, 131
Thomas, Kevin, 152
Thomas, Robert, 145, 146
Thompson, Charles F., 90, 130
Titiner, Steven, 158, 159

U

U.S. Army Air Corps, 59, 74
Underground Railroad, 22, 24, 25
Union Pacific, 32
Unverzagt, George, 129

V

Van Allen, James, 18
Van Der Snick, J. Brick, 137
Vanderwater, William, 101, 103
Van Dyke, Irene T., 125, 126
Van Osdel, John, 23
Vanek, Gary, 124, 132, 156, 176
VanNortwick, John, 22
VanNortwick, Barker, House & Company, 22
Van Santen, James, 76

W

Wade, Jan, 7, 135, 138, 139, 140, 158, 159
Wade, Mark, 138
Wagner, John, 24
Wagner, L. R., 18, 21
Walter, Nadine, 114, 115, 116
Warlick, Doug, 158
Webster, Senator Daniel, 24
Weiler, Bernard, 118
Weiler, Dan, 161
Weiler, Rory, 137

Weiler, Wayne, 98
Wells, Charles Brown, 30, 31
Wertz, Barbara, 118, 119
West Central Illinois Legal Aid Society, 102
Western United Gas and Electric Company, 60
Wheaton, Charles, 18, 21
W. H. Howell Sadiron Works, 35
Wiederman, Joseph, 75
Wilcox, J. S., 21
Wilcox, Sylvanus, 20
Wilson v. Wilson, 15
Wilson, Delia, 22
Wilson, Isaac G., 17, 18, 20, 22
Wilson, Peter, Jr., 92, 124, 132
Wilson, President Woodrow, 60
Wingader, Thomas A., 97
Withers, Dan, 75, 88
Wolff, Wally, 152
Wolfson, Louis, 86
Wolowitz, David, 99, 100, 120
Woodfield Mall, 109

Y

Yates, A. J., 72
Youssi, Francis, 88, 95, 132, 156

About the Author

Writer and historian Bill Beck has more than two decades of experience writing about business history. He wrote his first history for Minnesota Power in 1985, and has more than seventy-five published books to his credit. Recent books include illustrated anniversary histories for Gehl Company in West Bend, Wisconsin; The Metropolitan Washington Council of Governments in Washington, D.C.; and the American Society for Therapeutic Radiation Oncology in northern Virginia. He is currently writing a 150th anniversary history for the American Dental Association in Chicago, Illinois.

Beck is a 1971 graduate of Marian College, Indianapolis, and did graduate work in American history at the University of North Dakota. Beck started Lakeside Writers' Group twenty years ago, following ten years as a reporter for newspapers in Minnesota and North Carolina and seven years as the senior writer in the public affairs department at Minnesota Power & Light Company in Duluth, Minnesota.

New York Street in Aurora looking west from Lincoln Avenue in 1893. The railroad viaduct has not been built. (Aurora Historical Society)